THE
FINANCIAL
ABUNDANCE
BLUEPRINT

A Black
Woman's Guide

to Achieve
Financial Literacy,

Build a
Successful Career,

and Break
Boundaries

AMANDA HENRY

Published by:
Ulysses Press
PO Box 3440
Berkeley, CA 94703
www.ulyssespress.com

ISBN: 978-1-64604-713-0
Library of Congress Control Number: 2024934565

Printed in Canada
10 9 8 7 6 5 4 3 2 1

Project editors: Shelona Belfon, Renee Rutledge
Managing editor: Claire Chun
Editor: Christopher Bernard
Front cover design: Amy King
Artwork: leopard pattern (cover) © Olga/AdobeStock; author photo (cover, page 306) © Lifetouch, LLC
Layout: Winnie Liu, Yesenia Garcia-Lopez

To my son, Jonathan Jr., my greatest blessing and my heart. The moment you came into this world, everything shifted, and I was reborn into a stronger, wiser, and more driven version of myself. You are my legacy, and everything I do, I do for you.

To my younger self, who needed this wisdom back then— don't worry, not only did we survive, we thrived.

To every melanated, first-generation woman striving to break generational cycles, build wealth, and live abundantly—continue to defy gravity and let your magic shine.

"For God has not given us a spirit of fear, but of power and of love and of a sound mind."
—2 Timothy 1:7

CONTENTS

SIDE B

BUILDING YOUR FINANCIAL SYSTEM

EXPLORING PASSION, PURPOSE, AND POTENTIAL

INTRODUCTION: THE JOURNEY TO FINANCIAL ABUNDANCE

If you told me decades ago that I'd be where I am today, working for brands like Google, Verizon, and BET Networks, achieving career success, and empowering women to build wealth, I might have thought you were dreaming too big. My journey began as a first-generation college grad. Since then, I've worn many hats in my career, including roles in sales, project management, and corporate training; I achieved milestones that once felt out of reach: growing my 9-5 income to over $250K, paying off $65K of debt, and saving my first $100K by 27. Now, I'm on track for financial independence in my early 30s. But back then, little Amanda had no idea what it would take to be here today, and as the saying goes, "If only I had known back then what I know now…" I choose not to live life with regrets and stand on business with my decisions; however, I'm not immune to acknowledging how some lessons don't always need to be learned through experience. The sharing of wisdom, blueprints, instructions, etc., can be a game changer and an accelerator in each of our lives—which brings me to you.

If you've found your way to these pages, chances are you're on a quest for something more. Perhaps you're a Black woman, a trailblazer navigating the complexities of being a first-generation college grad and/or professional. Maybe you're an everyday middle-class individual striving to transcend socioeconomic boundaries, or simply someone who loves exploring the wisdom hidden in new authors. My story, much like yours, is one of envisioning a future life so vividly, feeling it, hearing its call, yet having no clear path to reach it.

I am a '90s baby, a Millennial from a typical middle-class family who got sold the American dream. Work hard, excel in school, go to college, get a job, and voila—the dream will unfold. Fast forward to 2020, a pandemic reshaping the world, with the dream fading away. As you read this, perhaps you feel echoes of your own struggles and aspirations.

We're now in the 2020s, with technology, social media, and AI, yet feeling like we're playing catch-up. The weight of expectations from older generations and the disillusionment of younger ones are heavy on our shoulders. If you picked up this book after being attracted by the title *The Financial Abundance Blueprint: A Black Woman's Guide to Achieving Financial Literacy, Building a Successful Career, and Breaking Boundaries*, you're in for a unique journey.

Allow me to share a glimpse of my reality with you. I stand here as an ambitious, first-generation Black woman on the brink of achieving financial independence on a 9-to-5 corporate income. It's a journey that defies the conventional narrative, making me a unicorn in the realm of the American dream.

In an era where hope seems fleeting, I want this book to be a testament to what's possible. It's a nod to my fellow sistas, my colorful cousins, and all trailblazers navigating a path to a better life. It's not a dig at previous generations, but an acknowledgment of the reality of being an adult today.

This book is a declaration of reclaiming and redreaming. I'm not chasing the American dream; I'm passionate about cultivating and living my own dreams. And I want to help you do the same, to move from surviving to thriving. For the ambitious professional Black woman in the corporate world, this book is a guide to living in abundance on a 9-to-5.

So, here's a mindset renewal for my Future Financially Free Corporate Queens/Kings/Royals: living an abundance-filled life on a 9-to-5! The American dream may have evolved, but I'm living proof you can craft your Abundant Life within the confines of a 9-to-5.

I realized that the path to financial abundance wasn't laid out in the neatly packaged dream I was sold. It required a different mindset, a unique approach. It was during this revelation that the idea of "The Financial Abundance Blueprint" (tFAB) began to take shape as a guide to achieving financial literacy and abundance, building a successful career, and ultimately breaking boundaries to what's possible as we navigate this thing called life.

Financial abundance is the state of having significant financial resources, granting you the freedom to make choices, ensuring your security, and facilitating positive contributions to both your personal and societal well-being. As you'll see, the definition of financial abundance has four components, three of which extend beyond money itself. Let's dive deeper into each:

→ **Wealth Accumulation:** This includes having significant financial resources to afford your lifestyle, however defined by you.

→ **Freedom of Choice:** This includes the freedom to pursue your passions, travel, invest in your personal development, and make decisions based on your personal fulfillment—essentially acquiring time-freedom, and a work-optional lifestyle!

➥ **Peace of Mind and Security:** This comes when you have enough resources to cover current expenses, save for the future, and withstand unexpected financial challenges. "Peace of mind and security" emphasizes the importance of financial stability for overall well-being.

➥ **Generosity and Impact:** Beyond personal gain, financial abundance is the ability to make a positive impact on others. It involves having the resources to contribute to charitable causes, support loved ones, or make a difference in your community.

Divided into three core sections, *The Financial Abundance Blueprint* aims to guide you through prioritizing self-awareness, navigating the corporate workplace, and building your financial system as the three pillars to curate an abundant life on a 9-to-5. And if the section titles don't give it away, this book is crafted to resemble a '90s Deluxe Album, complete with Side A and Side B. Remember those? It felt like two albums packed into one. Well, this book carries that same vibe. My Corporate Queens are about to learn how to thrive in their careers and maximize their money to unlock an abundant life on a 9-to-5.

Section 1: The Prelude— Exploring Passion, Purpose, and Potential

Here, we'll delve into personal stories, reconnect with your true self, define your goals, and understand your Abundant Life vision. We'll embark on an exciting yet potentially anxious exercise of being genuinely honest about what you want out of life. It's easy to say, "I want 10 million dollars," but breaking down what your day looks like when money isn't an obstacle will require a journey of introspection.

In this section, we'll also explore the superpower of "self-awareness," which is essential for ambitious women seeking to excel in the corporate world on their terms. Utilizing my PSA Framework will play a crucial role in helping you understand yourself better, especially in how you show up in the workplace and the decisions you'll make moving forward. By "show up" I'm speaking to how you carry and conduct yourself in the office. Corporate America can be compared to working in Hollywood, filled with actors, actresses, production, and more! Everyone is playing a role, some reflective of who they truly are, and others just making do for the needs of the movie. In either case, you are in the driver's seat, deciding how you want to "show up" in the workplace, and it's okay if that shifts during various seasons of your career.

The next part of this section ties everything together. We'll walk away knowing our goals—and we'll be in tune with our superpowers and what might be our kryptonite in the workplace. Now we need to bring this knowledge together through personal branding. Knowing something inside yourself is one thing but the ability to communicate it outwardly is something else. When done correctly, personal branding sets you up nicely for everything to follow.

Lastly, we'll discuss how to dominate your day like the Corporate Queen you are, ensuring productivity over mere busyness. Using my R&B Hit List Prioritization Matrix you'll optimize your workload and maintain your sanity effortlessly!

Section 2: Side A—Navigating Your Corporate Environment

Let me take you back to a moment in my corporate journey, a moment that changed everything. I was navigating the corporate landscape, surrounded by unwritten rules that seemed to favor a select few. As a Millennial Auntie to Gen Z, I realized the injustice of keeping these rules hidden. Speaking of which, why are previous generations so hell bent on young folks having to "get it out of the mud," like they had to? Wouldn't it make more sense to provide the next generation with the lessons we've learned so they can pick up where we left off and keep moving society forward? Maybe this is wishful thinking for the masses, but personally, I plan to do my part!

As a first-generation individual, breaking into these spaces is challenging enough; it shouldn't be harder to stay there. Specifically, as Black women, most of us have a strong work ethic, having worked twice or even three times as hard to get where we are, in comparison to our peers. Yet, because of these unwritten rules, many of us end up confused and disappointed when our careers are not progressing at the same trajectory as our peers. Therefore, in this section, I'll share stories of my own corporate struggles and triumphs, revealing my EMBODY Framework. It's time to make the unofficial rules official, bold, and accessible to all!

So, what's the EMBODY Framework? It's a simple yet comprehensive guide to playing the corporate game with ease and essentially shines a light on those unwritten rules! Many young professionals of color enter the workplace believing that just simply doing their job is enough, when sadly that's only a small fraction of what needs to happen to have a successful career. As a recovering workaholic turned top performer, trust me when I say we're no longer working ourselves to the brink of burnout for these corporations. This doesn't mean we won't deliver great work or lean into execution excellence, but as an authentic top performer, I'll show you how to show up strong with consistency, how to deliver and interact with key stakeholders, and ultimately how to navigate the corporate workplace with ease.

Achieving financial abundance as a Corporate Queen requires career success to grow your 9-to-5 bag, which we'll then multiply to hit our financial goals as we explore Side B!

Section 3: Side B—Building Your Financial System

Picture a pyramid—a 9-to-5er's Wealth Pyramid. Yes, your girl has a framework for everything because I believe in structure and easy-to-follow instructions. What good is personal success if it can't be replicated?

The financial framework described in this book is tailored for those working in the corporate space. It's designed to help young adults transitioning into their first full-time job or those who've worked for a few years but still lack a full understanding of how to maximize their compensation.

In this section, we'll cover the basics: your spending plan, your saving plan, and managing debt, if you have any. More importantly, we'll dive into investing in a musical way that makes sense for the everyday melanated queen. Oh, and I won't forget to highlight the thousands of dollars often left on the table in corporate benefits!

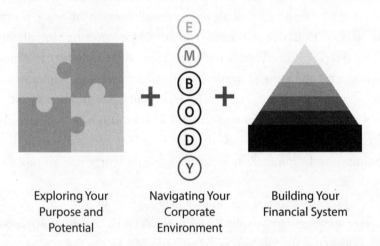

| Exploring Your Purpose and Potential | Navigating Your Corporate Environment | Building Your Financial System |

So, here you are, standing at the gateway to a new understanding of maximizing your 9-5 corporate experience and the income that comes with it! Think of me as the big sis you never had—or maybe you did, but she didn't know how to play the corporate game or multiply the money that came with it.

As we journey through this blueprint, my vision is for anyone who reads this book, dedicates time to its activities, and engages with the content, to walk away with three key outcomes:

➥ **Confidence and Self-Awareness:** You'll know yourself, understand what specific skills you bring to the table, and be confident in how to leverage your unique strengths.

➥ **A Corporate Playbook:** You'll understand how to show up in the corporate world, working smarter vs. harder, so career success is far more likely minus the burnout.

➥ **A Realistic Financial Plan:** You'll have a tangible, step-by-step plan that empowers you to make value-based decisions in your personal finances, ultimately creating the abundant life you desire.

tFAB in Action: Preparing for Your Abundant Journey

Now, before we dive headfirst into the sea of wisdom and revelations that await, let's make sure you're equipped for this transformative expedition. Here is your first set of action items for the Financial Abundance Blueprint (tFAB) journey:

Note-Taking Tools: Whether it's your trusty physical notepad and pens, a digital tablet, or any other preferred method of note taking, have your tools ready. Throughout our journey, you'll come across mini activities designed to elevate your understanding and spark introspection. Jotting down your thoughts, goals, and reflections will turn this reading experience into a personal odyssey of growth.

Growth Mindset: As you delve into the Tracks, bring with you a curious spirit and an open heart. Envision your abundant life without holding back. It might be closer and more attainable than you think. Allow the words to resonate and guide you on this transformative journey.

A Private Promise: If, by the end of this book, you find yourself transformed—more confident, more aware, armed with a realistic game plan—make a private promise. Promise not just to me, but most importantly, to yourself. Commit to sharing the invaluable lessons learned with a friend or family member who could benefit from this blueprint. Let the ripple effect of knowledge and empowerment begin with you.

I'm thrilled to embark on this journey with you Corporate Queens! Get ready for stories, some funny, some filled with heart lessons that had to be learned, but ultimately, a blueprint to hit the ground running. So, if you're ready to learn how to thrive in your career, manage, multiply, and ultimately maximize the money that comes with it, enabling you to cultivate and enjoy your financially abundant life, it's time to turn on Track 1.

ABUNDANCE ON A 9-TO-5

Do you remember your first taste of the abundant life? For me, it was November 2021, when vacationing in Cabo with my husband. Living on the West Coast, I can tell you a last-minute trip to paradise felt surreal, like a luxurious escape where every need was catered to at an all-inclusive Hard Rock resort. As we lounged by the pool, soaking in the sun and serenity, it struck me: this must be God's original intent for us. Not in a preachy way, but it was reminiscent of Adam and Eve in paradise, where they enjoyed each other's company, nature's beauty, and the fruits of the land before things went awry.

Now, you can read the Bible on your own time to find out what happens next, but the point is, I truly believe that it was our original intent as humans to live in paradise. Paradise can look different for everyone, but for me, it means living a life of ease. When I say a life of ease, I don't mean a life without challenges, but one where I'm not filled with anxiety or stress about how bills are going to get paid, what I'm going to cook for dinner, or what my next big project is. A life of ease is being able to exist and enjoy, filled with gratitude for what I currently have, while also feeling limitless and going after even more.

This Track is called "Abundance on a 9-to-5" because I want to reset the standard. The American Dream, as it has been historically known, is no longer relevant for today's Americans or for humans in general. I'm proud to be a part of the Millennial generation that is focused on redefining things for ourselves and our family legacy, whatever that looks like for us.

However, across all generations, particularly Gen Z and the upcoming Gen Alphas, there are young people who don't feel the same level of motivation. And if I'm honest, I'm sure some Millennials and members of older generations are struggling too. There's a growing sense of hopelessness in our society that doesn't sit right with me. There's also a loud conversation about how one corporate job isn't enough. While I do believe in having multiple streams of income as a financially smart move, it shouldn't be a requirement. Folks should be able to support themselves, at least the necessities with some frills here and there, on their 9-to-5 income. Because let's also be real here: Who has the energy to work multiple jobs while balancing all of life's responsibilities?! We, the people, are tired. When we talk about abundance on a 9-to-5, we're looking at how we can live the life we dream of, supported or at least funded by our traditional jobs. You'll hear me talk about corporate jobs specifically because that's my lens and area of expertise.

Okay, let's just cut to the chase. This is going to get real informal, real quick. But before we dive into the stories I'll be sharing in this book, here's a quick intro. First off, I'm an Aries, so you know I'm going to give it to you straight. I'm the eldest daughter with two younger brothers—hello, older sister syndrome! I'm in my early 30s, married for over eight years to my college sweetheart, and we recently welcomed our first (and last) child.

Transitioning from young adulthood to full-blown adulthood was quite the adventure. I'm a first-generation college graduate and corporate professional, which is a fancy way of saying I had wonderful parents who did their best with the tools they had, but for the path I wanted to blaze, I had to forge my own way.

Navigating adulthood in this ever-changing world can be a whirlwind. I graduated from the Wharton School at the University of Pennsylvania (yay Ivy League!) with over $40,000 in student loan debt. Add a new car because I moved to a new city for my first "big girl" job, and I was $65,000 in debt just from doing what we were all taught: go to school, get a good job, and advance your career to pay for the lifestyle you want.

I was doing everything "right," but as a first-gen professional, I didn't know the unwritten rules of the corporate world. That's why they're unwritten, because if everyone knew them, we'd all be successful. And we know that's not how society works. Capitalism loves its winners and losers. I don't necessarily agree with that, but the Aries in me must call a spade a spade.

And let's not forget, being a young Black woman in these corporate spaces didn't make things any easier. But here I am, a decade in, more senior than ever, with experience across various industries. I'm 1,000% confident in how I show up in the workplace today, and I pour that knowledge back into others.

Graduating with student debt is one thing, but knowing what to do next is another. You need to start paying back those loans, but who teaches you about budgeting, debt repayment strategies, or how to make your money work for you through investments? When I started getting my finances in order, I realized my career growth and financial health were intertwined. And I questioned why we all must struggle and suffer. Spoiler alert: we don't.

This is a good time to mention that I'm a Christian. I love Jesus. I love the Lord. And I wouldn't be where I am without His favor and grace. You can do all the right things, but having the Big Guy Upstairs on your side is a game-changer! I mentioned that because I knew there had to be a way to live an abundant life with just my 9-to-5 income. He ain't just put us on this giant rock to suffer. That's why I coined the term "Abundance on a 9-to-5." I want all my Corporate Queens and Kings to see the light at the end of the tunnel. Despite the craziness of the world, some folks will still thrive in their careers, finances, and lives. I'm not just talking about billionaires like Elon Musk or Jeff Bezos—they're in a completely different league. I'm talking about everyday millionaires and thousandaires next door who work regular 9-to-5 jobs just like me. We did it through consistent, intentional actions over time. It's not easy, but it's definitely worth it!

Cultivating Abundance in Corporate America

So Sis, if we're going to talk about living an abundant life based solely on your corporate income, I have to ask you a question and set some expectations. "What is the life you're trying to live?" I ask this with true sincerity. This book is infused with the vibes of the '90s because, honestly, I never left that decade—it's part of the life I'm personally trying to live, LOL! Remember those albums with, like, 24 songs, feeling like two separate albums with a side A and a side B? Well, that's the vibe of this book. It's written for you, my future financially free Corporate Queens. We have these two sides to us, and they both need to shine.

Side A of this book, or the first half, is going to walk you through navigating the corporate workplace. So many folks from different communities aren't prepared when they start their first full-time job. They don't know the unwritten rules, and because of some aspects of their identities or culture, they might never understand these rules without someone, a mentor or an ally, letting them know and bringing them into the fold. Without this knowledge, they'll likely struggle to show up effectively in the workplace, which means they'll struggle to earn promotions and increase their pay. You see the sad cycle, right? So, Side A is my attempt to write down those unwritten rules, or as many as I can fit into these pages. If we're going to have a life of abundance on our 9-to-5 jobs, we need to make sure our jobs aren't stressing us the heck out. Knowing how to navigate the corporate world successfully, efficiently, and effectively will make our time at work filled with more gratitude and fulfillment versus being plagued by the Sunday scaries every week. I'm pretty sure the former sounds better, and we'll explore that through my **EMBODY** Framework.

Side B of this book is the other side of the abundance equation. This half delves into financial literacy topics like budgeting, debt payoff, investing, and some other fun things I won't spoil just yet. As a first-gen professional, I didn't understand all that was at my disposal even within my early corporate experiences. And as they say, "Time is money," but more importantly, "Time is the one resource you can't replenish." When it comes to making your money work for you and seeing the benefits, having more time for that money to work its magic is key. But if you don't know better, you can't do better, and that's what Side B is all about. We'll explore this through the lens of the 9-to-5er's Wealth Pyramid and Your Prosperity Investing Playlists (yPIP) frameworks.

So, I ask you again: What is the life you are trying to live? Are you really clear on what that needs to look like for you? Do you understand what it requires from a monetary perspective? The title of this book might have been misleading. It's called *The Financial Abundance Blueprint*, which might make you think it's all about money. And yes, money is definitely half of it. But the heart of my message is that having a life full of fulfillment is still possible with your day-to-day job, assuming you're making at least a livable wage. I want folks to be re-inspired and filled with hope that their dream life is within reach. Now, if your dream life involves being on a yacht twice a day, we'll have a bit more work to do. But from what I understand, most everyday Americans have simple joys that should be accessible to them, no questions asked.

Now, let's take a moment to get really centered on what our Abundant Life looks like so we can curate it and bring it to life. I'm not going to give you a miracle remedy on how to do this, but I will offer some tactical, realistic steps you can put into action. I can honestly say that I'm very close to my full Abundant Life. Let's be real—there are levels to it. Right now, I'm at Abundant Life Tier 2, and Tier 3 is right around the corner.

With that, it's time to introduce a special feature in the upcoming Tracks: Abundant Chronicles, which delve into themes of life, career, and wealth. In these spotlight moments, I offer candid and transparent stories from my "adulting" journey. My aim is to provide insights that resonate with ambitious Black women, first-generation college graduates, and young professionals of color. These narratives not only showcase the experiences that have shaped the wisdom in this book but also reflect my desire to have known more so I could have done better. Now, I'm sharing these lessons to help you all navigate your own paths!

Abundant Life Chronicle: Your Dream Life Within Reach

Let me tell you about a remarkable young woman I had the privilege to coach. From our very first session, it was clear she had a solid financial foundation, but she didn't realize just how close she was to achieving her abundant life.

During our second session, a pivotal moment occurred. As we combed through her budget, she had an epiphany. She was already

The Financial Abundance Blueprint

in a far better position than she had ever imagined. Sure, she had some debt and room to grow her income, but she was on the brink of hitting that magical $100,000 net worth milestone. And we all know what happens after that—hello, compound interest!

As we delved deeper into her finances, she realized she wasn't just surviving; she was thriving. She had enough to cover her bills, enjoy her life, and still have room to dream. It was during this budget review that she began to share her real aspirations: traveling half the year, having a home base in her city to stay close to family, and truly living her best life.

I challenged her, as I challenge you now, to write down those dreams and research their costs. She accepted the challenge, and within a few weeks, she discovered that she was only a few years away from making her dream life a reality. It was a crazy thought, but all it took was defining what her dream life looked like in the first place.

That moment was incredibly empowering for her, and for me as well. Seeing her photos now, living her abundant life, fills me with pride. It's a testament to the power of clarity, intentionality, and taking actionable steps toward your dreams!

Visualizing Your Abundant Life

So, let's ask again: What life are you striving to live? This book is your guide to unlocking the boundless potential of abundance, all fueled by your 9-to-5 job. Through career development and financial education, you'll uncover the path to transforming your dream life into reality. But here's the kicker—the journey begins with you, right here in this Track.

We're kicking things off with a potent visualization technique. You may have encountered similar exercises before, but now it's time to delve deep and paint a vivid picture of your vision—your North

Star. This exercise is about envisioning your ideal day and life. Don't hold back. Be honest and dream big.

Take a moment to craft a detailed description of your ideal life. Divide it into categories that resonate with you—whether it's family, career, health, travel, or leisure. Envision your perfect day from dawn to dusk. What do you do upon waking? How do you fill your day? Who accompanies you? What emotions do you experience?

This vision will serve as your guiding light throughout this book and beyond. It's the driving force behind your commitment to your career journey, your financial discipline, and your commitment to personal growth. When faced with challenges, this clear vision will propel you forward.

In a world often beset by systemic obstacles and the daily grind, possessing the energy to dream and the clarity to pursue that dream can make all the difference. Your dream life isn't mere fantasy; it's a tangible goal awaiting realization through deliberate action. Let's embark on this journey together, with your vision of abundance illuminating every step of the way.

Visualization Exercise: Defining Your Abundant Life

Step 1: Create a Peaceful Environment

Find a quiet, comfortable space where you can relax without interruptions. This will help you focus and fully engage in the exercise.

Step 2: Gather Your Tools

Have a notebook, pen, or digital device ready to jot down your thoughts. You might also want to have some inspirational music playing in the background if it enhances your creativity.

Step 3: Close Your Eyes and Imagine

Take a few deep breaths, close your eyes, and imagine your perfect day. Think about every detail, from the moment you wake up to the moment you go to bed. Let your mind wander to all the possibilities without any limitations.

Step 4: Write Down Your Vision

Open your eyes and start writing. Break down your vision into categories such as family, career, health, travel, and leisure. Describe each aspect of your perfect day with vivid detail.

Sample Categories and Questions to Consider:

- **Family:** Who are you spending time with? What activities do you enjoy together?
- **Career:** What is your job? What achievements are you proud of?
- **Health:** How do you prioritize your physical and mental well-being? Which activities invigorate you?
- **Travel:** How often do you travel? Where do you venture? What experiences do you seek?
- **Leisure:** How do you unwind and have fun? What hobbies or interests do you pursue?
- **Finances:** What is your financial status? How do you manage your money? What financial goals have you achieved?
- **Personal Development:** What skills are you cultivating? How do you foster personal growth?
- **Relationships:** What friendships and connections do you cherish? How do you nurture those bonds?
- **Spirituality:** How do you connect with your spiritual side? What practices help you feel grounded and fulfilled?
- **Community:** How do you contribute to your community? What causes are you passionate about?

- ⟿ **Home Environment:** Describe your ideal living space and its ambiance.
- ⟿ **Legacy:** Describe the impact you want to leave on the world and how you desire to be remembered.

||||||||||||||||||||||||||||||||||||||||||||||||||||||||||||||||||||||||||||||||||||||||||||||||||||||||||||||||||||||||||||||

Abundant Life Chronicle:
My Abundant Life Vision

Remember, your vision is uniquely yours, but here's a glimpse of mine. As I awaken each morning, I make my way downstairs for breakfast in our kitchen nestled within our three-story home, situated likely somewhere in the South. This isn't just any breakfast; it's a spread of my favorites—French toast, eggs, bacon, and potatoes—the works. Our home is more than just a dwelling; it's a sanctuary where we gather for family game nights and entertain guests in our cozy, lounge-style basement.

After breakfast, I devote 45 minutes to a gym session, ensuring my body stays in peak condition. I'm a member of a fancy studio, where I enjoy rocking a cute workout outfit while having fun in class with the other gym girlies.

Reuniting with my husband and son, we embark on a new adventure each day. My mornings might involve delving into an online course that piques my curiosity. The flexibility of home-schooling allows us to travel and explore different cultures, transforming every city into a vibrant classroom. One month we might be exploring the ancient ruins of Rome, the next we're relaxing on a beach in Thailand. Afternoons are for park picnics and delightful lunches at local cafés.

While my husband and son have some quality bonding time, I dedicate some hours to nurturing my thriving home business. Striking that work-life balance is key, and it allows me to be a successful entrepreneur and a present mom. Evenings are filled with quality family time, from planning delicious dinners to deciding on our next spontaneous escapade: maybe a trip to the movies, a

The Financial Abundance Blueprint

night of laughter at a comedy show, or even a last-minute flight to a tropical paradise.

Taking care of myself is a must. Regular massages and facials keep me feeling rejuvenated, and hey, treating myself to a luxurious Coach bag every once in a while is part of the fun. But abundance goes way beyond material things. Giving back to my community through volunteering brings immense joy and leaves a positive legacy. We're also committed to building generational wealth, so our son will be financially literate by 18. Of course, financial education is an ongoing journey, and he'll be learning valuable money-management skills from a young age. This is just a glimpse into my vision of abundant living. Now it's your turn, Queen!

tFAB in Action: Establishing Your North Star

In this tFAB in Action moment, our focus has been on shaping your abundant life vision, a guiding north star that directs every decision onward, leading you toward its realization. Here are your action items:

Visualize Your Perfect Day: Take a moment to envision your ideal day from start to finish. Who are you spending time with? What activities bring you joy and fulfillment? Imagine every detail, from the moment you wake up to the moment you go to bed.

Craft Your Abundance Manifesto: Draft a written document outlining your ideal life across various dimensions, such as family, career, health, travel, leisure, finances, personal growth, relationships, spirituality, community, home environment, and legacy. Keep it somewhere accessible for regular reflection and reinforcement of your goals.

THE POWER OF SELF-AWARENESS

Ready to unlock the key to leveling up in both life and work? Let's talk about self-awareness, a game-changing tool for navigating the workplace with ease as your authentic self. Self-awareness is the conscious understanding of one's own character, feelings, motives, and desires. It's about knowing what makes you tick, what ignites your passion, and what might trip you up.

Imagine this: You're at work, and everything just clicks. You're fully aware of your strengths and where you could use some support. You handle challenges with ease. That's the magic of self-awareness—it's your built-in GPS for your career. When you're in tune with your capabilities and limitations, you can make savvy decisions and set realistic goals.

As Corporate Queens, having a strong sense of self-awareness is the foundation for successfully navigating the corporate workplace. It's about owning our space, knowing our worth, and not being afraid to show up as our true selves. Self-awareness helps us see where we shine and where we need to put in a bit more work. This isn't just about getting ahead; it's about thriving in spaces with people who might not always look like us or understand our experiences. It's about bringing our full selves to the table and making sure our voices are heard.

As we delve into this Track, take a moment to reflect on your own path. What are your strengths? Where do you see room for growth? How can self-awareness empower you to achieve your goals and cultivate a fulfilling, impactful career? Let's dive in and harness the power of self-awareness to pave the way for success and satisfaction in all you do.

Drop Your PSA: Personal SWOT Analysis

When was the last time you embraced your PSA? That's how I usually introduce this framework at a corporate training. PSA stands for Personal SWOT Analysis, and it's an amazing tool for boosting your self-awareness as a Corporate Queen! I used to think I was the only one on to this concept, but it turns out there are others who've also discovered its relevance for personal career growth.

Back in the 1960s, researchers at Stanford Research Institute developed the SWOT analysis—focusing on Strengths, Weaknesses, Opportunities, and Threats—to assess internal capabilities and external factors affecting potential for success. Initially for businesses, it's now a key tool in personal development.

For us Corporate Queens charting our career paths, the Personal SWOT Analysis is like a guiding light. It helps us understand ourselves better and thrive in the workplace. By identifying our strengths—like our unique skills, leadership traits, or cultural insights—we can stand out and make meaningful contributions. Recognizing our weaknesses opens up opportunities for growth and skill development, empowering us to overcome challenges and enhance our professional capabilities. And when we spot opportunities within our field or organization, we can strategically apply our strengths to advance. Being aware of external threats such as industry trends or workplace dynamics enables us to plan ahead and adapt, ensuring we stay resilient and keep growing in our careers. Through the SWOT analysis, we can align our personal goals with our organizational objectives, paving the way for success rooted in self-awareness and strategic thinking.

When you're ready to conduct your PSA, consider your Strengths, Weaknesses, Opportunities, and Threats in the context of your current role and organization. It's all about understanding your unique value and where you might need a little extra support or training. It's about embracing our flaws, leveraging our strengths, and always seeking ways to grow. I always say, "I know my weaknesses, but guess what? You'll never know what they truly are!" It's all about being in tune with ourselves and proactively seeking ways to shine in the workplace.

TRACK 2: PSA
(PERSONAL SWOT ANALYSIS)

The Financial Abundance Blueprint

Strengths

In the "Strengths" segment of your SWOT analysis, it's all about identifying what makes you stand out and excel in your current role. Here, you'll pinpoint your innate talents, honed skills, and personal attributes that not only streamline your work but also perfectly align with the demands of your position. By honing in on these strengths, you'll unveil the areas where you effortlessly thrive, empowering you to make meaningful contributions with ease.

Guiding Questions to Uncover Your Strengths:

→ What natural talents do I possess, or what skills have I cultivated over time?

→ Which projects or tasks do I find inherently manageable or straightforward?

→ What unique skills or knowledge do I possess that sets me apart?

→ Which aspects of my job or projects bring me the most joy or fulfillment?

→ Where do I receive consistently positive feedback or recognition from colleagues or supervisors?

→ How do my strengths align with the objectives and priorities of my team or organization?

→ What notable achievements or successes have I attained that demonstrate my strengths?

Weaknesses

In the "Weaknesses" section of your SWOT analysis, it's crucial to identify areas within your current job where you may face challenges or encounter tasks that are less enjoyable. This introspective process allows you to pinpoint specific aspects that may require improvement or further development. By recognizing these weaknesses in relation to your role expectations, you can strategically plan to enhance your skills and overcome any obstacles, ultimately fostering professional growth and achievement.

Guiding Questions to Uncover Your Weaknesses:

➥ What tasks or activities do I find challenging or frustrating?

➥ Which aspects of my job do I tend to avoid or procrastinate on?

➥ Are there skills or areas of knowledge that I lack and need to develop?

➥ What constructive feedback have I received on areas needing improvement?

➥ What personal traits might be holding me back in my role?

➥ Are there any professional or technical skills I need to acquire or update to keep up with my role?

Opportunities

In the "Opportunities" section of your SWOT analysis, focus on identifying ways to contribute value to your organization by leveraging your strengths. This analysis helps you identify potential advancements and strategic growth areas where you can excel effortlessly, positioning yourself as a top performer. By recognizing and seizing these opportunities, you not only enhance your professional impact but also create space to work on your "weaknesses" or areas needing improvement in the background.

Guiding Questions to Uncover Your Opportunities:

➥ How can I address team or organizational challenges by leveraging my strengths?

➥ What upcoming projects align with my strengths and interests?

➥ What gaps or needs exist within my team or organization that I could fill?

The Financial Abundance Blueprint

➡ Can I propose a new initiative that leverages my strengths and benefits the organization?

➡ Are there opportunities for me to collaborate with colleagues from other departments to broaden my experience?

Threats

In the "Threats" section of your SWOT analysis, it's time for a moment of truth. Here, you'll uncover specific threats that could potentially hinder your career advancement or professional growth. By honestly assessing potential obstacles and challenges, you empower yourself to navigate them effectively. This analysis provides a valuable opportunity to identify potential roadblocks and develop proactive strategies to overcome them, ensuring you stay on track to achieve your career goals. Remember, this is the section where you look beyond your current role and consider the broader landscape of your career path and aspirations.

Guiding Questions to Uncover Your Threats:

➡ What environmental factors impact my productivity, such as changes in leadership, team culture, or employee turnover?

➡ Are there specific tools or technologies in my industry that I lack proficiency in?

➡ Do I require additional education, such as a degree or certification, to advance within my company?

➡ Are there technological advancements that could render my current skills obsolete?

➡ Are there any personal circumstances that could potentially impact my professional growth?

➡ What internal policies or politics could hinder my progress?

➡ How do my long-term career goals align with the stability of my current organization?

Job Crafting: Shape Your Role toward Automatic Success

As Corporate Queens, you will find job crafting offers you a strategic tool to refine your role with purpose and precision. By consciously aligning your work environment with your strengths, interests, and values, you'll cultivate a professional landscape that's primed for you to succeed in. Utilizing your identified strengths through this analysis allows you to strategically navigate your professional journey. Identifying tasks that leverage your strengths not only enhances productivity but also reinforces your value as an essential contributor to your organization.

Moreover, the PSA serves as a guide in addressing areas for improvement and growth. Proactively identifying weaknesses enables you to seek out opportunities for development through training, mentorship, and collaboration. Additionally, recognizing and addressing your weaknesses protects you from taking on "special projects" that may not align with your strengths and end up being more trouble than they're worth. This proactive approach not only mitigates potential challenges but also accelerates our professional advancement, equipping you with the skills and knowledge needed to excel in your role.

Ultimately, the PSA acts as a compass, guiding you in refining your role and interactions within your professional environment, positioning you to consistently surpass expectations and cultivate a workplace environment that's shaped for your automatic success!

Abundant Life Chronicle: Leveraging Strengths as an Anti-Sales Salesperson

"What do you mean I need to focus on quantity and cold call as many businesses as possible?" That was my reaction when I joined a new sales team, transitioning from a role where I never even saw myself as a salesperson. My career journey had taken me through various sales titles such as account strategist, digital strategy lead, and senior account executive, but I never fully embraced the traditional sales persona. I didn't subscribe to the typical stereotypes of being pushy or transactional.

From the outset, I knew my strength lay in building trust quickly. While my peers focused on mass outreach, I saw an opportunity to delve deeper. Instead of inundating potential clients with calls, I immersed myself in research. I dug into their business goals, dissected their customer journeys, and crafted compelling narratives backed by data. By the time I made contact, I wasn't just selling a service; I was presenting a partnership they couldn't refuse.

This approach paid off. Quarter after quarter, I consistently ranked among the top performers on the team. It wasn't just about hitting targets; it was about leveraging my strengths and crafting my role to align with what I excelled at naturally. It was a lesson in self-awareness—knowing where I shine and having the confidence to lean into it.

Beyond personal success, this journey taught me the power of leveraging my Personal SWOT Analysis. It wasn't just about overcoming weaknesses; it was about strategizing how to use my strengths to reshape my job and achieve exceptional results with less effort. It's why, even as I launched training programs to elevate others' sales skills, I found myself not just teaching sales but transforming how we approach it. That's the power of self-awareness and job crafting in action, becoming an authentic top performer, guided by knowing and using my strengths.

tFAB in Action: Mastering Self-Awareness

This tFAB in Action moment has been focused on harnessing self-awareness through your Personal SWOT Analysis as a key advantage for excelling in your job. By understanding the unique blend of your Strengths, Weaknesses, Opportunities, and potential Threats within your current role, you can strategically leverage this awareness to navigate challenges and strategically position yourself for success as you navigate the workplace and propel your career forward with confidence. Here are your action items:

Conduct Your Personal SWOT Analysis: Perform a thorough SWOT analysis focusing on your current role. Identify strengths aligning with job requirements, pinpoint weaknesses, explore opportunities for leveraging strengths in career advancement, and identify external threats to long-term career goals.

Adjust Your Daily Reality through Job Crafting: Using your SWOT analysis, pinpoint areas in your daily tasks where you can apply your strengths to save time and effort. Aim to spend more time on activities that play to your strengths while seeking out resources to address your weaknesses and work on improving them.

Request Feedback and Reflect: Actively seek feedback from peers, supervisors, or mentors to understand your strengths' contributions to your team's goals, and areas that need improvement. Reflect on feedback to refine your level of self-awareness and adjust your approach for maximum professional impact.

SHAPING YOUR PERSONAL BRAND

Do you Corporate Queens ever wonder what you're known for in the workplace? Seriously, what do people think or say about you when you're not around? Believe it or not, they're definitely saying something! It's time to take control of your story and own your personal brand. Personal branding is all about crafting a clear and compelling narrative that showcases your unique value and leaves a lasting impression. It's about defining how you want to be perceived professionally and making sure you're consistent in every interaction. Remember, "Your personal brand is being built in the workplace, with or without your help." Translation: You better be in the driver's seat to make sure your brand is what you want it to be and represents you as desired! There are four core components to keep in mind when cultivating your personal brand: your Personal Brand Statement, your Elevator Pitch, your Personal-Life Details, and your Authentic Self. Let's dive into each of these and explore how to establish your personal brand!

Your Personal Brand Statement

Your Personal Brand Statement is like your personal mission statement—it succinctly captures the essence of who you are and what you stand for. Why is it crucial to have one? Because it brings clarity and focus to your life. Your Personal Brand Statement helps you define your long-term vision and mission. What impact do you want to have on the audiences that matter to you, both personally and professionally? What values do you want to embody as you pursue your goals? By answering these questions, you gain a clear understanding of your core values, which form the foundation of your personal brand.

This exercise is about being honest with yourself. You don't have to share your Personal Brand Statement with others if you're not comfortable doing that. It's about having a deep understanding of who you are and what you believe in. This clarity naturally influences how you interact with others, approach your work, and navigate your career.

So, start by reflecting on your experiences, decisions, and actions. What consistent interests, skills, or character traits have shaped your journey? How do these connect to your mission, passions, and objectives? Crafting your Personal Brand Statement sets the stage for a more intentional and authentic presence in both your personal and professional life. Ready to create your own? Here's a template to kickstart your journey.

Personal Brand Statement Template:

➥ **For [Target Audience/Group]:** Identify who you are aiming to impact or connect with (e.g., employers, colleagues, clients).

➥ **I will make a difference by offering [Unique Value]:** Describe the specific and memorable value you bring (e.g., skills, services, expertise).

➥ **Among all [Competitive Cohort]:** Highlight the group you are competing with, emphasizing your distinctive attributes.

➥ **Because of [Distinctive Capabilities]:** Detail the unique skills, experiences, personality traits, and credentials that enable you to deliver your value.

Here is my Personal Brand Statement:

"For ambitious young women of color seeking to thrive both personally and professionally, I will make a difference by offering insightful career coaching, personalized financial strategies, and empowering tools that cultivate and sustain an abundant life. Among all career and/or finance coaches, I stand out because of my unique ability to combine deep financial acumen, my personal journey of going from $65,000 in debt to financial independence through my 9-to-5 income, and a genuine passion for helping other young women have the corporate blueprint I didn't have. I bring more than 10 years of experience as a first-generation college graduate turned consistent top-performing corporate professional, with a proven track record of significantly growing my income through skill development and strategic opportunities, and a relatable approach as a Black woman who understands the challenges faced by young women of color transitioning into adulthood."

Your Elevator Pitch (i.e., Introduction)

Crafting a compelling elevator pitch is essential for Corporate Queens who aim to stay ready so they don't have to get ready when opportunity comes knocking. This concise yet impactful summary offers a glimpse into your professional identity while allowing room for personal touches, setting the stage for genuine connections and future opportunities.

Your elevator pitch serves as a powerful tool to leave a lasting impression on new colleagues, potential employers, or networking contacts. It enables you to succinctly articulate your unique value, skills, and career goals, ensuring each interaction is purposeful and memorable. Tailoring your pitch to different audiences allows you to highlight aspects of your background that resonate most with them, making every encounter more meaningful.

Key elements of an effective elevator pitch include being both concise and impactful, encapsulating your educational background, notable achievements, and specialized skills. This comprehensive approach gives others a clear understanding of who you are and why you're passionate about your chosen path.

Mastering your elevator pitch empowers you to confidently navigate professional settings, build meaningful connections, and showcase the authentic blend of skills and experiences that define your personal and professional journey. Ready to create your own? Here's a template to get you started.

Crafting Your Elevator Pitch:

→ **Start with a Hook:** Begin with a concise and engaging opening that captures attention and introduces yourself.
Example: "Hi, I'm [Your Name]. As a [Your Current Role or Aspiration], I bring [Unique Trait or Expertise]."

→ **Highlight Your Expertise:** Summarize your key skills, experiences, and achievements relevant to your audience.
Example: "With [Number] years of experience in [Field/Industry], I specialize in [Specific Skill or Area of Expertise]."

→ **Unique Selling Proposition:** Mention what sets you apart from others in your field or industry.
Example: "I'm known for [Distinctive Skill or Achievement], which allows me to [Impact or Benefit]."

→ **Personal Touch:** Optional but encouraged, add a personal detail that aligns with your professional narrative.

Example: "Outside of work, I'm passionate about [Interest or Hobby], which fuels my creativity in [Field/Industry]."

↳ **Call to Action or Future Aspiration:** Conclude with a statement that invites further conversation or highlights your career goals.

Example: "I'm excited about [Future Goal or Initiative], and I'm eager to connect with others who share my passion for [Field/Industry]."

Here is my Elevator Pitch:

"Hey there, I'm Amanda Henry, your go-to Senior Corporate Trainer and Instructional Designer. I'm all about helping teams and individuals shine in their professional journeys. With over a decade of experience and a love for continuous learning, I deliver corporate workshops that don't just teach but inspire. Picture this: dynamic sessions filled with industry and role-related expertise, interactive learning activities, and maybe a sprinkle of '90s R&B jams and pop culture vibes to keep it fun. Whether I'm coaching emerging leaders or refining seasoned teams, I thrive on creating transformative learning experiences that inspire confidence and achievement. Let's collaborate to elevate your team's potential and make your corporate training dreams a reality."

Your Personal-Life Details

Incorporating personal-life details into your personal brand can significantly enhance your professional relationships and opportunities. When people connect with you on a personal level, they're more likely to trust you, enjoy collaborating with you, and see you as a multifaceted individual. This is crucial because, as the saying goes, people often prefer to hire and promote those they know, like, and trust.

However, it's essential to approach this with intention and discretion. You have control over what personal details you choose to share. Oversharing or disclosing information that makes you uncomfortable can have unintended consequences, as workplace information can spread quickly. What you share should align with your comfort level and the professional image you want to project.

Safe topics for sharing include hobbies such as travel, movies, sports, TV shows, and music. These topics are generally light-hearted and can help build connections without delving into overly personal matters. For instance, discussing favorite travel destinations or recent movies you've enjoyed can foster rapport while maintaining professionalism.

Remember, you're not obligated to share photos or videos of your personal life, even if you have a new addition to your family. Your privacy and comfort should always come first. By carefully choosing what you share, you can cultivate genuine connections and strengthen your personal brand without compromising your boundaries. This approach allows you to showcase your personality and interests positively while maintaining a professional demeanor.

Personal Life Details Talk-Track:

↪ **Initiate with a Neutral Topic:** Start the conversation with a topic that's light and universally relatable.
Example: "Hey [Colleague's Name], did you catch the latest episode of [Popular TV Show/Movie]? I thought it was pretty interesting!"

↪ **Transition to a Personal Detail:** Once you've established a comfortable conversational flow, subtly introduce a personal detail that aligns with the topic.
Example: "Speaking of shows, I've been binging on [TV Show] lately. It's my go-to to unwind after a busy day."

↪ **Share in Moderation:** Share enough to show your personality and interests but avoid going into too much detail.

The Financial Abundance Blueprint

Example: "I love exploring new series. It's a great way to relax and recharge. What about you? Any recommendations?"

→ **Respect Boundaries:** Always be mindful of the other person's reactions and cues. If they seem uninterested or uncomfortable, gracefully shift the conversation back to work-related topics or common interests.
Example: "Actually, if it's okay to switch gears here, I wanted to ask your thoughts on [relevant work topic/another shared interest]. What do you think?"

→ **Follow-Up Appropriately:** If the conversation goes well and you find common ground, you can always follow up later on related topics.
Example: "I remember you mentioned you're into [Hobby]. Have you tried [Activity] related to that?"

Your Authentic Self

Bringing your authentic self to work is crucial for fostering a sense of belonging and fulfillment in your professional life. However, it's equally important to recognize that not every aspect of your identity needs to be shared in the workplace, especially if you're not comfortable or if the environment is toxic. As women of color, there may be parts of our identities that we prefer to keep private, reserving them for trusted circles like family and close friends.

This is why we emphasize the importance of crafting your personal brand statement, elevator pitch, and personal life topics intentionally. These tools help you determine how much of yourself you want to bring into the workplace while maintaining authenticity. Consistency is key here; your actions and narratives shape how others perceive you, and by staying true to yourself, you can establish a strong personal brand that aligns with your values and goals.

Remember, your personal brand is not just about how you want to be known but also about how you make others feel through your interactions and experiences. If your current brand isn't reflecting your true self or isn't yielding the desired results, you have the power to change it. By consciously deciding what you want your personal brand to look like and consistently showing up as that person, you can influence how others perceive and engage with you. Over time, your authentic self will shine through, and others will come to know and appreciate the real you.

However, it's equally important to recognize that not every environment is conducive to embracing your authenticity. In some cases, you may find yourself in a toxic work environment that hinders your ability to show up as your true self. If you realize that an organization is not conducive to your growth or well-being, it's essential to plan your exit strategy. While financial considerations will be covered in "Side B" of the book, the key point here is that it's okay to explore other options if the current company doesn't align with your values and goals. Your mental and emotional well-being should always take precedence, and finding a workplace where you can thrive authentically is essential for your long-term success and happiness.

Abundant Career Chronicle: My Brand Was Built without Me

The concept of personal branding really hit home for me through two key experiences during my corporate journey. At Verizon, I joined the Women's Employee Resource Group, where I met Karin, a standout figure known for her intentional personal brand. Soon, I realized that Karin showed up exactly as she appeared in her event program photo, her outfit, makeup, and hairstyle all perfectly aligned. Curious, I asked her about it.

Karin explained how her consistent look was a deliberate choice, reinforcing reliability and trustworthiness in her professional persona. Inspired by Karin, I decided to establish my own signature look at corporate events—leopard print and rose gold. This unique style reflects the vibrant energy I bring to my work under my brand Living In The Abundance (LITA). While it may not match my professional headshot, it has become a distinctive part of how I present myself.

On the flip side, my experience at Google taught me another valuable lesson in personal branding. In a routine meeting, my manager mentioned positive feedback from another manager named Max, someone I hadn't met yet, let alone had any interaction with. Though I was grateful this manager had wonderful things to say about me, it also gave me pause to reflect on the influence our managers' peers have on our career trajectory. This realization underscored that our personal brand is continually shaped by every action and interaction, whether intentional or not.

These encounters with Karin and Max have deeply shaped my understanding of personal branding. They've shown me that while we can't control everything, we can significantly influence how others perceive us by consistently embodying our authentic selves. This means being mindful of every interaction, ensuring our actions align with the professional image we want to project.

Ultimately, personal branding isn't just about how others see us, it's about how we choose to show up, authentically and consistently. By embracing our unique style and values, we not only build a credible professional reputation but also create opportunities for growth and meaningful connections in our careers and beyond.

tFab in Action: Establishing Your Personal Brand

This tFab in Action moment has been about actively defining and strengthening your personal brand. By proactively shaping how others perceive you, you ensure alignment with your values and professional aspirations. Here are your action items:

Craft Your Personal Brand Statement: Develop a clear and concise statement that encapsulates your values, strengths, and career objectives, providing a guiding light for your professional journey.

Perfect Your Elevator Pitch: Tailor a captivating introduction for various audiences, effectively showcasing your unique skills and ambitions to leave a memorable impression in any professional encounter.

Integrate Personal-Life Details with Purpose: Share carefully chosen personal details, such as hobbies and cultural interests, to foster authenticity and connection while maintaining professional boundaries.

Embrace Your True Self: Stay grounded in your values and personal brand, maintaining consistency in your actions and narratives to authentically resonate with others.

Evaluate and Adjust Your Brand: Continuously monitor how others perceive your brand, refining your narrative based on feedback and evolving career aspirations.

DOMINATE YOUR DAY: PRODUCTIVITY HACKS

All right, Sis, let's get real for a minute. Your well-being at work? It's all on you, 1,000%. Sure, there might be supportive managers and some helpful policies, but when push comes to shove, you're the one steering the ship. I once had a video go viral where I called out the backwardness of Corporate America. I highlighted how many so-called "top performers" struggle to navigate the system successfully. See, being a top performer often means you're drowning in tasks, but let's be honest: there's a huge distinction between being busy and being truly productive. So, let's figure out how to thrive sustainably, without burning out.

Think of corporate life as one giant game of Monopoly mixed with Uno and a little bit of chess. Once you know the rules, it can actually be fun to play, or at minimum, you have a chance at finding success and winning your way! As future financially free Corporate

Queens, our goal is to ace the workplace game so effortlessly that we have the mental bandwidth to focus on maximizing our earnings for financial freedom. Even if you love your job, there's always room to work smarter, not harder. And trust me, as a recovering workaholic and consistent top performer, I know the struggle firsthand. I've learned the hard way the importance of balance while maintaining a personal brand for always executing my work at a level of excellence.

Mastering productivity in the workplace boils down to these key elements: workload and task prioritization, time management, and organization. Think of it as setting up systems or routines that help you maximize your efforts and efficiency.

Workload and Task Prioritization

In an upcoming Track, we'll delve into aligning your role priorities with your manager's expectations. But for now, let's focus on maintaining your sanity while juggling numerous tasks. Enter in the prioritization matrix, inspired by Dwight D. Eisenhower, the 34th president of the United States. In a 1954 speech, Eisenhower quoted an unnamed university president who said, "I have two kinds of problems, the urgent and the important. The urgent are not important, and the important are never urgent."

Fast forward to today, and the prioritization matrix is a task management tool that helps individuals organize their to-do lists based on urgency and importance. Urgent tasks demand immediate attention and have clear consequences if not completed promptly. On the other hand, important tasks may not be urgent but are crucial for achieving your long-term goals.

Let's explore each quadrant of *our newly rebranded Prioritization Matrix,* a.k.a. the R&B Hit List to unlock its full potential in managing your workload.

The Financial Abundance Blueprint

THE R&B HIT LIST
(PRIORITIZATION MATRIX)

High

IMPORTANCE

SCHEDULE "Vision of Love" (Mariah Carey) These tasks are important for your long-term vision but can wait. Schedule them for later, like focusing on the "Vision of Love" for your project's future.	**DO** "Dance with Me" (112) These tasks are mission-critical and require your immediate attention. Get ready to "Dance with Me"! Focus your energy and handle this business right away.
ELIMINATE "No Scrubs" (TLC) These tasks are neither urgent nor important—they're just time wasters. Get rid of them like you would in "No Scrubs." They have no place in your best friend's ride!	**DELEGATE** "Right and a Wrong Way" (Keith Sweat) These tasks are important, but they don't require your superstar skills. Delegate them the "Right Way," clearly communicate expectations, and empower your team to shine!

Low ——————————— URGENCY ——————————— High

Quadrant 1: Do
"Dance with Me" (112)

Demanding immediate attention, Quadrant 1 tasks are the essential *high-importance and urgent* ones. Missing these critical objectives could have significant consequences for your key goals. Often requiring prompt action, they prevent delays or negative impacts on other projects and deadlines. The consequences for missing these well-defined deadlines are clear.

But Quadrant 1 goes beyond immediate needs. These tasks frequently contribute to larger projects and initiatives. Completing them on time keeps the overall project on track. Successfully tackling these high-visibility tasks showcases your skills and reliability, potentially leading to better career opportunities. *So, just as the infectious beat in "Dance with Me" compels you to move, let these top priorities get you grooving!*

Quadrant 2: Schedule
"Vision of Love" (Mariah Carey)

Not urgent, but important, Quadrant 2 tasks are the building blocks of your long-term vision. These tasks contribute to your key objectives but don't require immediate attention. The good news is they're not pressing...yet. Many urgent Quadrant 1 tasks were likely once Quadrant 2 tasks that didn't get scheduled properly.

That's why Quadrant 2 deserves your attention after tackling critical Quadrant 1 tasks. By *scheduling* these important tasks in advance, you take a proactive approach to managing your time and workload. Consider all the things that need to happen to complete tasks in this quadrant and map it out accordingly with proper milestones and deliverables. This prevents them from becoming urgent later and causing stress or last-minute scrambling.

Think of it as crafting a "Vision of Love" for your projects. By dedicating time to them now, you lay the groundwork for future success.

Quadrant 3: Delegate
"Right and a Wrong Way" (Keith Sweat)

Important, but not urgent, Quadrant 3 tasks offer a golden opportunity for delegation. These tasks contribute to your goals but don't require your unique expertise. By effectively delegating them, you free up your time and energy for higher-priority work. Remember, there's a "Right and a Wrong Way" to delegate.

Effective delegation is about more than just assigning tasks. *Clear communication* is essential. Ensure your peers and/or cross-functional partners understand the task's purpose, expectations, and deadlines. Provide them with the resources and support they need to succeed.

Delegation empowers your peers to develop their skills and take ownership. When done right, it's a win-win situation! You free up your time for crucial tasks, and your peers gain valuable experience and confidence. *So don't let these important tasks become a burden; delegate them the "Right Way" and watch your peers shine!*

Quadrant 4: Eliminate
"No Scrubs" (TLC)

Neither urgent nor important, Quadrant 4 tasks are the ultimate *time wasters*. These tasks offer no value and contribute nothing to your goals. They're like "No Scrubs." They have no place in your busy schedule! Ruthlessly eliminate these Quadrant 4 tasks. *Don't be afraid to say "no" to requests that don't align with your priorities.* Remember, nobody's checking to see if these trivial tasks get done.

If you're unsure whether a task belongs in Quadrant 4, consider delegating it. Delegation can free up your time for important work and potentially offer a learning opportunity for another person. This allows you to focus on your goals and achieve greater success!

If you're new to the Prioritization Matrix, give it a try. I'd recommend at the start of every week, map out all your tasks among the four quadrants and see where everything falls. You'll probably be surprised to find out you were spending way too much time on a task that didn't deserve it. Speaking of which, here's my secret weapon for peak productivity: a streamlined, *two-quadrant approach* focused on *planning and delegation*. Let's call it the "R&B Hit List Remixed"! This approach keeps me on top of my game and feeling productive.

THE R&B HIT LIST "REMIXED"
(TWO-QUADRANT PRIORITIZATION MATRIX)

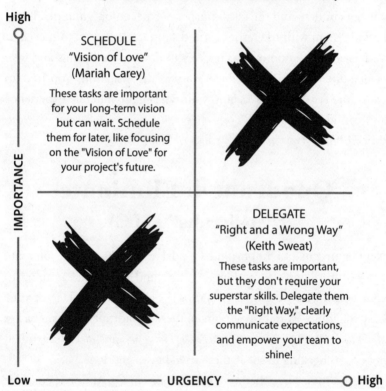

High

IMPORTANCE

SCHEDULE
"Vision of Love"
(Mariah Carey)

These tasks are important for your long-term vision but can wait. Schedule them for later, like focusing on the "Vision of Love" for your project's future.

DELEGATE
"Right and a Wrong Way"
(Keith Sweat)

These tasks are important, but they don't require your superstar skills. Delegate them the "Right Way," clearly communicate expectations, and empower your team to shine!

Low —————— **URGENCY** —————— **High**

Why This Works:

➥ **Self-Awareness Is My Superpower:** Knowing my strengths and weaknesses allows me to accurately estimate task durations. This proactive approach ensures I schedule tasks effectively, avoiding the dreaded "urgent" category altogether.

➥ **The Power of Delegation:** Let's face it, we can't all be superheroes in every situation. That's why delegation is my best friend. By delegating tasks that fall outside my zone of genius, I free up valuable time and energy to focus on what I do best.

➥ **Flow State, Activated:** This system keeps me in a state of *flow*. By minimizing urgency and focusing on tasks that leverage my strengths, I experience reduced stress and heightened productivity.

While the original prioritization matrix is a great tool, the two-quadrant approach can be even more powerful. After you've gotten comfortable with the matrix, *challenge yourself to eliminate "urgency" from your reality altogether, if possible!* Remember, somebody else's poor planning shouldn't become a forced fire drill on your end. By mastering planning and delegation, you can proactively manage your workload and keep stress down, allowing you to navigate the workplace with more ease.

Time Management

Effective time management in the workplace is the pinnacle driving force behind my ability to work smarter, not harder. In this next section, I'm going to break down different ways you can adopt this approach to optimize your workflow. I liken it to being in my groove, listening to my favorite '90s R&B jams on a Walkman.

For my Gen Z friends, a Walkman was the OG portable music player, basically a cassette tape player with headphones, before everything was on our cellphones. The concept behind it? Total

Jams, Zero Distractions. That's exactly the vibe we're going for with these '90s-inspired time management hacks to help you conquer your workday and crush your goals without losing your mind. If you have had much experience in the corporate world, you've probably been on the receiving end of some of these time management hacks. Let me share a few examples:

➵ Have you ever noticed someone's calendar filled from end to end with blocks of time where specific tasks might be described (such as "Weekly Team Meeting" or "Sync with Carol"), while others are marked "Private" or just "Busy"?

➵ Maybe you've tried to book some one-on-one time with a senior leader and had to go through an admin or use a specific appointment booking tool.

➵ Or maybe you couldn't connect with a peer one-on-one because they had DNS, "Do Not Schedule," blocks for an entire day?!

➵ Speaking of which, you might even see blocks on someone's calendar for "Commuting time" as they travel to and from the office.

➵ Oh, and what about those folks whose presence at meetings seems very coveted? They rarely attend, but when they do, they bring something insightful to the conversation.

These are prime examples of slaying time management, where someone is taking control of their schedule to boost productivity and dodge the stress of corporate B.S. I'm not saying you can avoid it all, but you can at least significantly reduce it so you're navigating the workplace with greater ease. Now I'm going to share a few ways you can infuse this strategy for yourself to work smarter and even more systematically!

Calendar Management

Treat your calendar like your ultimate mixtape, carefully curated to maximize focus and minimize distractions. Your calendar isn't just a tool; it's your daily playlist that sets the rhythm for your productivity. By carefully scheduling and protecting your time, you can create a structure that supports your goals and reduces stress.

Part of protecting your time includes leveraging "Do Not Disturb/Schedule" blocks on your calendar. These blocks should be nonnegotiable, allowing you to dive into important tasks without interruptions or at least be able to take a lunch break in peace. An alternative is to create "Ask Before Scheduling" blocks, which may feel more inviting if the idea of setting these boundaries makes you anxious. It's like having uninterrupted listening time to your favorite album. Pure focus and pure productivity was one of the benefits of the Walkman, in which listening to your music was the only option!

Lastly, consider leveraging appointment slots or direct booking methods to streamline scheduling and avoid the cycle of recurring social meetings that may not be the best use of time. This allows you to prioritize meaningful engagements while efficiently managing your time.

Meeting Etiquette and Saying No

Think of this as hitting the "pause button" on unproductive meetings. Unnecessary meetings can drain your energy and steal precious time. By politely declining, you free up your schedule for projects that truly need your expertise. This is a powerful move that allows you to prioritize your most important tasks and avoid getting bogged down in meetings that don't contribute to your goals.

That said, declining meetings can feel daunting, especially early in your career. However, it's a powerful skill that can save you significant time and mental energy. Plus, we've all attended a meeting that could have been an email or we simply felt like a pointless fly on the wall. It's always a great idea to confirm the meeting's purpose and agenda with the meeting organizer. If your presence isn't crucial, peace out and focus on tasks that matter. This helps ensure your time is used efficiently and that your presence truly adds value. It also sends a message that you value your time and the time of others, and helps establish a culture for others to do the same.

Flow State

Understanding when and how you work best is crucial for achieving a state of flow. It's not just about managing your calendar but optimizing your workflow to match your natural productivity rhythms. Identify your most productive times and the environments that enhance your concentration, then create these ideal conditions. Schedule focused work sessions during peak times, minimize distractions, and be clear about what your environment needs to help you stay in the "zone" and produce your best results.

To maintain your flow, manage interruptions by closing unnecessary tabs, muting notifications, and arranging your workspace to support focus. Additionally, communicate your preferences and boundaries with your manager and teammates to ensure a conducive work environment. (We'll delve into this further in Track 8.) For me, staying intensely focused means blasting "The Show Goes On" by Lupe Fiasco on repeat and tackling my heaviest tasks in the evenings, as I'm a night owl. Yes, I recognize this is "outside normal working hours," so I make sure to set up my day and calendar to support my personal flow state, and that's all I'll say on that.

Work-Life Balance

Effective time management isn't just about work. By scheduling personal time and maintaining boundaries, you avoid burnout and create a healthy work-life balance. Just as you'd set time aside to listen to your favorite tunes, set time aside for activities that recharge you! This means not only scheduling breaks and leisure activities but also

The Financial Abundance Blueprint

being firm about not letting work encroach on your personal time. Be proactive in communicating your boundaries with your manager and peers and try to stand firm on them. If you don't honor your boundaries, neither will your colleagues.

Organization

Effective time management is only as powerful as the organization that supports it, ensuring that your productivity strategies are complemented by a well-structured environment and systematic approach. Keeping your work life organized is key to navigating the corporate world with ease and efficiency. One effective strategy is to "templatize" your work processes. By creating reusable templates for such tasks as presentations, reports, and emails, you streamline your workflow and focus more on content rather than formatting. This not only ensures consistency in your work output but also saves valuable time that can be better spent refining your message for specific audiences. Remember, not everything needs to be reinvented every time; embrace the power of rinse and repeat!

Maintaining a well-structured digital and physical filing system is another essential organizational tactic. Digitally, organize your files into clearly labeled folders with intuitive naming conventions for quick retrieval. Use bookmarks or tab groupings to manage frequently accessed websites or links efficiently. Similarly, keep your physical workspace clutter-free by sorting and filing papers, using trays or folders to categorize ongoing projects and reference materials. A tidy workspace promotes productivity and fosters a clear mindset conducive to effective decision-making and task execution. After all, time is precious, and maximizing it to the fullest is paramount for success in the corporate world.

Abundant Career Chronicle:
Elevating Recurring One-to-Ones
to Purposeful Connections

As a mentor and advocate for junior employees of color in my workplace, I often find myself in the role of guiding others through their professional journeys. After our initial sessions, many express a desire for more frequent meetings. Initially, I embraced these requests, setting aside dedicated time on my calendar for monthly catchups. Thursdays became my go-to, with back-to-back sessions filling my calendar. I wanted to be a reliable resource, an "Auntie" to others in the company, providing support and guidance to those who needed it most.

However, over time, what started as structured mentorship sessions often morphed into casual chats without a clear agenda. While I cherished these connections, I began to realize that these impromptu meetings, sometimes lasting hours, were draining my time and energy. As a busy professional balancing multiple responsibilities, I knew I needed to reclaim control over my schedule.

This realization prompted a significant shift in how I approached mentorship. I transitioned from automatically scheduling recurring meetings to setting up appointment slots on my calendar. Now, colleagues interested in connecting with me must take the initiative to book a one-on-one session. This change ensured that those seeking mentorship were intentional about their needs, coming prepared with specific agenda items and situations they wanted help with navigating.

While this shift meant some colleagues may have fallen out of touch, I've come to understand the importance of prioritizing my own well-being and productivity. I've learned the importance of setting boundaries and safeguarding my time. After all, being productive doesn't mean saying yes to everything. It's about making intentional choices that support my personal and professional growth. So, in the rare event my schedule does get packed, I'm committed to making every minute of it count.

tFAB in Action: Cultivating Your Productivity Systems for Workplace Success

This Track's tFAB in Action moment has been about cultivating your productivity system so you're set up to thrive in your 9-to-5 job. Because when we navigate the corporate world with ease, we minimize stress and maximize impact, allowing us to focus on what truly matters: leveraging those corporate coins for financial freedom and work-optional status. Here are your action items:

Create Your R&B Hit List: Start by listing and categorizing your weekly tasks into the four quadrants of the prioritization matrix: Do, Schedule, Delegate, and Delete. Focus on closing out your Do tasks first, then prioritize tasks in the Schedule quadrant to prevent them from becoming urgent. Delegate or delete tasks that don't align with your priorities.

Templatize Your Work Outputs: Streamline your workflow by creating templates for recurring tasks, such as presentations and reports.

Optimize Your Calendar: Take control of your schedule by creating dedicated time blocks for priority tasks. Use appointment slots for one-on-one connections. Be selective about attending meetings, prioritizing those with clear agendas that demonstrate your need to be present.

Organize Your Workspaces: Maintain clear digital and physical filing systems for efficient document management, whether it's organizing your digital files into labeled folders or decluttering your physical workspace with trays and folders!

Evaluate and Adjust: Regularly review and adjust your time management strategies based on feedback and evolving priorities. Stay adaptable and open to change, continuously refining your approach to ensure continued efficiency and effectiveness in your work.

NAVIGATING YOUR CORPORATE ENVIRONMENT

INTERLUDE: THE EMBODY FRAMEWORK

As a new mother, I often marvel at the simple yet profound act of watching my son learn to walk. Each wobbly step he takes reminds me of the journey we all undertake in life, navigating through unfamiliar terrain, facing challenges, and striving for growth. It's fascinating how toddlers approach this milestone with a fearless determination, stumbling and falling, yet always getting back up to try again. And while their innocence shields them from the weight of failure, they still rely on the guidance and support of their parents or guardians to navigate this significant milestone.

When my son took his first steps, it was a monumental moment for him, a game-changer in his young life. I can only imagine the mix of excitement and trepidation he felt, eager to explore this new skill but also fearful of the unknown. As he stumbled and sometimes fell, causing moments of panic, he persisted, fueled by his innate curiosity and the assurance of having mommy and daddy there to guide him.

Reflecting on this journey, I see parallels between my son's experience and the challenges many of us face as first-generation college graduates and ambitious professionals navigating the corporate world. My son had the unwavering support of his parents to guide him through the process of learning to walk, but many of us lack that same level of guidance as we navigate the complexities of our careers.

For my son, having mommy and daddy to guide him meant he could learn to walk faster and with less risk. Success seemed almost guaranteed, as long as his legs worked and he had someone to catch him if he stumbled. Yet, as adults, many of us find ourselves navigating the corporate landscape with little to no guidance, relying on trial and error to find our way.

This lack of guidance can have profound implications for our careers, hindering our ability to reach our full potential and achieve our goals. Without a clear roadmap or mentorship, we may find ourselves stumbling along, unsure of which direction to take or how to overcome obstacles.

Just as my son's journey to walking required guidance, so too does our journey through the corporate world. With the right support and mindset, we can navigate the challenges ahead and stride confidently toward our goals.

Abundant Career Chronicle: DEI and the Family Workshop

During my tenure at Google, I spearheaded a workshop around diversity, equity, and inclusion, titled "DEI & the Family." This workshop was deeply personal to me, as it allowed me to intertwine my journey as a first-generation college graduate and corporate professional with my identity as a Millennial Black woman. The workshop aimed to shed light on the intricacies of my background and how it shapes my presence and experiences in the corporate space.

The workshop began with an exploration of the evolving dynamics of modern families. We moved beyond the conventional nuclear household model to embrace the diverse structures that define families today. As a first-generation college student, I shared my experience of navigating higher education, particularly at an Ivy League institution. We watched a poignant media piece featuring four students from varied backgrounds, all grappling with their identities while navigating the challenges of academia.

I then shared my personal journey with the participants, highlighting the challenges I faced similar to those students. Despite my determination to succeed, I lacked crucial guidance on navigating college life. For instance, I didn't realize the importance of connecting with professors during office hours until much later in my academic journey. My experience underscored the significance of mentorship and guidance, especially for individuals like myself who were charting unfamiliar territory.

Throughout college, I juggled multiple jobs to alleviate the financial burden on my family. Despite the hardships, I persevered, securing internships at renowned companies such as Disney, Viacom, and Verizon. However, transitioning into full-time employment posed its own set of challenges, resetting many of the lessons I had learned along the way.

As I concluded the workshop, I emphasized the enduring wealth gap and financial literacy challenges faced by many individuals, even after securing well-paying jobs. My journey served as a testament to the ongoing struggle to bridge these economic disparities and empower future generations to thrive in the corporate world and ultimately in the area of their finances to close the wealth gap, which so greatly differs in communities of color vs. white counterparts.

So, why do I share that example? Because we're about to embark on a roadmap for navigating your workplace. The reason I'm so passionate about the EMBODY Framework I've built is because guidance often makes the difference in achieving success. As I reflect on my university experience, I realize I lacked guidance, despite my parents doing their best with what they had. It was up to me to figure things out and push forward. However, I've witnessed cycles in families where individuals almost break free but face setbacks. Determined to progress, I've spent a decade learning invaluable lessons and strategies for navigating the corporate world as a Melanated Millennial Corporate Queen. Yet, these lessons were learned sporadically, and at times, I wish I hadn't needed to learn them on my own, the hard way. The EMBODY Framework is my way of distilling everything I've learned into an easy-to-understand guide; in fact, putting those "unwritten rules" down on paper. Unwritten they shall be no more! I want you, my fellow ambitious Black women, first-gen college grads, and young professionals of color, to take this framework and apply it step by step, starting from the moment you accept your first job offer.

The EMBODY Framework

The EMBODY Framework is a simple yet powerful guide on how to effectively navigate the workplace. We'll dive deep into each core area, ensuring you gain a thorough understanding of its principles. But let me provide you with a high-level overview of what this framework entails and the reflections you'll encounter along the way.

Now, you know how in the corporate world everything seems to have an acronym? Well, the EMBODY Framework is no exception. Although, I'll admit, it's a bit unconventional, as we work through it from bottom to top, a unique approach that may seem a tad confusing at first glance. But trust me, it's intentional, as we build upon foundational elements that are applied later on:

THE EMBODY FRAMEWORK

(E) verything and Everybody Else

(M) anaging Up, Across, and Beyond

(B) oard

(O) f

(D) irectors

(Y) our Performance

(Y) Your Performance

"Y" stands for Your performance: the very reason you were hired and the key to receiving your paycheck every two weeks. Unfortunately, many early-career professionals, especially those from disenfranchised backgrounds, lack clarity when it comes to performance management in the corporate world. There has been a generational shift in what it means to excel at work and fulfill your responsibilities. We'll delve deeper into this later, but the main takeaway is the importance of setting yourself up for success by delivering on your commitments and understanding how to achieve work-life harmony, whatever that may mean to you.

(B) (O) (D) Your Board Of Directors

"BOD" stands for your Board Of Directors, a.k.a. your professional tribe at work. These are the individuals who are invested in your success and play a crucial role in supporting you along your career journey. You can use any term you prefer to refer to these individuals, but the bottom line is that maintaining a strong professional network is essential. As the saying goes, "It's not just what you know, but who you know," and this holds true in navigating the ever-evolving job market. Your network can significantly impact your career trajectory, so nurturing these relationships is vital for long-term success.

Ⓜ Managing Up, Across, and Beyond

"M" stands for Managing Up, Across, and Beyond, also known as aligning your impact with the priorities of your leadership and peers. Think of it as self-advocacy and personal branding taken to the next level. While your work should ideally speak for itself, the reality is that your manager has numerous responsibilities beyond just overseeing your work. This section focuses on how you can ensure that the narrative you want about your contributions is effectively communicated to your leadership. It's about strategically managing your relationships with superiors and peers to ensure your value is recognized and your impact drives organizational goals.

Ⓔ Everybody and Everything Else

"E" stands for Everybody and Everything Else. This section encompasses various aspects of corporate dynamics that may not neatly fit into the previous categories. It's where we address miscellaneous topics, including the nuances of corporate politics. Additionally, it's crucial to focus on tasks such as updating your resume and LinkedIn profile, expanding your professional network beyond your Board Of Directors, and gaining clarity on your future career trajectory.

There you have the core of the EMBODY Framework. As I stepped into the corporate world in 2014, I quickly realized that success wasn't solely about merit; there were unwritten rules dictating how to navigate one's career. It's an unfair reality. The challenges faced by companies often stem from not having the best talents excel in these spaces. Simply getting there isn't sufficient; understanding the game's rules is crucial for effective play.

And let's not forget, the Financial Abundance Blueprint is tailored for young adults who rely on their career as their main source of income. A significant portion of this blueprint revolves around mastering the corporate landscape because, truth be told, if we can't sustain and increase our 9-to-5 income, our ability to generate wealth diminishes. This book is crafted with all my Corporate Queens in mind. Now, let's dive into the first topic of the EMBODY Framework, which revolves around Performance Management. Turn on Track 6!

MASTERING PERFORMANCE MANAGEMENT

So, you got the job offer—yay! We love that for you! But now the real journey begins as you prepare to start in just two weeks. You probably have a lot of things top of mind, such as: Will you like your new team? Are you ready to learn a new corporate culture? Can you actually do the job? That last question can feel daunting, but it's a common concern.

There's often a disconnect between what's written in the job description and what you'll be held accountable for once you start. Plus, Corporate America is ever evolving, with team transitions, layoffs, and sometimes a new manager within your first month. Despite this uncertainty, there are strategies to remain in control of your performance and ensure you're focusing on what truly matters. As I often say, there's a huge difference between being productive versus being busy. In Corporate America, it's not hard to look busy, but are you really getting the important work done?

Often, we see that the busiest people, people we call the "Top Performers," are the ones getting passed up for promotions. However, this isn't just a fluke; there's a reason behind it. We'll touch upon this more in Track 8 as it relates to Managing Up, Across, and Beyond, but there's a more crucial step that needs to be addressed first. We must start with performance management as the foundation of our EMBODY Framework for navigating the corporate workplace, because everything stems from that. There's a common saying from one of my previous employers that resonates in this moment: "Focus on your core, then the more."

In your early days at a new job, there are a few core questions you need to prioritize getting answers to:

1. Do you understand the job you were hired for?

2. Who does what well on your team?

3. What is your manager's definition of a job well done?

During your first 30-60-90 days, you'll want to focus on answering these questions to lay a solid foundation for your performance management. Let's break these down because understanding the *why* behind performance management is crucial before diving into the *how*.

1. Understanding Your Role: As we said above, there's often a gap between what's written in the job description and what's actually expected day-to-day. Performance management hinges on having a clear understanding of your role to ensure you're productive rather than just busy. Often, "top performers" in the workplace don't get promoted as fast as others because they're over-indexing in busyness rather than targeted productivity. Knowing your job inside and out helps you streamline your efforts and shine where it counts.

2. Knowing Your Team Dynamics: Understanding who does what well on your team is crucial. Even if you're unclear about your own role, someone else on the team might have similar responsibilities and can offer guidance. Earlier Tracks focused on identifying your superpowers and skills, but it's equally important to leverage the strengths of those around you. Success in the workplace isn't just about what you know, but also who you know and how their knowledge can support your journey.

3. Aligning with Your Manager's Expectations: Understanding your manager's definition of a job well done is key. Your standards might differ from theirs, and aligning these expectations is crucial for your success and well-being. This alignment ensures that you meet or exceed their expectations in a sustainable way, positioning you favorably for future opportunities.

Abundant Career Chronicle: My First Two Weeks as a Verizon Intern

Let me take you back to the spring of 2013, where I found myself sitting in my dorm room at the University of Pennsylvania (UPenn), anxiously contemplating my future. As many of you know, the internship you secure during the summer before your senior year often becomes your gateway to full-time employment. For me, this was particularly critical because I had accumulated over $40,000 in student loans to attend this prestigious Ivy League university. I had already interned at BET Networks via Viacom the previous summer, but I decided not to return there. Time was running out, and despite applying to numerous positions, nothing seemed to stick. The internship recruiting process at UPenn was intense, like interviewing on steroids.

Little did I know that things were about to turn around in a way I couldn't have imagined. I had applied for a marketing internship at Verizon, being a die-hard marketing major. Unfortunately, I didn't get the marketing position. However, they offered me an internship on a different team, the Operational Excellence Team. Looking back, this was the best thing that could have happened to me. Having an operations background has been invaluable in my career. This is why I emphasize productivity and efficiency so much—it's rooted in operations. However, at the time, I had no idea what Operational Excellence entailed, but I embraced the opportunity wholeheartedly.

This internship had a unique summer camp vibe, with many interns, especially from minority backgrounds, living together in a dorm. Half of the interns came from a college in Puerto Rico, which was a fantastic cultural exchange. I even improved my Spanish that summer! Enter Mr. Chu, my manager. He was incredibly smart, and while I didn't know what his expectations were of me initially, I knew I had to excel because my future student loan payments depended on securing a full-time job!

I was assigned a project involving documentation around text analytics software, essentially decoding customer sentiments and emotions from written responses, which reminds me of early AI and ChatGPT technology and gives me a chuckle as I recall this experience now. I dove into the project, working diligently, and to my surprise, I completed it within the first month. This was an assignment Mr. Chu expected to take most of the summer, from June to August.

Imagine the shock, both mine and his, when I delivered a high-quality work product so quickly. It was a lesson in performance management that I hadn't yet mastered. There's a balance in under-promising and over-delivering without being excessive. Throughout my years in corporate, I've learned that projects often take longer because the team is managing performance strategically, ensuring they meet expectations while pacing themselves appropriately.

Despite this early misstep in performance management, I thoroughly enjoyed my internship. I forged lasting friendships thanks to the summer camp atmosphere, and finishing my project early allowed me to dive into numerous Learning and Development trainings, sparking my interest in the L&D space. I also got involved in Employee Resource Group initiatives, expanding my network early on. Being recognized as a superstar early on also didn't hurt when it came to securing a return offer.

Looking back, I wish I had known the performance management strategies I'm about to share with you. It would have certainly influenced how I approached my internship. But, in the end, it all worked out, and the lessons I learned have been invaluable. Now, let's dive into those key strategies that will help you navigate performance management effectively in your own careers.

For first-gen young adults or corporate professionals from minority backgrounds like myself, there are truly unwritten rules to corporate life, particularly in the critical area of performance management. To help put pen to paper on these unwritten rules, I've created a tool that I call PAGES (Prioritization Alignment, Growth, Effort ÷ Skills).

PAGES will serve as your guide to mastering performance management in the corporate environment. This tool will break down the essential elements you need to focus on to excel in your role and navigate your career path effectively. As a quick aside, in the corporate workplace, you should document everything (I call it "keeping *pages* of your receipts," which we'll talk more about that later). Now, back to the topic at hand: performance! Here's the game-changing formula for performance management:

> **Performance Management = Prioritization Alignment * Growth * (Effort ÷ Skills)**

Prioritization Alignment

Performance management boils down to how well you align yourself with the most critical tasks, projects, or initiatives set by your manager or senior leadership. It's about taking ownership and accountability for what you prioritize and when you tackle it. Think of it as curating the perfect playlist; you want to make sure you're jamming to the right tunes at the right time.

Ensuring alignment with your priorities is crucial to avoid burning out on tasks that nobody really cares about. Imagine being known as the go-getter who always has a dozen things on their plate. I once had a white peer and ally tell me, "Amanda, you're doing so much! Why not drop a couple of those tasks for a month and see if anyone notices?" Spoiler alert: nobody did. While this might not be your exact experience, it's a common challenge for many young women of color in the corporate world.

We've all heard stories of colleagues drowning in their workload, taking on more and more tasks without considering their own bandwidth. The issue often lies in neglecting the crucial aspect of prioritization alignment in performance management. I've been there too, with new projects added to my already overflowing plate or being asked to pick up the slack for a struggling team member.

But here's the thing: You have the power to push back. The next time your manager wants to add something to your plate, try responding with, "Thank you, [manager's name], for considering me for this opportunity. I would love to help the team out. However, I'm already at capacity with my current projects. Could you help me understand which items I should deprioritize to make space for this new initiative?" This response not only keeps you in control but also showcases your prioritization skills, a must-have for any Corporate Queen who aims to navigate the workplace with ease. It also puts the decision back in your manager's hands to provide clarity on how you should be spending your time; because everything can't be a priority!

The Process for Establishing or Regaining Alignment in Your Priorities

1. Start by jotting down your priorities for the month, but limit yourself to no more than 10. If you're juggling more than that, chances are some items don't belong on your list. Let's differentiate between being busy and being productive. Write down everything so we can assess what's on your plate.

2. Once you have your list, define the objectives for each item. What does success look like? Ensure your objectives are quantifiable with timelines. Remember the SMART goal-setting acronym: Specific, Measurable, Actionable, Realistic, and Time-bound.

3. Identify the stakeholders who care about each priority. This could include your manager, your skip-level manager (i.e., your manager's manager), or cross-functional stakeholders from other teams. Knowing who's invested in each task helps you understand its importance.

4. Provide a status update for each item. Are you just starting, in progress, or completed? Since most items will likely be in progress, consider adding a secondary indicator to track progress more precisely.

5. Reprioritize your list. The most critical items should be at the top, while the less important ones should be lower down. This exercise helps you focus on what truly matters.

6. Bonus: Map out your list using the R&B Hit List Prioritization Matrix we learned about in Track 4, to help put a visual to your analysis.

Now that you've got your list ready, it's time to tackle that one-on-one with your manager. You might find that some tasks disappear, others get handed off to someone else, or you realize you're further along than you thought on a project. Also, it wouldn't hurt to bring your R&B Hit List Prioritization Matrix to serve as a visual aid behind your recommendations on how you prioritize your tasks moving forward! But no matter what, after that chat, you should feel both clearer and more confident about where to put your energy.

For bonus points, take your top five items to your next quarterly one-on-one with your skip-level manager. Discuss how your priorities align with theirs, showcasing your proactive approach to drive organizational goals, and to get on their radar. With clarity on your prioritization drive toward organizational goals, you're ready to move on to the next aspect of our Performance Management formula.

Growth

When it comes to Performance Management, the growth aspect is about how your current role and the projects you're working on align with your long-term career goals. Early in my career, I approached my work as a Jill of all trades, a spin on the quote, "Jack of all trades, master of none, but oftentimes better than master of one." This means having a broad range of abilities rather than being an expert in just one area. I leaned into this mentality heavily, acquiring as many skills and corporate experiences as possible to build my skillset. Eventually, I shifted from a "Jill of all trades" generalist to a specialist as I advanced in my career and became a Senior Corporate Queen myself. This growth aspect seeks to answer the following question: As you tackle a role or a specific project, what are you seeking to gain from the experience?

For example, when I started at Google as an account strategist in sales, I knew I was there for a good time, not a long time. To advance as a senior marketing professional (my original career north star), I needed sales experience. My goal was to learn what I could about sales, acquire relevant skills, and add them to my overall marketing résumé. I focused on hitting quotas, not becoming an expert at sales.

If my goal had been to become a sales manager, I would have taken the role more seriously. Well, the joke was on me since I ended up pivoting into Sales Enablement and the Learning and Development space instead. But hey, everything always works out in the end...right?

Knowing my career north star helped me focus my efforts. This clarity allowed me to navigate the corporate landscape strategically rather than getting bogged down with tasks that didn't serve my ultimate career aspirations. I made a conscious decision to avoid extra projects that didn't align with my long-term marketing goals at the time, even if they seemed like great opportunities on the surface. This approach meant saying no to certain assignments or initiatives, even if they were prestigious or came with high visibility. It's about playing the long game and understanding that not every opportunity is the right opportunity.

Many people in the workplace fall into the trap of taking their jobs too seriously when, in reality, these roles are often just stepping stones. They invest all their energy into every task, trying to excel at everything, which can lead to burnout and a feeling of being overwhelmed. It's crucial to recognize that not every project needs to be a career-defining experience. Sometimes, the role you're in is simply a means to an end, a way to gain valuable experience, earn a paycheck, and build a network that will support you in your future endeavors.

Now that we have our priority-aligned list that's manager-approved, let's do a growth reflection exercise:

1. Identify Your Top Three Projects: Start by pinpointing the top three projects you're currently working on. These should be the ones that hold the most weight in your day-to-day responsibilities.

2. Assess for Growth Opportunities: Do any of these projects provide natural opportunities for you to grow in a skill set that aligns with your long-term career trajectory? Reflect on each project and determine if there's a chance to develop a specific skill that will be beneficial for your future goals. This would be a good time to revisit your PSA output from Track 2 for inspiration and direction.

3. Set Specific Growth Goals: If a project does offer a growth opportunity, write down the specific skill sets you can develop. Then, assign a growth goal for each one. Be clear about what you want to achieve and how this project will help you get there.

4. Evaluate Your Current Circumstances: Decide whether your current personal circumstances enable you to take on these growth goals at this moment. Consider your workload, personal life, and overall capacity.

5. Update Your PDP (Professional Development Plan): If you're in a position to pursue these growth goals, add them to your PDP. A PDP is a personalized roadmap, typically created in collaboration with your manager, that outlines goals, skills, and strategies to support your career growth and professional development within an organization. Outline the steps you'll take to achieve these goals and the timeline for each.

6. Acknowledge and Revisit If Necessary: If you find that you're not currently able to take on these growth goals, acknowledge it to yourself. Be okay with your decision and plan to revisit it later when your circumstances might be more favorable.

I can imagine that step four of this growth reflection exercise caught some of you off guard. We're fortunate to live in a time where we can have authentic conversations about balancing our careers and our personal lives. Historically, Performance Management made us believe we must do everything our manager says, regardless of our well-being. The growth element is crucial because it provides space for humanity in this conversation. Let's explore a couple quick examples of what this looks like in practice:

➡ **Growth Activated:** Jane oversees the launch of new software as a program manager, involving four sub-projects with cross-functional teams. She aspires to be a People Manager. Jane will use this opportunity to develop skills in providing written feedback and influencing others—critical for her career goals.

➥ **Growth Deactivated:** Jane is in the same program manager role but has taken on caregiving responsibilities for her nephew for the next six months. Jane focuses on completing her assignments and takes on nothing more during this time. In six months, Jane plans to have a PDP conversation with her manager about stretch opportunities when she'll be in a position to take them on.

In summary, taking these steps ensures that you're always moving forward, whether by actively developing new skills or by planning for future growth when the time is right. This structured approach helps you stay focused on your career trajectory while balancing your current responsibilities and personal well-being. It's okay to go above and beyond on certain projects if it aligns with your long-term goals. But it's also okay to acknowledge when you don't have the capacity or desire to do more. Once we align our priorities and growth goals with our work, we can move on to the next crucial aspect: the contrast of efforts and skills.

Effort ÷ Skills

This is going to be the biggest game-changer in how you approach your career. As a recovering workaholic turned top performer with ease, let me tell you, it is so important to understand the effort required to get the job done and how your skills align with that. It's the reason we began this book focusing on your self-awareness as the key. Because once you know your own superpowers, your strengths, and your kryptonite, the way you see every future work assignment will shift!

Let's get into Effort ÷ Skills. What do we really mean when we say that? Given that we already know our top five priorities and where we want to gain more experience, we're now in a place to be very intentional about how we get the work done. Before I get into the ABCs of Workload Execution, it is time for another Abundant Chronicle. And this one, y'all, when I was going through it, it hit home.

||||||||||||||||||||||||||||||||||||||||||||||||||||||||||||||||||||||||||||||||||||||||||||||||||||||||||||||||||||||||||||||||||||||||||||||||||||||

Abundant Career Chronicle:
Miss Doin' Too Much

Imagine walking into a conference room with your manager after a promotion cycle, only to hear that you didn't have to do everything you did to get promoted. I wish I were making this story up, but unfortunately, it's true. Let me backtrack real quick.

After joining Google as an account strategist in sales, it quickly became apparent that I was under-leveled. I was surrounded by some great people, but the majority of them were only a few years removed from college. Here I was with years of experience under my belt and only a few classes away from completing my master's degree.

Anyways, I joined the organization and got to work. I figured out my approach to the role and was quickly seeing success. Thankfully, I also had some great people in my corner, and that led to my next role. After six months in the first role, I made a lateral move to the Accelerated Growth Team and quickly established myself as a Top Performer. I was doing anything and everything they threw my way. I wanted to get promoted quickly because being more senior on a sales team meant a larger commission percentage. I was already killing it, so in my mind, I was leaving money on the table until I got my leveling up.

Needless to say, I was crushing my sales quota while doing fifty-eleven side projects just to build up my portfolio. Meanwhile, my peers were doing less than half as much. And well...y'all know what happens next....We all get promoted. Yay! Celebrations...right?!

Well, now we can go back to when I walked into the conference room to hear the news officially from my manager. Of course, he's excited to share the good news, and heck, so am I...I want to know what that new money is going to look like. At this point in my financial independence journey, I was already debt-free, so the increase would be going toward accelerating my financial goals. But yeah...he shares the numbers and then he says, "You know, Amanda, you didn't have to do all that to get promoted...I mean, it definitely didn't hurt, but it wasn't necessary." To which I replied something along the lines of, "Yeah...that sounds good...but I'm not sure if I believe you."

Keep in mind, my manager was a real one, super supportive of me, always gave me credit and moments to shine, and was truly invested in my success. That said, I'm sure I took a minute or two to educate him on the nuanced realities of being a Black woman in Corporate America. At the end of the day, we'll never know if I was doing too much or just enough vs. my peers. But I did learn a valuable lesson that I've since transformed into the ABCs of Workload Execution.

The ABCs of Workload Execution

Let's delve into our ABC's of Workload Execution, a benchmark for determining how much effort you need to exert in relation to the skills you've acquired over time; the final piece of our performance management equation. In case you forgot, let me refresh your memory:

PERFORMANCE MANAGEMENT (PAGES)

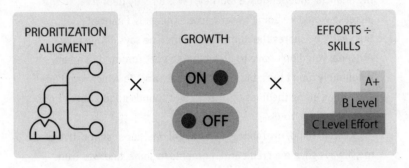

There's a quote out there that says you're not paying me for the time it takes me to get the job done; you're paying me for the years of experience I've acquired that allow me to do the job efficiently. This idea resonated with me when I made a (perhaps) controversial video in 2024, stitching together a clip from another content creator who questioned why we still give 100 percent effort at these jobs.

At the time, there was a lot of talk about burnout in the workplace. People were working extra hard, putting in long hours, and the paychecks didn't necessarily add up to the effort. Moreover, because of layoffs in recent years, folks were feeling extra insecure and thus were giving far more to their jobs than what they were getting back. Not to mention, raises were averaging around 2 to 3 percent, so the math was not adding up.

In my response video, I highlighted how depending on tenure in your career vs. understanding of your skills vs. having clarity on your priorities, that you likely do not need to give these jobs 100 percent of your effort. And this is not to be confused with providing subpar output. Again, as a recovering perfectionist and workaholic known for execution excellence, it's important to understand that execution excellence does not mean burning out in your role or giving 100 percent. It's about applying everything we've covered thus far and putting it into action.

This is why we say, "effort divided by skills." Once you have your priorities in alignment and understand the growth aspect, you're left to determine how much effort you need to exert, and that is a function of your skill set as it relates to those first two items. Those of us who are more tenured in our careers and working in roles that are in alignment with what we're great at will find that our acquired skills make tasks easier to execute. Hence, my execution excellence may only require 50 percent of my effort due to my skill set, while someone newer into their role or career overall may need to give closer to 100 percent. It's crucial to understand these first two buckets to decide what level of output and effort is required of you.

The ABCs of Workload Execution reference my high school days, and given that Corporate America often feels like a school popularity contest anyway, it kind of makes sense. The question I want you to ask yourself when you bring this whole equation together is: What level of output is required of me at this time? Your answer may also depend on whether you want to climb the corporate ladder or have specific timelines in mind for a promotion, etc. Either way, you'll want to tap into our ABCs...as easy as 123....You see what I did there?!

ABC Workload Execution Benchmark

Imagine you were to stay in your role at your current company. What does success look like? Using my ABC framework, define What it means to earn a C, a.k.a. doing the bare minimum requirements. What does B level output look like, a.k.a. going above and beyond? Finally, what does A level output look like, a.k.a. being the blueprint for others to follow and ultimately demonstrating consistently that you're promotion ready?

C Level: Just as in high school, the question becomes: What is necessary to pass the class, or in this case, to simply meet expectations? This can often be seen as doing the bare minimum or, alternatively, quietly quitting your job. But if you have your priorities in alignment, and you're very clear on the growth you want to pursue from this initiative or the lack thereof, you're really just answering the simple question: What do you need to do consistently every single day to not get fired? I get it; for recovering perfectionists, workaholics, and top performers like myself, the idea of just doing the bare minimum may seem foreign and unnatural. But it's important that you at least understand what this would look like in case your situation changes and you need to pull back for a little bit just because of your personal life or to protect your mental health.

B Level: Once you've defined C level, now we take it up a notch. What would it look like to go above and beyond within reason? I think of this as doing what's expected of you and adding a little razzle-dazzle on top. This could look like hitting all of your project goals but doing it in a shorter time frame or without needing all of the resources you were provided. At this stage, you're being seen as a solid contributor, someone with potential for leadership on the team, but again, you're doing this on your terms without the burnout. You get to decide how much you want to go above and beyond because, again, you've mapped this out and made yourself a playbook to decide how you want to execute and, more importantly, when and how often.

A Level: At this stage, you know what the bare minimum looks like, and you know what it means to do a little B+ razzle-dazzle. Defining what A level should look like is key to mapping out your entire journey and career goals. A-level work is what you'll want to preserve for promotion time or when you want that new leadership position. And more importantly, when you want to signify growth and your ability to perform at the next level. This is when you are essentially pulling out all the stops!

As you engage in this exercise of defining your output levels, strive for specificity and practicality and consider quantifying your efforts to make things crystal clear. For instance, if you're in sales, you might outline a specific number of sales calls or aim for a percentage attainment ranging from 100 percent to 300 percent, hypothetically speaking.

The reason behind delineating these three levels is crucial. If you come out swinging at the A level within your first 30 days, you risk setting yourself up for failure or burnout. Promotion and leadership opportunities are often extended to individuals demonstrating influence, authority, and potential for growth. Starting with the bar set too high may inadvertently constrain your future progression. I've had countless conversations with members of the LITA community expressing frustration due to feeling boxed in by their early success. Remember, when stepping into a new role there's a season of onboarding for a reason. Whether you're being formally trained or not, there's typically a grace period of 30 to 90 days for acclimation. Use this time to familiarize yourself with your role, meet your team, and understand the workflow. While it's important to seek small wins to establish your brand, going too hard too soon might set an unrealistic standard that could be challenging to sustain in the long run with unintended consequences.

So there you have it. PAGES is your new favorite acronym as you strategize your performance, or the Y of our EMBODY Framework:

> ### Performance = Prioritization Alignment
> ### * Growth * (Effort ÷ Skills)

But wait! We need to dive into the dual significance of PAGES. While it's our powerful framework for enhancing performance management, it also emphasizes the importance of documentation, or as I like to call it, keeping your receipts! Maintaining documentation of your work and how you accomplish tasks is crucial. The aim is to ensure that all of us Corporate Queens are recognized and rewarded not just for what we achieve but also for our collaborative spirit and approach to work. Now, let's discuss a few valuable resources to help us keep our PAGES always up to date.

Let's talk about the importance of documenting your career journey, or as I like to call it, your Abundant Accomplishments. There are several key reasons why this matters, and here are a few that come to mind:

1. Résumé Updates: With the multitude of tasks and projects you'll undertake in your role, it's vital to keep a record of your accomplishments. This makes it easier to update your résumé when needed, ensuring you don't overlook significant contributions you've made to the business. Even seemingly small projects could be relevant for specific job opportunities in the future.

2. Cover Your A\$\$ (CYA): Apologies for the blunt language, but it's crucial, especially for people of color in the workplace. Despite efforts to improve racial equity and experiences, the reality is that we're not there yet. Having a documented record of your achievements and proof of negative incidents helps protect you in case of discrepancies or misunderstandings.

3. Promotion and Salary Discussions: When it comes to advocating for yourself in discussions about promotion or salary increases, having concrete evidence to back up your claims is essential. Simply stating that you deserve a promotion or a raise without any supporting and quantifiable evidence won't be as effective. Your documented accomplishments provide impactful proof of your worth to the organization.

By maintaining an Abundant Accomplishments record, you not only ensure that you're recognized for your hard work but also empower yourself in career advancement discussions. It's a proactive approach that sets you up for success in navigating your professional journey. Here are a couple of options I recommend, but feel free to choose what aligns best with your preferences. The key is to establish a system or process that allows you to be consistent in documenting your accomplishments:

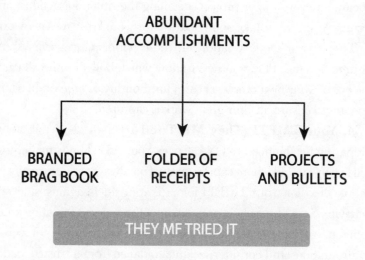

ABUNDANT
ACCOMPLISHMENTS

BRANDED
BRAG BOOK

FOLDER OF
RECEIPTS

PROJECTS
AND BULLETS

THEY MF TRIED IT

1. Your BBB (Branded Brag Book): Your BBB, or Branded Brag Book, is your chance to shine like the Corporate Queens you are. Think of it as the public-facing showcase of your career triumphs. Picture it: a dynamic PowerPoint presentation or slideshow highlighting your major wins, tailored to specific roles or projects. Don't hold back: include your quantified impact, perhaps a case study, images of praise, or even snapshots of those well-deserved awards. Whether it's for internal promotions or external recruitment, your Branded Brag Book should tell a story about who you are and what you're capable of!

2. Your FOR (Folder Of Receipts): This is where you stash quick snippets and screenshots of praise or recognition you've received. It's your safety net, ensuring you're ready for anything. Keep emails from senior leaders, Slack messages from peers, or photos of workshops you've led. These "receipts" add social proof and validation when seeking promotions or salary increases. They're also handy for updating your Branded Brag Book. And on those rough days, they serve as a reminder of your accomplishments and impact.

3. Your PAB (Projects And Bullets): Take the time to document every major project, detailing the situation, actions, and results. Yes, it may take some extra effort, but trust me, it's worth it. This is your secret weapon for those performance reviews and résumé updates. Plus, you never know which bullet point will catch the eye of your next employer. Aim for monthly or at least quarterly updates to ensure all your great work is captured!

4. Your TMFTI (They MF Tried It): Now, let's talk about preparing for the need to CYA, Cover Your A$$. Unfortunately, we still live in a world where experiences aren't always rosy, especially for people of color. Your TMFTI folder is your shield against sideways behavior. Save screenshots or print out written documentation when someone treats you inappropriately. Send recap emails for verbal confrontations and consider seeking guidance from a trusted leader. While we hope you rarely need to use your TMFTI folder, it's better to be prepared.

As we wrap up our discussion on PAGES (performance and documentation), it's crucial to emphasize the need for consistency in this practice. Thriving in the corporate world isn't just about achieving success, it's about finding balance and sustainability. I want you to feel like you're flowing effortlessly through your workday. Sure, there will be intense moments, but it shouldn't feel like you're constantly drinking from a fire hose. That's where your monthly check-ins come in handy. Take the last Friday of each month to reassess your priorities, ensuring they align with both your manager's expectations and your personal growth aspirations.

Be honest with yourself about where you're at. Are you in a season where you can push harder and take on more growth opportunities, or do you need to dial it back to maintain balance? With your priorities and growth goals in mind, evaluate whether your current efforts align with your skill set. Once you've had this honest conversation and mapped out your path, it's like navigating with Apple Maps. You know your destination, your route, and how much fuel you'll need. And hey, make sure your radio is tuned to some smooth Keith Sweat tunes for the journey because with this level of clarity and intentionality, success feels like a smooth ride. Who can do it like you? Nobody, Baby!

Performance Challenges in the Workplace

Navigating performance challenges in the corporate world can sometimes feel like a rollercoaster ride. Maybe you've encountered a manager who struggles to define priorities or align expectations, leaving you drowning in a sea of tasks. Or perhaps you've found yourself on the receiving end of a Performance Improvement Plan (PIP), which can feel like a one-way ticket out the door.

Let's address the elephant in the room: PIPs. These are often the first step toward termination, and while turning things around is possible, it's essential to have a reality check. Here are some questions to guide your reflections if you're facing a PIP:

→ **What specific areas of my performance need improvement?**

Clarity is key here. Understand precisely where improvement is needed to focus your efforts effectively.

→ **Do I agree with the feedback and assessments provided?**

Take a moment to reflect on the feedback. Is there a misunderstanding, or do different perspectives exist? Clearing this up is vital for your next steps.

➡ **What steps can I take to meet the outlined goals and expectations?**

If you're committed to staying in your role, create a plan of action. Set measurable objectives, seek support, and adjust behaviors as needed.

➡ **Do I have the necessary resources and support to succeed?**

Assess your access to resources and support. Advocate for what you need or seek resources independently if necessary.

➡ **What opportunities exist outside of my current role, and how do they align with my skills and career aspirations?**

If you decide that your current role or team no longer aligns with your career aspirations, it's time to explore other opportunities. Start by looking within your current company for roles in different teams or departments that might better fit your skills and career goals. This internal reflection is crucial because, if you decide to pursue another opportunity within your company, you will still need to address the PIP to maintain your employment.

On the other hand, if you realize it's time to move on from the company altogether, begin exploring roles outside your current organization. This gives you the flexibility to take a more relaxed approach while continuing in your current position, knowing you are preparing for a transition.

➡ **What support networks or resources can I tap into for career guidance and job search assistance?**

Conduct thorough research on potential roles and companies. Network with professionals in your desired field to gain insights and uncover hidden opportunities.

The Financial Abundance Blueprint

Create a strategic action plan to pursue these opportunities. This might include updating your résumé, preparing for interviews, and reaching out to your network for referrals and advice.

Facing a PIP can be daunting, but it's not the end of the road. Your next steps depend on whether you want to stay and improve or explore opportunities elsewhere. Remember, maintaining control over your decisions puts you in the driver's seat of your career journey. At the end of the day, performance management is just one piece of the puzzle when it comes to thriving in the corporate world.

tFAB in Action: Performance Management

This Track's tFAB in Action moment has been all about getting your performance management system in place. I know I sound like a broken record, but again, set yourself up for success so you're consistently productive rather than just busy, maintaining a sustainable work-life harmony. Remember, we need to keep our 9-to-5 income growing to build wealth toward financial abundance! Here are your action items:

Strategize Your Performance with PAGES

➥ PERFORMANCE = PRIORITIZATION ALIGNMENT * GROWTH * (EFFORT ÷ SKILLS)

➥ **Establish a Recurring Check-in with Your Manager**: This ensures you're always working on the right priorities and meeting their expectations.

- **Treat Every Assignment as a Mini Project**: Give this project a clear objective, success metrics, and timelines to ensure you're always exceeding expectations.

- **Always Keep Your "ABCs" Top of Mind when deciding how you approach "Effort/Skills"**: Remember, not every assignment requires A-level outputs; C's get degrees too!

- **Keep Your PAGES Handy**: Document everything. In other words, "keep your receipts," just in case someone tries to challenge you.

ESTABLISHING YOUR BOARD OF DIRECTORS

All right, Corporate Queens, let's keep it real. We all know that working hard, having expertise, and sharing your knowledge are nonnegotiables. We've all got our seat at the table for a reason, and proving yourself is just the beginning. But let's channel the wisdom of that African proverb that says, "If you want to go fast, go alone. If you want to go far, go together." There will come a time when your career's upward trajectory will hinge on the support and influence of others. Yes, Sis, it's not just about what you know, but who you know, especially as you climb into the mid and senior phases of your career.

Imagine managing your career like a business or corporation, where you are the Chief Reputation Officer. Your job is to shape your personal brand and ensure that every interaction you have exceeds the expectations of your "customers": your colleagues, managers, and industry peers. However, just as a corporation has a board of directors to guide its strategic direction and decision-making, you need your own "personal board of directors," which we'll call Your Tribe for simplicity from here on out.

Your Tribe isn't just your network; it's a carefully curated group of people who support your professional (and personal) success, no matter your career stage. These are your mentors, peers, and allies, who understand your unique challenges and champion your success. Whether you're a newbie navigating the corporate world or a seasoned pro, here are some recommended tribe members to consider:

- **The Mentor:** This is your experienced guide. They've been there, done that, and are eager to share their wisdom and insights. Mentors offer insights, share knowledge, and help you navigate professional challenges and opportunities.
- **The Sponsor:** This is your career champion. Sponsors promote your visibility within your organization or industry. They use their influence and networks to open doors, advocate for your growth, and provide opportunities for advancement.
- **The Career Coach:** This is your help-me-overcome-career-hurdles guide. A career coach helps you navigate specific career challenges, transitions, and opportunities. Through formalized sessions, coaching focuses on setting and achieving goals, overcoming obstacles, and developing essential skills for career success.
- **The Confidant:** This is your trusted sounding board. Someone you can confide in, vent to, and get honest feedback from. Confidants often form lasting bonds and provide enduring support beyond the workplace.
- **The Connector:** They may not be your bestie, but they're valuable networking assets. Connectors can introduce you to new people, provide referrals, and help you build mutually beneficial relationships.

This begs the question: can one person serve in more than one role in your Tribe? The short answer is yes! There's a quote I heard once: "A coach talks to you, a mentor talks with you, and a sponsor talks about you." That said, depending on the level of seniority, access, and influence a person has, someone who initially falls into the Mentor camp could also take on the role of Sponsor. If you're fortunate enough to develop a mentor relationship with someone who is a senior leader in your organization, that's an ultimate win-win situation since they'll already be well aware of your brand, impact, achievements, and career goals. It'll be that much easier for them to advocate for you both publicly and privately. Below is a personal story about how my Tribe showed up for me and led to a major move in my career.

Abundant Career Chronicle: The Unplanned Lateral Career Move

Who would have thought that a seemingly small decision between joining the Accelerated Growth Team (AGT) or the Engage Team would have such a monumental impact on my journey at Google? Spoiler alert: I ended up choosing AGT in 2018. But let me tell you, getting to that point wouldn't have been possible without the invaluable guidance of my mentor, Lawrence. Lawrence was a standout sales leader at Google and a fellow Wharton alum. One of the connectors in my tribe suggested I connect with him early on, and boy, am I glad I did!

Now, let's rewind a bit. At the time, I wasn't particularly keen on either team. I was wrapping up my master's degree from Boston University, feeling pretty comfortable in my current role, and basking in the glow of a fantastic manager. Why rock the boat, right? But as it turned out, I was under-leveled in the organization and needed eventually to spread my wings. Plus, a member from my onboarding class was cheerleading for AGT every chance she got, even though I still wasn't interested in making a move.

Thankfully, I had Lawrence in my corner, offering up some game-changing advice. After weighing the pros and cons of both roles, he dropped this nugget of wisdom on me: "Pursue Both Roles." I was shocked to hear that—pursue both roles? I wasn't even sure I wanted either of them! But Lawrence knew what he was talking about. He encouraged me to throw my hat in the ring, get people talking, and then make my choice. And you know what? It worked. I landed offers from both teams, ultimately choosing AGT. But here's the kicker: the manager from the Engage Team later became a sponsor for me, opening up new opportunities down the line.

Those three years I spent on AGT were transformative to my career in ways I don't have time to cover. What matters now is, I wouldn't be here without Lawrence's guidance and that's the power of a Mentor and building your Tribe!

Now that we've outlined the key individuals you should have in your Tribe, the next question arises: How do you find and cultivate these relationships? This can be particularly challenging for introverted individuals.

Introducing the Drive-Thru Method to Networking

So, if you really knew me, you'd know my very first job was at McDonald's, stacking those checks and making memories that lasted through my college years. Now, if you're not familiar with the fast-food scene, let me break it down. Before mobile apps took over, ordering food came down to two options: the Drive-Thru or Dine-In. The Drive-Thru crowd preferred a quick order and exit, avoiding interaction. On the flip side, Dine-In patrons didn't mind the wait and often enjoyed their meal in-store. Now, what does McDonald's have to do with professional connections, you ask? Well, as a career coach, I often get asked about finding mentors and sponsors in new organizations. Enter my Drive-Thru Method.

Here is how the Drive-Thru Method to Networking works:

1. Schedule a 15-minute chat, starting on the hour (:00) or half-hour (:30) mark.

2. Prepare two to three thoughtful questions.

3. Follow the recommended Chat Flow.

Gratitude: Begin by expressing gratitude for their time and sharing why you reached out. Whether you heard great things about them or someone specific recommended them, let them know.

Your Intro: Provide a brief overview of your journey. Share who you are, your background (especially if you're new to the organization), and what you're currently focusing on in your role.

Their Intro: After your introduction, express interest in learning more about their journey. Invite them to share their experiences, perhaps by saying, "I'd love to hear more about your journey to XYZ..."

Meaningful Questions: Once introductions are complete, dive into your prepared questions. These questions should spark meaningful conversation and allow you to learn more about their perspectives, experiences, and insights. Here are a few examples to get you started:

→ Career Path Inspiration: What inspired you to pursue your career path, and what key factors have contributed to your success along the way?

→ Professional Growth: How do you stay current with industry developments and ensure continuous professional growth?

→ Proud Projects: Could you share a project or initiative you're particularly proud of leading? What were the key takeaways from that experience?

→ Work-Life Balance: What are your thoughts on maintaining work-life balance while pursuing ambitious career goals?

→ Organizational Priorities: What are the top priorities or initiatives you're focused on driving within the organization over the next six months?

→ Role Contribution: How do you envision "my role" contributing to the success of these priorities within your organization?

4. Always follow up with an email thanking them and highlighting key takeaways.

5. Aim to schedule another meeting one to two months later.

Use that opportunity to follow up on the takeaways discussed in your previous correspondence.

My Drive-Thru Method to Networking is tailor-made for our Corporate Queens, offering a swift and effective way to build meaningful connections in the workplace. It's a game-changer for a few key reasons. Firstly, it's quick and to the point, with just enough time for introductions and a couple of questions. This shows respect for the other person's time, especially if they're more senior. Plus, scheduling 15-minute slots at the :00 or :30 hour is intentional. For introverts, the idea of a 30+ minute coffee chat can be daunting. But with this method, the conversation is concise, and there's no pressure to extend beyond the allotted time. If the connection is strong, you can always continue, but if not, no worries, it's over before you know it.

Secondly, the follow-up email is where the magic happens for our Corporate Queens. Expressing gratitude and sharing key take-aways is crucial for turning a new connection into something more meaningful. Remember, mentors provide wisdom, while sponsors advocate for you behind closed doors. Building these relationships takes consistent engagement over time, whether it's acting on advice from a mentor or sharing your progress with a sponsor. This ongoing interaction is essential for both parties.

You might be wondering, how do I know if someone is a mentor or sponsor for me in the workplace? It's not always crystal clear, but you'll recognize it through their actions or feedback from others. Throughout my career, I've mentored several young professionals, and in most cases, we didn't explicitly label it. Instead, I knew based on our interactions; they sought advice, scheduled time to connect, and followed up on our discussions. That's how they made me their mentor. Similarly, by consistently engaging with others using the Drive-Thru method and extending conversations when appropriate, you'll naturally build relationships with mentors in your tribe.

Identifying sponsors is a bit trickier and often involves third-party validation. This means someone else lets you know how someone went to bat for you. To confirm if someone is a sponsor, seek feedback during a promotion cycle. Promotion decisions often hinge on the influence of specific groups advocating for their direct reports and others they sponsor. When I went up for promotion, my manager made it clear that everyone in the room supported me without question. Feedback from managers and leaders praising your work or how you handle situations is a strong indicator of sponsorship. These moments show that someone believes in you and your brand, setting the stage for future success.

As we wrap up, remember to be deliberate and thoughtful in your interactions with colleagues. Office dynamics are often more interconnected than we realize, and you never know who's connected to whom. So, always treat everyone with kindness and respect. It's a simple yet powerful way to navigate the corporate landscape successfully.

tFAB in Action: Cultivating Your Tribe

This Track's tFAB in action moment was about diving into the practical steps of assembling your personal board of directors, also known as your Tribe, and actively engaging with them to advance your career. Here are your action items:

Identify Potential Tribe Members: Take a moment to assess your network and identify individuals who could serve as mentors, sponsors, career coaches, confidants, and connectors. Consider their expertise, experience, and potential to contribute to your professional growth.

Schedule Drive-Thru Meet and Greets: Utilize the Drive-Thru Method to Networking detailed in this Track. Arrange brief yet focused meetings with potential Tribe members, armed with thoughtful questions to guide the conversation. Don't forget to follow up afterward with an email expressing sincere gratitude to solidify the connection.

Expand Your Professional Network: Actively seek opportunities to broaden your professional circle by attending industry events, joining relevant organizations, and connecting with peers in your field. Cultivate relationships with connectors who can facilitate introductions and collaborations, opening doors to new opportunities.

Establish Ongoing Relationships: Prioritize the cultivation of ongoing relationships with members of your Tribe. Schedule regular check-ins and follow-up meetings to maintain momentum and deepen your connection. Express gratitude for their support and guidance, and actively seek their input and advice as you navigate your career path.

MANAGING UP, ACROSS, AND BEYOND

Many of us were raised to believe in the meritocracy of hard work and the idea that diligence and dedication will inevitably lead to success. We imagined ourselves climbing the corporate ladder, earning promotions, and enjoying the rewards that come with them. But the reality of Corporate America often proves more complex. While diligence is essential, the truth is that your work won't always speak for itself. You must advocate for it, ensuring that the right people recognize its value. This is the essence of Managing Up, Across, and Beyond, which is ensuring that those who need to be aware of your contributions are informed.

Managing Up: Cultivating a Positive Relationship with Your Manager

There's a powerful quote that says, "People don't leave bad companies, they leave bad managers." This sentiment rings true in many workplace experiences. While toxic or ineffective managers undoubtedly exist in every organization, there's often a window of opportunity to shape and improve the manager-employee dynamic from the outset. This is the essence of Managing Up.

Managing Up is not about merely tolerating or enduring a difficult manager; it's about proactively cultivating a positive and mutually beneficial relationship. At its core, Managing Up involves establishing a constructive partnership with your manager, where both parties understand each other's perspectives and are committed to driving the success of the business in a healthy and productive manner.

Here are five essential elements for building a strong partnership with your manager:

1. Building Rapport with Your Manager

This might seem obvious, but you'd be surprised! Getting to know your manager as a person (within professional boundaries, of course) is crucial. I've experienced managers who kept their personal lives private, and others where the lines blurred a bit too much. The key is finding common ground and shared interests that foster rapport. Remember those interview questions about your personality? Think of building rapport as an extension of that process. People enjoy working with (and promoting!) those they connect with. And the most important connection you can build at work? With your manager.

Your manager has their own career goals, challenges, and life situations. However, the level of personal information shared goes both ways. This is a professional setting, so maintain appropriate boundaries. Remember, info shared in a one-on-one setting rarely stays there in the workplace. The goal here is to find a comfortable balance where you can get to know your manager, not everything about them, but enough to build a strong working relationship. This is key to success in your role.

2. Prioritization Alignment

Building on what we learned in Track 6, aligning your priorities with your manager's is critical for both your performance and success. Understanding how your work contributes to their goals is key to shining together. Many organizations set goals at the leadership level, cascading down to individual contributors. However, it's easy to get sidetracked by cool projects that offer personal learning opportunities, even if they're not aligned with your manager's priorities. This can lead to unexpected performance reviews. Remember, being productive is about doing the right things, not just being busy.

To ensure you're consistently working on the most impactful tasks, schedule regular check-ins with your manager. This open communication allows you to discuss new projects and their alignment with your manager's goals before diving in. By highlighting how your work contributes to the bigger picture, you showcase your understanding of their priorities and solidify your role in achieving them. This collaborative approach fosters alignment and sets up both of you for success.

3. Ways of Working Preferences

The next critical aspect, following prioritization alignment, is establishing a clear understanding of both your and your manager's working preferences. By doing so, you create an efficient and collaborative work environment, reducing miscommunication, and fostering a stronger relationship. Clear alignment on how you'll work together minimizes the chances of micromanagement and ensures smooth collaboration from the start. Here are some tips for aligning working preferences with your manager:

→ **Open Communication:** Initiate a conversation with your manager to discuss preferred communication methods, such as email, phone calls, Slack messages, video calls, or in-person meetings. Understanding each other's preferences can prevent miscommunication and ensure urgent matters are addressed promptly. Be honest about your preferences and maintain consistency in your communication approach.

→ **Active Listening:** Pay attention to your manager's communication style and adapt accordingly. While you don't need to match their style completely, finding a middle ground ensures effective communication. Whether it's through live meetings or asynchronous emails, aim to meet halfway to enhance collaboration.

→ **Setting Boundaries:** Communicate your work preferences, including preferred working hours, breaks, and availability for meetings. Establishing boundaries helps create a conducive work environment and allows your manager to support your well-being. Reflect again on the Time Management strategies shared in Track 4.

→ **Feedback Delivery Approach:** Understand how you prefer to receive feedback, and communicate this with your manager. Similarly, grasp your manager's preferred feedback method. Openly discussing feedback preferences can facilitate constructive communication and foster mutual understanding. Whether it's written feedback followed by a discussion or another approach, prioritize what works best for you while remaining open to your manager's needs.

4. Demonstrating Initiative

A positive relationship with your manager hinges on taking ownership of your work, being proactive, and embracing accountability, especially in challenging situations. While it can be tempting to go along with the status quo in the workplace, exceptional managers value more than mere compliance. They appreciate employees who demonstrate initiative, creativity, and a commitment to continuous improvement, which are qualities synonymous with a growth mindset.

Demonstrating initiative means being a self-starter, ready to exceed expectations and explore new opportunities for growth. It involves innovating in your approach and actively seeking solutions rather than simply identifying problems. This proactive mindset not only earns recognition but also positions you as a valuable contributor within the organization.

However, it's essential to be intentional about when and how you showcase initiative. Drawing from insights in Track 6 (Mastering Performance Management), ensure that your actions align with your career goals and workload constraints. By strategically demonstrating initiative, you can maximize its impact while safeguarding against burnout or exploitation.

Abundant Career Chronicle: What Is Your Unique Value Add?

Now, let's delve into the 5th Element of Managing Up your manager, one that warrants its own narrative: your Unique Value Add (UVA). When entering a new team or organization, possessing a clear UVA is vital for standing out and making meaningful contributions. Your UVA encompasses a blend of skills, experiences, and perspectives that distinguish you from your peers. But the question remains:

What exactly is your Unique Value Add? How do you set yourself apart within the team?

Let's rewind to a pivotal moment during the pandemic, around the 2020–2021 timeframe. Naturally inclined toward mentoring and fostering growth, I discovered an opportunity to formalize my role as a career coach within the organization. The company offered a compelling program where employees could volunteer as coaches, guiding others through various topics and skill sets.

I became a sought-out coach for new hires during their onboarding phase and tenured employees seeking career advancement. Interestingly, regardless of experience level, one of the most frequent questions was: "How do I effectively manage my relationship with my boss?" Even seasoned employees grapple with managing their manager. Beyond the tips I previously shared (getting to know your manager, aligning priorities, setting communication preferences, and demonstrating initiative), there's a final, mission-critical step: identifying a gap you can uniquely fill on your team.

Here are the golden questions I share with my coaching clients (and you!):

➼ What is everyone's superpower on the team as it relates to this role?
➼ What "superpower" is missing from the team?
➼ How do you see my skill set as a differentiator and value-add to help level up the team in a certain area?

These questions for your manager are not just conversation starters; they, and the answers to them, help you create a strategic compass to guide you toward maximizing your impact within the team. Your manager will undoubtedly appreciate your thoughtful inquiry, and even if they don't have an immediate answer, it serves as a catalyst for gathering valuable insights. Every role and team is unique, operating within different dynamics, from individualistic spaces such as sales to collaborative environments such as project management.

Knowing everyone's strengths equips you to navigate team dynamics seamlessly. You can identify subject-matter experts, the go-to people for specific questions, saving you time and ensuring you get the right advice. This knowledge also helps you carve your own space to shine. By leveraging your Unique Value Add (UVA) alongside your colleagues' strengths, you can make a distinct contribution to the team.

This understanding positions you for success across the organization. Imagine using this knowledge to propose a training relevant to your team's needs, with data to quantify its potential impact. Following a successful team rollout, you could then scale the training to your manager's peer's team, maximizing your impact and becoming a recognized asset across the organization.

Maximizing Your One-on-One's for Managing Up

Now that we've explored the key aspects of managing up, let's delve into the execution and where the magic truly happens: your one-on-one meetings with your manager. Regardless of their frequency, it's vital to recognize that your one-on-one meetings are for you. You should take ownership of the agenda and ensure that the time spent leaves you feeling aligned with your manager and empowered to fulfill your responsibilities. Top performing Corporate Queens utilize their one-in-one time with their manager to advance their narratives and priorities! Here's a recommended agenda outline for maximizing your one-on-ones effectively:

➥ **Warm Up with Small Talk (3–5 minutes):** Build rapport by catching up. Briefly discuss your weekend or a shared interest, fostering a personal connection alongside professional dialogue.

- ➥ **Highlight Your Wins (Majority of Time):** This is your moment to shine! Briefly outline your completed tasks and major victories in a clear, concise format (think bullet points) within the meeting agenda. This allows your manager to easily grasp your achievements and provides talking points they can use to showcase your work to your skip-level manager.
- ➥ **Proactive Roadblock Removal (As Needed):** Identify any challenges you face that require your manager's intervention. This demonstrates that you value their time and initiative, anticipating potential issues before they escalate.
- ➥ **Career Development (Every Six Months):** Schedule regular discussions (at least every six months) about your career path. Discuss skills you want to develop, opportunities you seek, and next steps toward your professional goals.
- ➥ **Roundtable for Manager's Input (Remaining Time):** Address any additional items your manager has on their agenda. By proactively addressing other topics beforehand, this section will likely be brief. Remember, aim to address everything proactively, minimizing surprises.

Managing Across: Engaging Your Manager's Peers and Cross-Functional Teams

"Managing across" entails nurturing connections with colleagues outside your immediate team or department. These relationships are pivotal for collaboration, knowledge-sharing, and, ultimately, bolstering your professional network. While it may seem daunting amidst your workload, it's essential to allocate time for both your tasks and relationship-building efforts.

You might be thinking, "How do I even find the time to build these relationships?" The answer lies in the "15-Minute Drive-Thru Method" introduced in Track 7. This method, used for internal team building, can be equally effective for managing across departments. Within your first 90 days, prioritize scheduling brief "drive-thru" chats with key colleagues who work closely with your manager. In many companies, performance reviews and promotions involve input beyond just your direct supervisor. Your manager's peers can significantly influence your brand perception and career trajectory within the organization as well.

Here are some conversation starters to guide your interactions:

➥ Tell me about your journey at [company name] → Encourages them to share their experiences and fosters a personal connection.

➥ What are your team's priorities for the next six months? → Demonstrates your interest in collaboration and potential areas for teamwork.

➥ How do our teams collaborate? Are there areas for improvement? → Shows you seek to understand existing dynamics and identify opportunities for stronger partnerships.

➥ Do you have upcoming projects needing extra support? → Shows initiative and willingness to contribute beyond your core responsibilities.

➥ Any advice for working with [manager's name]? → Provides valuable insights into your manager's working style and preferences.

By learning about their backgrounds and team dynamics, you not only establish rapport but also uncover potential avenues for collaboration and mutual support. Look for opportunities to contribute meaningfully to their projects or initiatives, showcasing your skills and willingness to collaborate across teams. Moreover, consistency is key in nurturing these relationships. Keep in touch regularly, even if it's just a brief check-in every few months. Your goal is to cultivate a network of allies who can vouch for your abilities and advocate for your professional growth.

Transitioning to managing relationships with cross-functional stakeholders requires a more strategic approach. Treat each task or project as a mini-project, applying project management principles to ensure clarity, alignment, and effective communication. By meticulously managing your work and interactions, you shape a positive brand-experience that aligns with your career objectives and leaves a lasting impression on those you collaborate with.

Project Managing for Stakeholder Engagement

Before diving into how I integrate project management principles into stakeholder interactions, let's briefly explore the theoretical framework. The Project Management Institute (PMI) offers a robust framework known as the Project Management Body of Knowledge (PMBOK), outlining essential processes and best practices. The project management process encompasses five phases: initiation, planning, execution, monitoring and controlling, and closing. Each phase offers tools to streamline processes and maintain focus, which prove invaluable for consistent, structured engagement with project teams and stakeholders.

Here are a few tools that I find applicable for all Corporate Queens to put into their toolkit for managing across the organization:

Project Charter

The first tool we'll integrate into our strategy for stakeholder excellence is the project charter. Typically, a formal document outlining project scope, goals, and objectives, along with budget, timeline, and deliverables, the project charter serves as a roadmap for success. However, I approach it as a mental checklist, ensuring clarity and alignment before taking on any initiative or deliverable.

For me, it's about preemptively understanding the assignment's purpose, the key outcomes expected by leadership and cross-functional partners, and critical milestones and timelines. I also consider what success looks like, seeking differentiated tiers of success from my manager to consistently exceed expectations. While I don't always provide a formal project charter to cross-functional stakeholders, I ensure alignment via follow-up emails outlining these key aspects. This proactive approach fosters clarity and alignment, setting the stage for successful collaboration and ensuring everyone understands the project's objectives and timeline. Ultimately, my aim is to underpromise and overdeliver, consistently meeting and exceeding expectations while maintaining focus and accountability.

Stakeholder Mapping[1] and Communications Plan

While informal chats and conversations are essential for building relationships with my manager's peers, engaging with cross-functional stakeholders requires a more structured approach. Stakeholder mapping involves identifying and categorizing stakeholders based on their level of power/influence and interest in the project. This visual representation provides valuable insights into how each stakeholder contributes to and impacts the project's success. By understanding their roles and perspectives, I can tailor communication strategies to address their specific needs and preferences. In practice, I compile a list of stakeholders and analyze their influence and interest levels to prioritize engagement efforts. This allows me to focus my communication efforts where they will have the greatest impact, ensuring that

---

1 Adaptation of (Mendelow 1981).

key stakeholders are informed and engaged throughout the project lifecycle.

STAKEHOLDER MAP

Manage Closely (High Power, High Interest): These stakeholders are crucial to project success. Engage them actively through detailed updates, consultations, and collaborative decision-making.

Keep Satisfied (High Power, Low Interest): While they have significant influence, their interest is limited. Provide periodic, high-level updates to maintain their support.

Keep Informed (Low Power, High Interest): Though they lack decision-making authority, their vested interest can drive advocacy. Share regular updates and involve them where appropriate.

Monitor (Low Power, Low Interest): These stakeholders have minimal impact and interest. Observe them periodically but allocate your primary focus elsewhere.

STAKEHOLDER COMMUNICATIONS PLAN (EXAMPLE)

Stakeholder	Category	Purpose	Communication Method	Cadence	Last Communication	Next Communication
Engineering Team	**Manage Closely**	Ensure team is on track and address any roadblocks	Check-ins (Meetings)	Daily	Aug. 2	Aug. 3
Executive Team	**Manage Closely**	Ensure continued alignment and buy-in from senior leadership	Status Reports (Email)	Weekly	Aug. 2	Aug. 9
Sales Team	**Keep Satisfied**	Ensure sales team is trained in new processes and can effectively sell the product	Status Reports (Email), Business Reviews (Meetings)	Weekly	Aug. 4	Aug. 11
Customer Support Team	**Keep Satisfied**	Ensure customer support team is prepared for upcoming changes and can effectively support customers	Business Reviews (Meetings)	Monthly	Aug. 2	Sept. 2
Marketing Team	**Keep Informed**	Ensure marketing team is prepared for upcoming changes and can effectively market the product	Business Reviews (Meetings)	Monthly	Aug. 4	Sept. 4
Finance Team	**Monitor**	Ensure project is on track financially and does not exceed budget	Status Updates (Email)	Quarterly	Aug. 4	Nov. 4

It's crucial to tailor your communication approach to meet the preferences of each stakeholder, ensuring that you engage with them at the appropriate level. For instance, if a senior director or VP is sponsoring the initiative you're working on, bombarding them with frequent bi-weekly meetings may not be the most effective strategy, as they may prioritize their time differently. Instead, crafting a well-articulated monthly email update can keep them informed while respecting their busy schedules.

However, effective communication goes beyond merely keeping stakeholders in the loop; it's about establishing consistency and reliability in your interactions. By providing regular updates and demonstrating the impact of your work, you reinforce your credibility and reliability. This approach fosters trust and confidence in your abilities, laying the groundwork for continued support and collaboration.

Project Closure

The "traditional project closure" phase provides a valuable opportunity to reflect on the project's journey, acknowledging its successes, challenges, and lessons learned. But for us, we should focus on creating artifacts that not only communicate the initiative's success but also provide visibility to leadership and stakeholders across the organization. Whether it's compiling a detailed report, creating a presentation, or developing case studies, these artifacts serve as tangible evidence of our contributions. For exceptional outcomes, these achievements may even find a place in our Branded Brag Book, ready for future reference and showcasing our capabilities!

These are just a few examples of how project management principles can be leveraged beyond traditional project management roles. By adopting these tools and strategies, you can consistently deliver top-tier performance and build stronger relationships with stakeholders, senior leadership, and peers alike. Remember, project management isn't just about projects; it's about achieving success through structure, communication, and a focus on results—all qualities that contribute to building a strong personal brand and enable the successful management of relationships across the organization!

Managing Beyond: Establishing Advocacy and Alignment with Senior Leadership

Having strong relationships with senior leaders is a major asset in any corporate environment. These leaders can become advocates and sponsors, championing your contributions and propelling you toward your career goals. As the corporate landscape evolves, with factors like remote work and AI impacting how we work, building strong relationships with senior leaders becomes even more critical. They can offer valuable guidance and support, protecting your interests when at a crossroads at various times throughout your career journey. Let's focus on building relationships with senior leaders who are one to two levels above your manager, often referred to as your "skip-level" leaders, folks more senior than your manager in your leadership chain of command, as mentioned earlier.

It's essential to approach meetings with senior leaders with intentionality and respect for their time. Aim for a 15- to 20-minute session (our Drive-Thru Approach works here too!), acknowledging the senior leader's busy schedule. Utilize their executive assistant or directly book office hours if available, ensuring convenience for both parties. Next, focus on crafting an agenda to ensure a productive discussion. Here's a suggested agenda for your skip-level meeting:

➥ **Introductions:** For a first meeting, spend some time introducing yourself (experience, role, etc.), using your elevator pitch to clearly communicate your value proposition. Allow the leader some time to share their background as well.

➥ **Performance Updates:** Highlight your accomplishments and wins, focusing on those most aligned with the leader's priorities. Showcase your impact on the broader organization.

➥ **Leadership's Top-of-Mind:** Actively listen to understand the leader's key priorities for the next six to twelve months. Learn what keeps them up at night and how your work aligns with their goals. Offer solutions or perspectives gleaned from your "on-the-ground" experience. If it's a follow-up meeting, come prepared to showcase actions you've taken based on the leader's previous guidance.

➥ **Career Development:** Discuss your career goals (at least once a year). Understanding your aspirations allows the leader to advocate for you and identify development opportunities. Their insights into the company's vision can help you make informed career decisions and avoid potential roadblocks as well.

With a strong agenda ready to go, you already know what happens next...powerful question preparation! Here are some examples to help get you started:

➥ Can you share your career journey and how you developed your expertise?

➥ What are our greatest challenges and successes as a team (or organization)?

➥ What key priorities are driving the team (or organization) forward?

➥ How can our team contribute to achieving the company's long-term goals?

➥ What skills or competencies do you believe are crucial for success in our industry?

➥ In your opinion, how can we better differentiate ourselves in the market?

➥ How can I further develop my skills within my role or grow within the company?

Keep in mind that throughout the conversation, you'll want to leave the door open to provide them with feedback and insights. You're in the coveted position of being on the ground and knowing the true challenges and opportunities in the organization. Lean into those moments to add value beyond your immediate role and provide insight and thought leadership to your skip-level to help drive strategic decision making.

As always, be sure to nurture the relationship by scheduling follow-up meetings to close the loop on previous discussions and share back positive outcomes that came from the leader's guidance. Aim to regularly connect with your skip-level leader every six months if possible. Remember, you are managing your brand narrative and establishing a positive experience with this key leader. By investing in this relationship, you position yourself for success and gain a valuable advocate for your career journey over time!

Connecting with senior leadership can seem quite daunting. The truth is, there are two sides to managing beyond with senior leadership. The first involves scheduling informal meetings every six months to touch base, share your wins, ask for wisdom, and follow up on feedback. If you're doing this, you're already ahead of the game. You'd be surprised how many people have never even met their skip-level director or VP on a one-on-one basis, even though most companies offer some form of opportunity to do so, whether it's through office hours or scheduling via an executive assistant.

However, there's another crucial aspect of managing beyond with senior leadership, and that's about creating moments of visibility that matter. Think of it as doing what you would have done anyway, leaning into your authenticity and greatness, but also creating moments where your senior leaders can see and benefit from your actions.

Abundant Career Chronicle: Creating Moments of Visibility

My first job out of college was at Verizon, a company that epitomized the stereotypical Corporate America culture: old, non-diverse, and quite rigid. Although the brand has improved since, there was still much progress to be made. I joined the company as a returning intern, having had a great experience the previous summer. The internship allowed me to connect with other young Millennials, particularly Millennials of color, in a corporation where the majority of employees did not look like us.

Upon returning full-time, I quickly got involved in Employee Resource Groups (ERGs), which are excellent for establishing a network, building connections, and serving in leadership capacities. However, most of Verizon's ERGs were focused exclusively on traditional communities such as women, veterans, or African Americans. Yet, as a young, Black woman working across four generations, I didn't feel adequately served by the existing communities.

So, with the help of some of my "corporate cousins," we utilized our internal social media platform to create our own community: the Millennial Community (MC). It was a safe space for all Millennials and our allies to connect, share thought leadership, and have lunch together.

A few months into creating this community, we had a new leader join the organization: Diego, the new Chief Marketing Officer. Diego brought a fresh perspective to the company's vision, particularly in marketing. Recognizing the importance of Millennials, he tapped into our to help illustrate the company's new brand positioning. One day, I received a phone call from one of his brand studio people, asking if I could recommend individuals from our community to participate in a video project to bring Diego's new brand-positioning to life.

I was floored. Something I had created based on a need and aligned with my true values had caught the attention of the C-Suite.

Long story short, my corporate cousins and I participated in the video project, which became a mini-series showcasing our new brand positioning. The videos were shown at the leadership level, and eventually, my director, Bill, called me into his office to commend me on the incredible work. He told me that all of the leadership (from the C-Suite on down) were being shown the videos, finally reaching the directors that day! Essentially, I became one of the most well-known people at Verizon. To bring this story to a close, during a quarterly town hall, the videos were shown to the entire company. As I watched from the front row, a VP sitting next to me turned and said, "Oh, that was you," to which I proudly replied, "Yes, that was me."

This story came from my decision to create a community to empower younger voices in the organization and my authentic partnership with corporate cousins, which led to a relationship with the Chief Marketing Officer. If this book were printed in color, I'd show our selfies together (yes, there are multiple from multiple occasions), and yes, we're connected on LinkedIn to this day! Oh yeah, quick sidenote, I also met the CEO the year prior as an intern and got a selfie with him—#PersonalBrandingForYa!

Keep in mind that managing up, across, and beyond is about establishing positive relationships and creating a consistent brand experience with the people you frequently interact with within the organization and those you want to have on your side. Even though that was a more extreme example, it still offers a three-step recipe for success:

1. Doing Great Work: Performing your core duties well and pursuing additional projects you're passionate about.

2. Visibility: Making sure the right people know about your accomplishments through intentionally curated and consistent communications appropriate for the stakeholders.

3. Amplification: Proactively seeking out ways to showcase your work to a wider audience, or staying ready for when an incredible opportunity comes knocking on your door!

tFAB in Action: Managing Up, Across, and Beyond

This Track's tFAB in Action moment focuses on setting yourself up for success by creating positive brand experiences with your manager, your manager's peers, cross-functional stakeholders, and senior leadership as opportunities arise. Here are your action items:

Establish Your One-on-One Cadence and Agenda: Ensure you're maximizing your time with your manager and driving your priorities forward. Be proactive in getting to know them, understanding their working preferences and how they prefer to deliver and receive feedback.

Engage with Your Manager's Peers: Schedule a 15-minute Drive-Thru session to start building relationships with your manager's peers. This will help broaden your network and support system.

Leverage Project-Management Best Practices: Use tools like a Project Charter, Stakeholder Mapping, and a Communications Plan to ensure a consistent collaboration experience with cross-functional stakeholders.

Align with Senior Leadership's Priorities: Seek opportunities to work on initiatives that align with the priorities of senior leadership (Director/VP level). Set aside time every six months to connect with them one-on-one to stay top of mind for career development.

Curate Recaps of Major Initiatives: After completing a major initiative, deliverable, or project, create a recap to include in your Branded Brag Book. This recap serves as a live artifact that key stakeholders can use to advocate for your contributions and increase visibility of your greatness!

EVERYTHING AND EVERYBODY ELSE: CORPORATE DYNAMICS

Believe it or not, we're nearing the end of Side A of our album (or should I say, book), where we've covered the major aspects of navigating the corporate world. Achieving Financial Abundance as a Corporate Queen means understanding the unwritten rules of the workplace to exponentially increase our income and fund our abundant lives. My goal for all of us Corporate Queens is to thrive in our careers and feel empowered in every corporate interaction! We prioritize work-life balance while excelling in our roles with grace and ease, no more Sunday scaries over here! The EMBODY Framework has equipped you to work smarter and systematically, ensuring your success without overworking and underpayment.

As much as I'd love to delve into every detail, obstacle, and experience, our time is limited. Hence, this Track, "Everything and Everybody Else," serves as a catch-all, offering one last dose of corporate wisdom before we transition to Side B of the book.

Expanding Your Network Internally and Externally

Your network is one of your greatest assets, directly impacting your career trajectory and financial success. While we've already covered the importance of building strong relationships with your manager and cross-functional teams, expanding your connections both inside and outside your organization is equally critical for long-term growth and opportunity.

Participating in Employee Resource Groups (ERGs) offers a strategic avenue to enhance your internal network. These groups not only provide support but also present opportunities for career growth, especially for young women of color navigating corporate landscapes.

Key Benefits of ERGs:

➥ **Leadership Opportunities:** ERGs often allow members to assume leadership roles, even at junior levels, facilitating the development of management skills and increased visibility within the organization.

➥ **Access to Mentors:** Through ERGs, you can connect with senior leaders who offer guidance and support, aiding in your professional development while removing some of the pressure to cultivate these relationships on your own.

➥ **Community and Support:** Engaging with colleagues who share similar backgrounds or interests fosters a sense of belonging and provides a platform for sharing experiences and resources. My first lateral move early in my career came from the referral of a great woman I connected with at an ERG event that blossomed into a friendship to this day.

Expanding your network outside your organization is equally crucial. Attending industry conferences and joining professional online communities can significantly enhance your external connections.

Strategies for External Networking:

➥ **Industry Conferences:** Participate in conferences relevant to your field to stay informed about industry trends and to meet professionals from other organizations. Active engagement in these events can lead to valuable insights and connections.

➥ **Online Professional Communities:** Join industry-specific forums, social media groups, and professional associations to interact with peers, share knowledge, and build relationships that can support your career objectives.

By integrating both internal and external networking strategies, you can establish a comprehensive support system that fosters personal and professional growth, keeping you informed and connected within your industry.

Crafting Your Digital Presence

As you expand your network both internally and externally, your digital presence becomes a powerful tool that shapes and amplifies your personal brand in today's tech-driven world. Platforms like LinkedIn and whatever comes next serve as your professional portfolio, not just a static résumé. Think of LinkedIn as your digital business card, a dynamic space to actively showcase your skills, achievements, and professional journey. Here are some tips on what to focus on and how to maximize your effectiveness:

➥ **Keep It Updated:** Regularly update your profile with new skills, certifications, and accomplishments. Share insights about industry trends and engage with relevant content to stay visible. Joining groups and participating in discussions can connect you with like-minded professionals and potential mentors.

↪ **Build Relationships:** Utilize LinkedIn's features to schedule virtual meetups or coffee chats. Networking is about building relationships that can unlock new opportunities, not just collecting connections.

↪ **Expand Beyond LinkedIn:** Your digital presence extends beyond LinkedIn, as recruiters, hiring managers, and future coworkers will assess how you represent yourself across all platforms. It's essential to be conscious of your online persona, given that anything shared can last indefinitely. To protect your privacy, think about blocking new coworkers or managers on personal platforms; friendships can develop after you've moved on from the company. Consider creating a personal website as a central hub for your portfolio, industry insights, or a professional blog. This allows you to control your narrative and present your brand cohesively. Remember, the digital platforms of today may not be around in ten years, #RipMySpace, so it's essential to stay adaptable and lean into evolving technologies. Embrace new trends and tools to keep your presence fresh and relevant, ensuring you're always a step ahead in your professional journey.

↪ **Consistency Is Key:** To really stand out, it's important to keep your brand consistent across all your digital channels. When your online presence is cohesive, it shows you're serious about your growth and helps others recognize who you are. A polished profile not only boosts your visibility but also gives off leadership vibes, opening doors to new opportunities. Think of it like this: when you show up consistently, it makes it easier for people to connect with your story and seek you out to establish mutually beneficial relationships.

Ready-to-Go Résumés

Your résumé tells the story of your career journey, highlighting your accomplishments, skills, and potential contributions to future employers. When tailoring your résumé for each opportunity, focus on showcasing relevant experiences and measurable achievements that align perfectly with the job description. Don't forget to sprinkle in keywords from the job posting to ensure your résumé gets noticed by applicant-tracking systems (ATS's) and human eyes alike.

When it comes to writing an eye-catching résumé, remember that each line item should tell a story that leaves the reader wanting more! Recruiters from Google suggest following this formula to illustrate your impact while in role: Accomplished [X] as measured by [Y], by doing [Z].

➡ **Accomplished [X]:** Start by highlighting your achievement or accomplishment. This could be a project completed, a goal achieved, or a problem solved.

➡ **As Measured by [Y]:** Next, specify how you measured this accomplishment. This could be in terms of such metrics as percentages, numbers, or timeframes.

➡ **By Doing [Z]:** Finally, describe the actions you took to achieve this result. This could include specific tasks, strategies implemented, or skills utilized.

Regularly updating and refining your résumé is essential to reflect your ongoing career growth, and newly acquired skills. This is where your Projects And Bullets from your Abundant Accomplishments documentation will come in handy, as discussed in Track 6! Whether you're actively job hunting or not, having an up-to-date résumé means you're always ready to seize unexpected opportunities externally or pursue internal advancements within your current organization.

Navigating Promotions

Navigating promotions is a pivotal aspect of career advancement that requires proactive career management and strategic planning. It's about demonstrating your value, increasing your visibility, and preparing yourself for higher responsibilities within the organization. Here's how to effectively navigate this process:

→ **Set Clear Career Goals:** Start by defining clear short-term objectives and long-term aspirations that align with your strengths and the organization's needs. Communicate these goals early and consistently, not just during the promotion cycle, to align with company priorities and demonstrate readiness for advancement. Collaborate closely with your manager to develop and execute a plan of action. This proactive approach ensures you're on track to achieve your goals, leveraging their guidance and support for effective career development. Regularly adjust based on feedback and evolving priorities to showcase your commitment to growth and readiness for new challenges. After mapping out your career advancement goals, it's essential to focus on "getting a slice of PIE": Performance, Image, and Exposure. Each element plays a crucial role in positioning yourself as a strong candidate for advancement in alignment with your goals.

→ **Performance:** Strive for excellence in your current role by achieving measurable results and exceeding expectations, documenting achievements and contributions to highlight your impact on key projects and initiatives. Utilize the PAGES Framework for performance management to support your promotion efforts: ensure tasks align with organizational priorities, emphasize continuous personal and professional development to demonstrate growth in specific skill sets, and apply skills diligently and consistently for visible and impactful contributions (Track 6). This is the time to crank out that A-level workload execution!

→ **Image:** Continue to maintain a professional image aligned with your career goals and organizational values. Consistently portray your skills, achievements, and demeanor, leveraging insights from Personal Branding efforts (Track 3). Now is not the time to start acting differently!

→ **Exposure:** Increase visibility by volunteering for leadership roles, participating in networking events, and engaging with senior leaders. Build a positive reputation and strong relationships across different levels of the organization. Utilize strategies from Managing Up, Across, and Beyond (Track 8) to ensure key decision-makers are aware of your contributions through your Branded Brag Book.

→ **Prepare for Promotion Discussions:** Thoroughly prepare by documenting your achievements, skills, and contributions systematically. Ask your manager about the promotion process and what documentation they require. If possible, take the opportunity to craft your promotion packet, the documentation used to make the case for your promotion, to ensure all your accomplishments are accurately captured. Clearly articulate how your strengths align with the role's requirements and the organization's strategic objectives, and all the impact you've made in alignment to those objectives!

→ **Post-Promotion Process:** Whether you receive positive promotion feedback or are advised on areas for improvement, it's essential to use the opportunity to grow. If you achieve the promotion, celebrate your success and enjoy the new raises or compensation that comes with it. If you don't get the promotion this time, seek clarity on areas for improvement and focus on developing the skills needed for future opportunities. Embrace both outcomes as part of your journey

The Financial Abundance Blueprint

toward achieving your career goals and continuing to grow professionally.

High-achieving Corporate Queens always strategize to secure promotions effectively. Remember, your highest leverage for compensation often begins when you first join a company. It's crucial to select roles and opportunities that align with your financial needs from the outset. This approach ensures you can focus on excelling at work without the stress of financial insecurity. While it's natural to desire more income, don't let it become the sole motivator or a tool for your employer to exploit your talents. Let promotions unfold naturally as you focus on meaningful growth and development in your career journey.

Navigating Corporate Politics and Microaggressions

Navigating office politics is a vital skill that involves understanding the informal power dynamics and social interactions that influence decision-making and career advancement. For individuals from underrepresented backgrounds, this journey can be particularly challenging. It requires not only mastering the organizational structure but also managing biases and microaggressions that can hinder professional opportunities and skew perceptions.

For example, consider a scenario where a talented Melanated Corporate Queen consistently contributes innovative ideas in meetings. However, those ideas are often overlooked or attributed to others. It may be necessary to strategically position oneself by following up with managers after meetings, highlighting contributions directly, and fostering relationships with influential colleagues who can amplify your voice.

Building strong relationships with mentors and allies is essential. These connections can provide invaluable support, helping you navigate the subtle nuances of office culture. Allies can advocate for you when you're not in the room, ensuring your contributions are recognized and valued.

It's also crucial to assert yourself confidently. This might mean actively participating in discussions, sharing your expertise, or volunteering for high-visibility projects that align with your career goals. At the same time, remaining attuned to the cultural dynamics at play is essential. For instance, understanding how to navigate different communication styles within your organization can help you build rapport and avoid misunderstandings.

Cultivating resilience and emotional intelligence is key to handling challenging situations and maintaining your integrity in the face of adversity. This might involve developing coping strategies for dealing with microaggressions, such as practicing self-affirmation or seeking support from trusted colleagues. Recognizing when to engage in difficult conversations about bias or discrimination and knowing how to do so effectively can empower you to advocate for yourself and others.

Ultimately, navigating corporate politics requires a blend of strategic awareness, strong relationships, and self-advocacy. By understanding these dynamics you'll be in a better position to cultivate success for yourself and a more inclusive workplace for all.

A Word on Microaggressions

Microaggressions are forms of discrimination that affect individuals from marginalized groups. They manifest as offhand comments, jokes, or actions that reinforce negative stereotypes. For example, saying, "You're so articulate for someone from your background" is a microinsult that implies surprise at someone's competence. Microinvalidations dismiss marginalized experiences, like claiming, "I don't see color," while microassaults involve explicit derogatory remarks or harmful behaviors, such as racist jokes or slurs.

The Financial Abundance Blueprint

These instances often stem from unconscious biases and cultural stereotypes, revealing more about the person making the comment than the recipient. Below are a few examples of typical microaggressions that occur in the workplace:

Racial Microaggressions:

➡ "You're so articulate for a Black person," implying that being articulate is unusual for Black individuals, perpetuating harmful stereotypes.

➡ "Where are you really from?" questioning the authenticity of someone's national identity based on their appearance.

Gender Microaggressions:

➡ "You're too emotional," directed at women in professional settings, undermining their credibility and reinforcing gender stereotypes.

➡ "You should smile more," a comment often directed at women, implying that their appearance should be more pleasing.

Sexual Orientation Microaggressions:

➡ "You don't look gay," a statement that invalidates someone's identity based on stereotypes about how LGBTQ+ individuals should appear.

➡ "That's so gay," using "gay" as a derogatory term, which is offensive and dismissive.

Disability Microaggressions:

➡ Saying "You're so inspiring" to someone with a disability, which can be patronizing and reduce their achievements to their disability.

➡ "I didn't expect you to be able to do this," underestimating someone's abilities because of their disability.

If you encounter microaggressions at work, it's important to take proactive steps. Acknowledge and validate your feelings. Keep detailed records of incidents, noting dates, times, locations, and what happened, and if possible, include witnesses. You'll want to have those receipts in your They MF Tried It folder in case things escalate. If it comes to that point, seek support from trusted colleagues or mentors in your Tribe that can provide advice and a safe space to discuss your experiences.

I've had to personally navigate this particular set of B.S. that comes with working in Corporate America more than I'd like to recall. However, early in my career I didn't have a name or comprehension of what was truly happening beneath the surface. I call it out here so that we can all be informed and understand what's truly happening and then be empowered to make decisions based on that knowledge. I never want any of my Corporate Queens to feel like their career is outside of their own hands.

If by chance you deal with this as a one-off that can be handled behind the scenes, then great, go ahead and address it and keep pushing forward. However, if unfortunately, you find yourself experiencing a constant toxic environment in this regard, then you'll need to take some time to reflect on your next steps. It's not fair that someone else's ill behavior toward you might result in you having to decide about your employment. But it's important to take that time to reflect because, if you do need to raise a case with HR, then you'll want to prepare for what that could mean in terms of your future at the company. Truth be told, you'll probably want to consider other places of employment because no one should have to work in such a toxic environment.

Managing Workplace Conflict

Managing workplace conflict is essential for maintaining a positive and productive environment. Office gossip can create a toxic atmosphere and strain relationships. It's vital to steer clear of gossip circles, as rumors can spread quickly and damage reputations. For my Corporate Queens, especially those from marginalized backgrounds, being dragged into corporate scandals is not an option. If you find yourself the target of gossip, address it head-on with those involved. Use your TMFTI receipts (They MF Tried It, Track 6) to support your side of the story and clarify any misunderstandings. Approach these conversations calmly and constructively, promoting transparency and open communication to prevent gossip from taking root and fostering a more supportive work environment.

Another challenge is when someone takes credit for your work. This can be incredibly frustrating, but there are ways to address it. If you're effectively managing up, across, and beyond (Track 8), the right stakeholders should recognize you as the true contributor. Leverage project management tools to track your key initiatives and document your contributions. This proactive approach not only establishes your credibility but also makes it harder for others to claim your work. By navigating these conflicts with tact and resilience, you protect your professional reputation and help cultivate a workplace culture rooted in honesty and mutual respect. While you may not be able to change the entire workplace ecosystem, you can ensure that your contributions are acknowledged and valued.

Dealing with Organizational Change

When a reorganization occurs, adaptability becomes crucial. Take the time to understand the new structure and expectations, while digging deeper to uncover the strategic objectives behind the changes. Engage with leadership and your network to clarify how your role fits into this new setup and identify potential opportunities or challenges.

Reorg-Ready Corporate Queens: Steps to Stay Strong and Pivot

➡ **Embrace Adaptability:** Stay open to adjusting your goals and strategies as changes unfold. Keep communication channels clear with supervisors and team members to ensure alignment.

➡ **Strategic Engagement:** Take advantage of opportunities to work closely with new managers, showcasing your skills and positioning yourself as an essential team member. Volunteer for cross-functional projects that align with evolving goals.

➡ **Purposeful Prioritization:** Use the Prioritization Matrix (Importance vs. Urgency) for effective planning. Define success with your manager, focusing on maintaining quality outputs. Protect your work-life balance to avoid burnout, especially in the aftermath of reorgs in which you may be expected to get more done with less folks around to do the work.

The Unfortunate Reality of Layoffs

Layoffs, similarly, are a challenging aspect of the corporate landscape, often driven by strategic shifts or economic pressures. It's vital to remember that your worth is not tied to these decisions. Whether you're navigating the aftermath of a downsizing or contemplating your next career move, approach this transition with resilience and a clear strategy. For those who remain in the organization, the "Reorg-

Ready" strategies are still applicable. For those facing layoffs, new dynamics come into play.

Layoff Bounce Back: Can't Hold a Corporate Queen Down

↪ **Embrace the Change:** Use this time for reflection and planning your next steps. When one door closes, another opens; keep your mindset open to new possibilities.

↪ **Check Your Finances:** Assess your savings and any severance packages to understand how long you can cover essential expenses.

↪ **Freshen Up Your Digital Profile:** Update your résumé, LinkedIn, and personal website to stay prepared for new opportunities.

↪ **Tap Into Your Network:** Reach out to industry contacts and former colleagues for support and job leads.

↪ **Learn and Explore:** Consider taking courses or earning certifications to boost your competitiveness. Freelancing or starting a side hustle can also provide a financial cushion.

By embracing adaptability and leveraging your support network, you can navigate the complexities of organizational change with confidence. Remember, every challenge is an opportunity for growth, and you have the power to turn adversity into a stepping stone for your future success.

Practicing Gratitude

While workplace dynamics can sometimes feel transactional, with favors exchanged and alliances formed, genuine expressions of gratitude transcend mere reciprocity. Taking the time to sincerely thank colleagues and team members for their support, whether through a personal note or public acknowledgment, not only strengthens bonds but also demonstrates respect and appreciation. When colleagues go above and beyond to assist you, a thoughtful note of appreciation can make a profound impact. Consider copying their manager to ensure their efforts are recognized at a higher level, reinforcing their value and dedication.

Moreover, many companies have formal gratitude or recognition programs in place. Utilizing these platforms, especially during your initial 90 days in a new role, can significantly enhance your integration into the team. Recognizing the efforts of others publicly through these channels not only acknowledges their contributions but also boosts their visibility and reputation within the organization, and we'll talk more on this in Track 14.

By nurturing relationships through sincere appreciation and strategic recognition, you position yourself for long-term career success and continue to build a strong network of support. In the words of Auntie Maya Angelou, "I've learned that people will forget what you said, people will forget what you did, but people will never forget how you made them feel."

Abundant Career Chronicle: Reflections on My Time in Corporate America

As a first-generation college graduate and corporate professional, entering the workforce presented its challenges, despite my early start with odd jobs and summer programs. My first real job at McDonald's at 16 was a stepping stone, but nothing prepared me for Corporate America as a triple minority: young, female, and Black to the core. The company I joined, despite its flaws, was a powerhouse I'd work for again. Yet, it embodied the Old Boys' Club of Corporate America. In 2014, when I officially entered the workforce, it was a time when four generations were working side by side, which was a learning curve for everyone involved. I remember those happy hours with colleagues, where the running joke was they'd been hitting the same spot for 25 years. I was just 22 then, so the idea of staying at one company for decades with the same routine seemed surreal.

Back then, corporate loyalty meant everything as you stuck around for the pension, a promise of stability and security that often defined your entire career path. It was common to spend decades at the same company, building up seniority and benefits that would see you through retirement. However, today's corporate landscape has shifted dramatically. The focus has shifted toward maximizing your time, skills, and pay within each role, recognizing that career growth and fair compensation often necessitate moving between companies. Loyalty now extends to the advancement of personal and professional development, where individuals seek new challenges, opportunities for learning, and equitable rewards that align with their evolving aspirations and skills. This dynamic environment encourages agility and adaptability, where each career move is seen as a strategic step toward achieving long-term success and fulfillment.

Reflecting on my career journey in the first half of this book brought back many emotions. There's truly no way to know all the things that come with transitioning into working adulthood except through firsthand life lessons or the secondhand wisdom shared by others. As a triple minority, each aspect of my identity brought its own set of hurdles, from navigating corporate politics and dealing with microaggressions (even changing my hair every two to three weeks became a topic of conversation) to securing those well-earned promotions. Navigating Corporate America isn't always smooth sailing. Like many of my Corporate Queens of color, I was taught to work hard, two or three times more than my counterparts, and that my work would speak for itself. However, as many of us eventually learn, that's not always the case.

Being able to translate my own firsthand workplace lessons into secondhand wisdom via the EMBODY Framework, to shine a light and put structure to the unwritten rules of corporate success, is fulfilling in ways I can't even put into words. Capitalism wasn't designed for everyone to succeed, but amid the challenges, there are winners. My aim for you, after reading this first half, is to equip you with the tools to be among those winners: play the corporate game strategically, secure more money, and move closer to Financial Abundance and Work-Optional Status.

tFAB in Action: Navigating the Workplace Like a Boss

This Track's tFAB in Action moment is all about mastering some of the unwritten rules and challenges that come with being in the corporate world. Here are your final action items from Side A of the book:

Expand Your Network: Build relationships internally and externally to support career growth and mentorship.

Craft Your Digital Presence: Curate a professional online profile that highlights your skills and attracts opportunities.

Optimize Your Résumé: Keep your résumé updated and tailored to showcase relevant achievements and skills.

Plan for Promotions: Remember to have a slice of PIE (Performance, Image, Exposure) when vying for promotions.

Manage Workplace Conflicts: Develop conflict-resolution skills and maintain your TMFTI receipts when challenges arise.

Adapt to Organizational Changes: Embrace change and navigate layoffs or reorganizations with resilience.

Practice Gratitude: Foster a mindset of gratitude to enhance resilience and happiness in your career.

BUILDING YOUR FINANCIAL SYSTEM

INTERLUDE: THE 9-TO-5ER'S WEALTH PYRAMID FRAMEWORK

Hey, Corporate Queens! Can we just take a moment to acknowledge and celebrate how far we've come together? In the initial Tracks, we delved into self-discovery, aligning ourselves authentically for success in both personal and professional realms. Thanks to the EMBODY Framework, we're equipped with the tools and strategies to navigate the corporate environment with ease, transitioning from mere survival to thriving in our 9-to-5 careers! We've strategically positioned ourselves to successfully secure the corporate bag and now we can transition our conversation toward maximizing that bag. However, financial abundance goes beyond income. It encompasses those core four aspects we explored early on: significant financial resources, choice freedom, peace of mind, and positive contributions all defined by you.

The notion of "significant financial resources" varies for each of us, setting the stage for our journey to Side B! Here, we'll explore managing and maximizing our coins using the 9-to-5er's Wealth Pyramid Framework. This book aims to change the narrative around financial literacy and wealth-building discussions, making them inclusive for underrepresented communities and those navigating the journey for the first time.

In true Amanda fashion, I aim to connect the dots. This book, centered on financial literacy, spent considerable time discussing careers and the unwritten rules to mastering the workplace, because everything is interconnected. Ambitious women need to know not only how to secure the bag (i.e., how to thrive in their careers) but also how to grow that bag (i.e., how to maximize their money). This seamlessly leads us to our next revelation: the Career and Money Journey (CMJ) Map.

The Career and Money Journey Map is a powerful tool for understanding how your corporate and financial experiences have flowed over time. This exercise is a moment of reflection, introspection, and celebration. I vividly remember preparing for a speaking gig for new college grads at a major tech company as part of their rotation program's development day summit. I crafted the CMJ Map to help these emerging leaders understand the importance of the financial tips I shared for maximizing their corporate compensation on their journey toward Financial Independence (FI) while providing a visual representation of what implementation of said tips can look like over the course of their career.

As Corporate Queens, it's crucial for us to acknowledge our achievements and to understand the intricate dance between our careers and our financial choices. Throughout our career journeys, there will be different priorities guiding our decisions that have financial implications. Sometimes you'll take on a new role purely for a raise in salary. Sometimes you'll take on a new role due to your

MY CARETER AND MONEY JOURNEY

2014 — Graduated from University of Pennsylvania with BS in economics and $43,000 in student loans (plus a $22,000 car loan)

2014 — Hired as a Customer and Business Intelligence Analyst at Verizon

2014 — Started paying minimums on student loans and car loans; started contributing 6% to company 401(k); began graduate school

2015 — Became a Consumer Insights Analyst at Verizon (lateral move)

2016 — Introduced to #DebtFreeCommunity on IG, beginning my Financial Literacy Journey

2016 — Promoted to Segment and Cultural Marketing Senior Analyst at Verizon

2017 — 401(k) employer contributions fully vested at Verizon

2017 — Hired as an Account Strategist at Google; moved from New Jersey to California

2018 — Became Digital Strategy Lead at Google (lateral move); no student loan debt

2018 — Graduated from Boston University with MS in global marketing management (with no new student loans!)

2019 — Promoted to Senior Account Executive at Google

2019 — Began maxing out 401(k)

2020 — Became a Partner Manager at Google (rotation in Italy); began contributing to and maxing out Roth IRA (Backdoor) & HSA (Family) accounts

2020 — Became a Sales Trainer at Google (lateral move)

2021 — Achieved Coast FIRE (retirement by age 65 guaranteed!)

2022 — Promoted to Senior Sales Trainer at Google; Boy Mom on maternity leave life stage changes or a location preference. Sometimes you'll stay in a role, longer than desired, because it provides greater flexibility for you to pour into other aspects of your life. As illustrated in my CMJ Map, you'll see how milestones in career and money decisions, and life in general, are all interrelated and ultimately a reinforcement that everything will work out over time. Not all milestones will happen in a linear way.

At first glance, it may seem like I've had a smooth journey, navigating multiple company cultures, earning promotions, making lateral moves, paying off student loans, and investing in retirement accounts. It's 2024 as I reflect on my CMJ Map and where it stands today, currently enjoying a career thriving with ease while seeing multiple six-figure gains in my portfolio, on the brink of financial independence, and it's all surreal. Small steps and humble beginnings manifested into something greater than even I thought possible so long ago. They say a picture is worth a thousand words, and that rings true here as there's certainly more to the story.

What?! you might ask. You hyped up your CMJ Map, and now you're telling us there's more to the story? Absolutely! I promised to keep it real, sharing both successes and hard lessons. Understanding the origin of the 9-to-5er's Wealth Pyramid is crucial to understanding why it's been so effective for myself, my clients, and the thousands of other professional young adults I've hosted workshops for on this very framework. If I had known these insights earlier in my adulting journey, I'd be even further along and closer to my goals.

My Money Story

My earliest lessons in personal finance came at a young age. I had to be in the single digits, definitely less than ten years old. My dad came up to me and my brother and told us to divide our money into thirds:

bills, savings, and spending. Thinking back on it now, it was essentially a lesson in budgeting 101, and it kind of made sense even for a young mind. My next money memory came from my aunt, who shared a more extreme approach: for every dollar you get, spend 50 percent and invest or save the other 50 percent. Honestly, looking back on it, her strategy was technically my first introduction into the FIRE Movement, which stands for Financially Independent, Retire Early. Although she never mentioned FIRE directly, the idea of aggressively putting aside a significant percentage of your earnings was certainly FIRE-ish. For my final and most impactful money memory, I reflect on my mom, who embodies abundant generosity and was always the first to help others. Through her example, she illustrated the importance of giving back in a way that's authentic to your financial goals while setting boundaries to protect yourself too. Little did I know it at the time, but these early lessons laid the foundation for my financial journey.

When I was old enough to get a real job, I did what any highschooler would do: apply for a job at McDonald's, of course! Now that $7.15 per hour seems like nothing in today's age of inflation, but back in 2008, you couldn't tell me a thing! I learned the importance of having a financial buffer and not splurging mindlessly. I would often have uncashed checks waiting for me even when payday came around.

Let me acknowledge my privilege real quick. I came from a middle-class two-parent household where all my basic needs were met and then some. I recognized, even as a child, what a blessing that was and still is today. So needless to say, part of the paycheck stacking came from not having grown-up responsibilities thrown on me as a teenage child. But even still, I clearly wasn't blowing the money shopping at the mall every weekend either, so give your girl a little bit of credit too!

Fast forward to college decisions, and best believe your girl had plenty of options, having been a high achiever with a strong GPA and all the extracurriculars stacked on my high school résumé. I got into nearly every college I applied to and secured some form of financial aid! When it came time to decide on where I would attend, I ended up turning down a full-ride scholarship to a local school and instead chose to attend the University of Pennsylvania, an Ivy League School, instead, which required me to take out over $40,000 in student loans. For context, as a future 1st Gen College student, I wasn't aware at the time of the Ivy League. I took a college-matching quiz that placed UPenn at the top of the list based on my educational aspirations and desired collegiate experience. Even at a young age, I've always been high into self-awareness, as we discussed in Track 3! I chose to attend the school that appeared best suited to meet my desires in a college education.

Looking back on it, I know I made the right decision, but from a financial perspective, one could certainly argue that the full-ride could have made better sense. Throughout my college experience, I found myself always working at least two jobs at a time since freshman year. The fall semester of my senior year, I was actually balancing four jobs at once! Though they were not full-time jobs, given everything else on my plate: full course load, dance team, business fraternity, basketball games, and the jobs too; it honestly felt like managing 60+ hours of work per week. Needless to say, I learned very quickly the benefit of having multiple streams of income as well as the importance of work-life balance. Your girl averaged less than five hours of sleep each night for three months straight...Unfortunately, because my knowledge of investing was quite limited (well, frankly speaking, it was nonexistent), I lost out on $10,000s of future growth; had I known, I would have put that money to great use.

Adding on to my early money lessons, the decision to take on the financial burden of loans raises an important perspective about goal alignment. Sometimes the required path, in alignment with your long-term goals, might require a few less optimal decisions and experiences in the short-term. Either way, we must remain focused on what's authentically in alignment with our Abundant Life desires, block out the noise, and stay on the path forward.

Graduating in 2014 with over $40,000 in student loans, I made financial decisions, such as getting a new car, that added another $20,000+ in financial responsibilities. Starting a full-time job at Verizon with a $54,000 salary, I entered the post-grad life, chasing the Millennial's American dream: work hard, live modestly, and pay off my loans. I even started grad school soon after in fall 2014, recognizing the importance of a master's degree for climbing the corporate ladder. However, at this point, I owed more money in student + car loans than what I made in a year, and that's before Uncle Sam took his cut in taxes.

In 2017, a game-changer entered my life. Ms. Arriaza, a colleague at Verizon, introduced me to Dave Ramsey and his book, *The Total Money Makeover*. While I don't endorse his platform today, he was the catalyst for my debt-free journey. His seven baby steps guided me to become debt-free in 2018, but building wealth was a challenge I'd take on through further self-education.

From 2017 onward, my journey became one of discovery, education, and empowerment in finances. Living In The Abundance (LITA) originally started as an Instagram page documenting my debt-free journey, later evolving into a community of 16,000+ individuals seeking to thrive in their careers and maximize their money through the collective sharing of tips and strategies. If I could speak to little Amanda with her minimal financial literacy, I'd let her know that, by 2024, when she's thirty-two years old, she'll have mastered the following lessons:

➥ You don't have to know everything, just be willing to learn something new every day and trust it's going to all work out.

→ You'll be Debt Free, having paid off $60,000+ in student loans and car payments.

→ You'll have figured out the Corporate Game, resulting in multiple promotions and securing multiple six-figure compensation.

→ You'll have achieved Coast FI, which means you already have enough money invested that, even if you don't invest another dime, your money will grow into enough for retirement at 65.

→ You'll maximize the heck out of your corporate benefits, resulting in $1,000s in incremental value each year.

→ You're on track to achieve Financial Independence status in your 30s!

→ You'll impact the lives of thousands of young professionals, guiding them with their careers and money journeys through your workshops and mentorship so they too can experience financial freedom for themselves and their families, creating a legacy that will resonate for generations to come.

The 9-to-5er's Wealth Pyramid Framework

The 9-to-5er's Wealth Pyramid Framework emerged from necessity. As a first-gen everything Black woman, my journey to full financial literacy took years of trial and error. The 9-to-5er's Wealth Pyramid (9-to-5er's WP) Framework offers a simple pathway to build wealth and achieve financial wholeness, customizable to individual goals for those work a typical day job, a.k.a. my Corporate Queens!

Visualize the 9-to-5er's WP Framework as your guide. The foundation, the first layer, is the literal base of the pyramid. Before building wealth, we need the freedom to do so; hence, the foundation. It gives us the peace of mind to let our money grow without constant withdrawals. In this layer, we'll tackle crafting your Prosperity Plan (budget), setting money goals aligned with your values, and creating realistic plans for saving and paying off debt.

Moving up the pyramid, divided into different sections, we'll explore the world of investing, remixed for the modern-day Corporate Queen's easy understanding! Investing is about making your money work for you to make you more money. We'll focus on organizing your money movement and optimizing your credit usage while providing strategies for navigating challenging financial conversations and decisions. Additionally, we'll explore ways to increase your income through multiple streams and maximize your corporate benefits for enhanced financial growth. By the end of Side B, you'll have a personal wealth-building plan ready for implementation. Just as we automate aspects of our careers, we'll do the same

THE 9-TO-5er's WEALTH PYRAMID

Brokerage

After-Tax
401(k) (Mega
Back Door Roth)

Traditional/Roth 401(k)
up to Annual Contribution Limit

Traditional/Roth
IRA

Health Savings
Account (HSA)

Traditional/Roth 401(k) up to Employer Match

The Foundation:
Prosperity Plan (Budget),
Savings Goals (Emergency Fund, Sinking Funds),
Debt Payoff Plan ("Snowy" Methods)

for maximizing our money, which should be as easy as building a '90s-themed music playlist on Spotify. Don't worry, that'll make sense by the end of Side B.

FAB in Action: Preparing for Financial Abundance

Before you embark on crafting a wealth-building plan, it's important you take some time to reflect on your history and relationship with money. Truth be told, you can have the best mentor, laid-out instructions, visual aids, etc., in the world, but if something on the inside won't "let you be great," then it needs to be dealt with. Living paycheck to paycheck isn't always about not making enough money; sometimes it stems from poor decisions that are the result of warped money mindsets. If you find yourself struggling to answer the questions below or experience intense negative emotions of sadness, or shame, or guilt, etc., I urge you to seek counseling or therapy in this area. YOU don't want to be the person holding YOU and Your Family back from a future of financial freedom (or at least financial stability). Here are your reflections-based action items:

1. Money Background: What is your earliest memory of money? How was money experienced in your family?

2. Money Mindset: How do you feel about your financial journey? Is it stressing you out, giving you security, or empowering you?

3. Financial Goals: What are your money dreams? Short-term and long-term?

4. Spending Habits: What types of purchases lead to you experiencing an increase in joy? Which purchases, alternatively, miss the joy-mark for you?

5. Emergency Preparedness: Life happens. Do you have that stash for unexpected moments? How are you handling those surprise money curveballs?

6. Debt Awareness: Who's knocking on your door because you owe 'em a little somethin' somethin'? How much do you owe them?

7. Savings and Investments: You shared your financial goals above. Help me understand how, if at all, you're progressing against them? Are your financial goals a line item in your budget?

8. Financial Education: How do you feel about money talk? Any financial lingo that's making you go, "Wait, what?!"

This reflection sets the stage for our journey toward financial abundance. As we explore the layers of the 9-to-5er's Wealth Pyramid, remember, it's not just about wealth-building; it's about crafting a life of abundance on your terms.

YOUR PROSPERITY PLAN

Let's dive into traditional budgets often seen as the financial equivalent of a strict diet, always saying "no" to the things you enjoy. But we can change that. The negativity around budgeting often comes from focusing on scarcity, which can feel demoralizing. Instead, let's embrace the Prosperity Plan. It's not about restrictions; it's a powerful tool to help you achieve your financial goals and build lasting wealth. Think of it as your roadmap to abundance, guiding you to make intentional choices with your hard-earned money.

Here's the magic: with a personalized Prosperity Plan tailored to your goals and lifestyle, you gain freedom. It's not just about making great money in Corporate America; it's about managing those funds effectively to create your most abundant life. Imagine directing your money toward what truly matters to you, guilt-free, while cutting out unnecessary expenses that bring you zero happiness. We'll keep it flexible and easy to use, integrating tools and strategies seamlessly into your life!

However, before crafting your Prosperity Plan, it's crucial to acknowledge the impact of money traumas, which often shape how you manage finances today. Think back to your early childhood experiences with money: Did you have enough money when you were growing up? Is money a source of power or fear? Are there concerns about falling back into poverty? These questions reveal how past financial experiences influence current behaviors. Money traumas manifest in various ways, affecting your ability to stick to budgets and make sound decisions. Challenges like impulse buying, unrealistic expectations, and inconsistent tracking can derail efforts. Social pressures, irregular income, and debt add stress, while complex financial terms complicate matters. Emotional spending driven by stress or boredom exacerbates financial challenges. Now is a great opportunity to revisit your reflections from Track 10's tFAB in action moment and consider whether you need to take further action. To address these issues and move toward financial freedom, consider these steps for overcoming money trauma:

→ **Acknowledge and Reflect:** Take time to understand how past financial experiences have shaped your beliefs and behaviors. This awareness can help you identify triggers that lead to unhealthy financial habits.

→ **Seek Professional Support:** Consider working with a therapist or financial counselor specializing in money trauma. They can provide insights and strategies to heal from past experiences and develop healthier financial habits.

→ **Educate Yourself:** Increase your financial literacy to build confidence in managing money effectively. Understanding financial concepts and strategies empowers you to navigate challenges and make informed decisions.

→ **Practice Mindfulness:** Cultivate mindfulness to observe your thoughts and emotions about money without judgment.

This practice can help you recognize patterns of behavior and develop more constructive responses.

→ **Set Realistic Goals:** Establish clear and achievable financial goals that align with your values and aspirations. Break them down into manageable steps to track progress and celebrate milestones along the way.

→ **Take Incremental Steps:** Start implementing practical strategies such as budgeting, saving, and debt repayment. Consistent effort and small changes over time can lead to significant improvements in your financial well-being.

Addressing money traumas is a critical step toward building a healthier relationship with money and achieving your financial goals. By confronting these challenges and adopting proactive strategies, you can overcome barriers, reduce financial stress, and pave the way for a more prosperous future. And hey? Picking up this book is a great first start on your journey to financial healing

Crafting Your Prosperity Plan

Crafting Your Prosperity Plan is all about being intentional with your hard-earned money, ensuring it brings you joy and aligns with your journey to financial freedom! Inspired by the iconic Missy Elliott song "Work It," here are the five elements to guide your Prosperity Plan:

→ What are you working with? (What is your Income?)

→ Where do you want and need to work it? (What are your Lifestyle Expenses?)

→ How do you want to work it going forward? (What is your Abundance Accelerator?)

→ When do you want to work it? (What are your SMART Financial Goals?)

➥ How are you going to keep working it because it's worth it? (How are you going to invest to achieve your Financial Freedom?)

To quote the first couple of lines of the song, "*Is it worth it? Let me work it. I put my thang down, flip it, and reverse it. Ti esrever dna ti pilf nwod gnaht ym tup i.*" Translation: Plan your financial goals and approach and then work your plan, as long as it's in alignment with what's worth it to you!

The point of crafting Your Prosperity Plan is that it is 100% You-Focused. You need to believe in your plan, or it's never going to stick. That's not to say you won't have mishaps along the way as life be lifin'. But if you're spending your money based on someone else's expectations, you're never going to get there. Let's delve into the first three elements now, leaving the rest for future Tracks.

1. What are you working with? (What is your Income)?

Let's start with the basics: your income. It's crucial to know exactly how much money you bring in and how frequently it arrives. Everyone deserves at least a livable wage to cover their basic needs, but sadly, that's not always the reality. Now, assuming you have a consistent income or even if it's irregular, here's a simple exercise to clarify things:

Create a table with three columns: "Income Stream," "How Often," and "How Much." List all your sources of income where money reliably enters your accounts or hands. For each income stream, jot down the average amount you receive and how often it comes in. Calculate your total monthly income based on these figures. Table 1 gives an example.

TABLE 1: INCOME STREAMS

Income Stream	How Often	How Much $
9-to-5 Corporate Job	Biweekly	$3,000
Side Hustle 1 (Lyft Driver)	Monthly	$350
Side Hustle 2 (Digital Products)	Quarterly	$1,500
Christmas Bonus (9-to-5 Job)	Annually	$500
What You're Working With Monthly Avg. (Income)		**$6,350**

You might notice, in Table 1, I didn't factor in all the irregular income, such as the digital product side hustle or bonuses. Why? Because when crafting your Prosperity Plan, we want a realistic view of what we're working with to cover our consistent monthly lifestyle expenses. Depending heavily on irregular income can skew our perception of what's sustainable. If your income fluctuates, consider planning around the minimum you can reliably count on. This approach ensures you're prepared for any financial curveballs. Plus, that additional irregular income will serve as a bonus to help accelerate progress toward your goals once you can officially count on it coming in.

Now that you've completed this exercise, you'll have a clear picture of your average monthly income. Whether you're pleasantly surprised or slightly frustrated, remember, this clarity is essential as we move forward. It's about facing our financial reality head-on and realizing where adjustments may be needed. Let's dive into the next steps with confidence, knowing we're building a plan that truly works for you.

2. Where do you want and need to work it? (What are your Lifestyle Expenses?)

Let's dive into your lifestyle expenses. At the end of the day, life is short, so you deserve to enjoy it and live in a way that brings you fulfillment. I prefer to call these lifestyle expenses rather than bills or spending categories because they reflect the life you're curating for yourself. For some, it might mean brunch every Saturday, a new outfit bi-weekly, and cozy nights at home. For others, it's about jetting off to exotic locations, indulging in enriching experiences, or building a nurturing home and family life. No matter your vision, every choice has its tradeoffs, and that's perfectly okay as long as it aligns with your values.

The key here is to understand your current lifestyle expenses to establish a baseline of where you are today. Remember, our current reality is not where we shall remain. Let's simplify this process with a handy table (see Table 2). If you find it challenging to estimate these costs, review your bank and credit card statements from the last three months. Most digital platforms categorize spending, giving you a clear view of your expenses. Use these averages as a baseline and adjust as needed to reflect your lifestyle.

TABLE 2: CURRENT LIFESTYLE EXPENSES

Current Lifestyle	Subcategories	How Much $
Housing	Rent	$3,000
	Utilities	$300
Transportation	Car Payment	$350
	Car Insurance	$150
	Gas	$250

The Financial Abundance Blueprint

TABLE 2: CURRENT LIFESTYLE EXPENSES

Current Lifestyle	Subcategories	How Much $
Food	Groceries	$400
	Restaurants / Takeout	$350
Personal Spending	Personal Care (Hair, Skin, Makeup)	$500
	Clothing & Accessories	$200
	Entertainment	$300
Debt Minimum Payment	Student Loans	$250
Experiences	Vacation / Travel	-
	Celebrations	$50
Miscellaneous	Everything Else	$200
Where do you want and need to work it? (Monthly Expenses)		$6,300

Remember, in Track 1, Abundance on a 9-to-5, I had you do a visualization exercise around your abundant life. Recall how I guided you to describe in detail a typical day, the activities you enjoyed, the people you spent time with, and more. Now is the moment to put that vision into concrete terms. Just like a client who realized she was within reach of her abundant life with some adjustments to her Prosperity Plan, I want you to experience that same breakthrough.

Take some time to translate your Abundant Life vision onto paper. Estimate how much each category of your Abundant Lifestyle will cost to bring to life.

TABLE 3: ABUNDANT LIFESTYLE EXPENSES

Abundant Lifestyle	Subcategories	How Much $
Housing	Mortgage	$4,500
	Utilities	$450
Transportation	Car Payment	$400
	Car Insurance	$175
	Gas	$375
Food	Groceries	$300
	Restaurants / Takeout	$800
Personal Spending	Personal Care (Hair, Skin, Makeup)	$1,000
	Clothing & Accessories	$100
	Entertainment	$100
Childcare	Daycare / Preschool	$1,000
Experiences	Vacation #1	$700
	Vacation #2	$550
	Celebrations	$50
Miscellaneous	Everything Else	$500
Where do you want and need to work it? (Monthly Funding)		**$11,000**

In the example provided in Table 3, their Abundant Life would require roughly forty percent more than their current spending. This figure might seem daunting but achieving the Abundant Life you envision often requires increasing income. However, it's promising to see that there are areas where funds can be reallocated from categories that don't align with the person's most abundant life, such as shifting money from the entertainment category (\$300 → \$100) and putting toward vacations (\$0 → \$200 out of the \$550 for #2) to start living closer to their abundant life sooner! This awareness can provide early momentum toward achieving your goals. Remember, the objective here is to visualize the gap between your current and desired lifestyles and then craft a plan to bridge that gap.

3. How do you want to work it going forward? (What is your Abundance Accelerator?)

Now that we've established what we're working with, our reliable income streams, and where we want and need to allocate those funds to sustain our current and desired lifestyles, it's time to focus on how we propel ourselves forward. This is where your Abundance Accelerator comes into play. Remember our earlier exercise where you visualized your Abundant Life? The key word here is "Your" Abundant Life. We're crafting a Prosperity Plan that aligns with what truly brings you joy and fulfillment, not what society dictates.

> ## Your Abundance Accelerator =
> ## Income – Lifestyle Expenses

This gap between your income and lifestyle expenses is where the magic toward your Abundant Life happens, which is why we call it your Abundance Accelerator. There's a financial principle that advises living below your means and investing the difference, and that's essentially what we're doing here, but with a touch of sparkle. Whether it's \$100 or \$1,000 a month, this surplus is what will enable you to not only create but also start living your Abundant Life.

This leftover money isn't just extra cash; it's fuel for your financial journey. It can be channeled into investments to generate more wealth, funding for a side hustle or business venture, or simply enhancing your lifestyle further, however you want to maximize those funds. We emphasize understanding our current lifestyle expenses up-front because it's crucial to spend intentionally on what truly adds value to your life. This includes prioritizing expenses aligned with your values and minimizing or eliminating those that don't contribute positively.

In Table 4, this Corporate Queen's total monthly income we can rely on is $6,350. Comparatively, her current monthly lifestyle expenses total roughly $6,300, leaving an initial Abundance Accelerator of approximately $50* (this is what we can consistently count on monthly). While this figure may seem modest, it's a starting point that reflects reality for many individuals striving toward financial stability and abundance. Furthermore, as is the case with this Corporate Queen's additional irregular streams (side hustles, bonuses), when those surplus funds come in, she can then allocate them to "accelerate" achieving her financial goals on a case-by-case basis!

TABLE 4: ABUNDANCE ACCELERATOR

Your Prosperity Plan (Summary)	How Much $?
Total Income	$6,350
Total Lifestyle Expenses	$6,300
Abundance Accelerator	$50*

And remember, where this number starts today is not where it will end. The first part of this journey equipped you with strategies to navigate the corporate world effectively. Understanding these dynamics enhances your ability to excel professionally, which can lead to higher income opportunities and accelerated financial growth. As income increases, your Abundance Accelerator grows, accelerating your path to Financial Freedom. When it comes to lifestyle expenses, mapping out the financial requirements of your desired life versus your current reality is essential for tracking progress and making informed decisions. Remember, everything in life involves tradeoffs. Saying Yes to one thing inevitably means saying No to something else, and that's not a bad thing, just a reality. Spend in ways that bring genuine joy and value to your life, not to impress others or meet societal expectations. Staying true to your values makes achieving financial goals and living your Abundant Life much more attainable and rewarding. Now that we've covered the first three foundational elements of your Prosperity Plan, let's explore some tools that will bring this plan to life.

Building Your Prosperity Plan Toolbox

Now that we've grasped the three primary elements of our Prosperity Plan: our Income (which we aim to grow over time), our Lifestyle Expenses (the cost of living), and our Abundance Accelerator (the difference between income and expenses, which funds our Financial Freedom goals—let's explore the tools that will bring this plan to life. This section, "Building Your Prosperity Plan Toolbox," equips you with essentials for a successful and sustainable prosperity plan.

First, you need a mechanism to track your expenses, especially in the early stages of this journey. If your abundance accelerator is negative (meaning you're spending more than your income allows), tracking expenses becomes crucial. Knowing exactly where your money goes helps you make informed decisions and adjustments. Digital tools such as budgeting apps (for example, YNAB and Nerd Wallet) offer user-friendly features for logging expenses, categorizing them, and generating reports. For those preferring a traditional approach, spreadsheets like Excel and Google Sheets allow for customization to fit specific needs.

Second, understanding your net worth is essential for a comprehensive financial plan. Your net worth represents a snapshot of your financial health by calculating the difference between your assets (such as savings, investments, and property) and your liabilities (debts such as car loans and credit card balances). Empower Personal Dashboard App, in my own experience, emerges as an invaluable digital tool for managing your net worth. Through its app and website, Empower provides detailed reporting and intuitive dashboards that allow you to monitor income streams, analyze spending patterns, and assess your net worth growth. By linking your bank accounts and credit cards, the platform automatically aggregates your financial data, offering a clear overview of major spending categories and financial trends. For those preferring a more hands-on approach, traditional methods such as using spreadsheets can also effectively track net worth. While more time-consuming initially, spreadsheets offer customization and flexibility tailored to your specific financial tracking needs. Regardless of the tool or approach, it's important to have that 360-degree holistic view of your personal finances. Tracking not only increases accountability but seeing your progress is a great motivator to keep going!

This third "tool" is optional but could be critical for folks where the money traumas are having a great effect on their money-management abilities (and that's okay, let's get the help we need!). Consider adding a financial coach or advisor to your toolkit, particularly if money management feels challenging. A coach can elevate your financial literacy, while an advisor provides strategic guidance to maximize your financial potential. While not essential, such support can be transformative, especially in the early stages of building wealth and understanding financial strategies.

Our final and fourth "tool" is to establish an accountability mechanism tailored to your lifestyle. This could vary based on whether you manage finances solo or with a partner. Regular financial check-ins biweekly or monthly are recommended to assess progress against goals and adjust spending as needed. Utilize your chosen tool (spreadsheet, app) to review planned versus actual spending, ensuring alignment with your Prosperity Plan, and make adjustments as necessary for future months. By assembling these tools and practices, you create a structured approach to managing your finances effectively, paving the way for achieving your Financial Freedom goals.

Putting Your Prosperity Plan into Action

Now that we've redefined budgeting as a Prosperity Plan, it's time to find the approach that best fits your lifestyle and financial goals. Just as everyone's journey to prosperity is unique, so too are the methods that can help you get there. To help you identify the ideal budgeting method for you, take the following quiz. It's designed to match your preferences and habits with the most suitable Prosperity Plan approach, setting you up for success on your path to Financial Freedom.

Abundant Wealth Chronicle: Prosperity Plan Quiz

1. How detailed do you want your budget to be?

A) Extremely detailed, tracking every expense

B) Moderately detailed, with clear categories

C) Simple, with broad categories

D) Not detailed at all; I prefer automation.

2. How much time are you willing to spend on managing your budget each month?

A) A lot of time; I enjoy tracking every penny.

B) A moderate amount of time; I can manage weekly check-ins.

C) Minimal time; I prefer a quick monthly review.

D) Very little time; I want it to be almost automatic.

3. **What is your primary financial goal?**

    A) Controlling spending and maximizing savings

    B) Balancing needs and wants while saving

    C) Ensuring I don't overspend on discretionary items

    D) Making sure I prioritize my financial goals first before anything else

4. **How do you feel about using cash for budgeting?**

    A) I mostly prefer digital transactions.

    B) I'm okay with some cash but prefer digital tracking.

    C) I'm comfortable using cash for most transactions.

    D) I rarely use cash; I prefer everything to be automated.

5. **How do you handle unexpected expenses?**

    A) I meticulously track unexpected expenses and adjust my budget accordingly to ensure every dollar is accounted for.

    B) I have a buffer category for unexpected expenses in my budget. I handle them as they come.

    C) I try to use my savings to cover unexpected expenses, but I don't stress too much if it dips into a specific spending category.

    D) I have a well-funded emergency fund as a safety net for unexpected expenses.

6. **How disciplined are you with sticking to a budget?**

    A) Very disciplined; I stick to every dollar assigned.

    B) Moderately disciplined; I follow my budget but with some flexibility.

    C) Not very disciplined; I struggle with overspending from time to time.

    D) More than disciplined; I reach my financial goals and live within my means.

7. **What's your preferred method of tracking expenses?**

    A) Manually recording every expense

    B) Using a budgeting app or spreadsheet

The Financial Abundance Blueprint

C) Allocating funds to categories and tracking broadly

D) Automating savings and going with the flow from there

8. How do you feel about setting and achieving financial goals?

A) I thrive on setting specific financial goals and meticulously tracking my progress toward achieving them.

B) I enjoy having clear financial goals, but I prefer flexibility in the path I take to reach them.

C) I focus on setting broad financial goals that allow for adjustments as my life evolves.

D) I prioritize automating my financial goals. Once set, I focus on living my life.

Congratulations on completing the Prosperity Plan Quiz to discover which budgeting method is most ideal to help you achieve your financial goals and ultimately achieve a life of Financial Abundance! Don't worry, we're going to review each of these methods in depth in a moment, but based on your responses, here's where you likely fall. If you:

Mostly Checked A's: Use Zero-Based Budgeting Method.

Mostly Checked B's: Use 50/30/20 Budgeting Method.

Mostly Checked C's: Use the Envelope Budgeting System.

Mostly Checked D's: Use either the "Pay Yourself First" Budget or the "No Budget" Budget Methods.

Now that you understand which Prosperity Plan method is most aligned with your personality, behaviors, and goals, let's dive into each of them in more detail. You can also find templates online to help you get started, leverage the digital recommendations from above, or simply create your own!

Zero-Based Budgeting Method

Zero-Based Budgeting is a highly detailed approach to managing your finances where every dollar of your income is assigned a specific purpose until there are no unallocated funds left. This method requires you to account for every dollar, ensuring that your income is fully utilized in a purposeful manner. The main advantage of Zero-Based Budgeting is that it provides a crystal-clear picture of where your money is going, allowing for exceptional control over your spending and savings. By meticulously tracking expenses and income, Corporate Queens can identify areas where adjustments may be needed to align with their financial goals. However, Zero-Based Budgeting can be time-consuming to maintain due to the detailed tracking it requires. It is ideal for Corporate Queens who want to maximize control over their financial resources and are willing to invest the time needed to manage their budget meticulously.

50/30/20 Budgeting Method

50/30/20 Budgeting is a straightforward and balanced approach to managing your finances by dividing your after-tax income into three main categories: 50 percent for needs, 30 percent for wants, and 20 percent for savings and debt repayment. This method simplifies budgeting by providing clear guidelines on how much to allocate to essential expenses, discretionary spending, and financial goals. The primary advantage of 50/30/20 Budgeting is its simplicity, making it easy to implement and maintain without extensive tracking. It offers a balanced approach that ensures essential needs are met (50 percent), provides for discretionary spending on wants (30 percent), and prioritizes savings and debt repayment (20 percent). However, the 30 percent allocated for wants might be excessive for those with

The Financial Abundance Blueprint

substantial debt obligations, and some Corporate Queens may find the lack of detailed tracking less suitable for their financial management style. The 50/30/20 Budget is ideal for Corporate Queens seeking a straightforward approach that promotes financial harmony and helps achieve both short-term enjoyment and long-term financial goals.

The Envelope Budgeting System

The Envelope Budgeting System is a more "hands-on" approach to managing your finances by allocating cash into physical envelopes designated for different spending categories. Each envelope represents a specific category, such as groceries, entertainment, or transportation. Once the cash in an envelope is depleted, spending in that category *should* cease until the next budget cycle. This method encourages disciplined spending and significantly reduces the likelihood of overspending by imposing strict physical limits on discretionary expenses. By using the envelope system, Corporate Queens gain greater control over their finances and develop a heightened awareness of their spending habits. It also promotes prioritization of financial goals by allocating specific amounts to savings envelopes. However, the envelope budgeting system can be inconvenient in a largely cashless society where many transactions are conducted online or automatically. It may require additional effort to adapt the system for expenses like bills and subscriptions. Despite these challenges, the Envelope Budgeting System is ideal for Corporate Queens who struggle with overspending and prefer a hands-on method of managing their money. It fosters financial discipline and accountability while promoting conscious spending and savings habits.

The "Pay Yourself First" Budget

The Pay-Yourself-First budget is a proactive approach to financial management that prioritizes saving and investing by allocating a portion of your income to these goals before addressing other expenses. This method ensures that your financial objectives are met first, fostering a wealth-focused mindset that can lead to substantial financial growth over time. By committing to this approach, Corporate Queens create a habit of prioritizing long-term financial health over immediate spending. The Pay-Yourself-First Budget requires careful management of the remaining funds to ensure that all necessary expenses are covered without falling into debt. It encourages Corporate Queens to live within their means and make deliberate choices about their spending habits. However, for those facing challenges such as high fixed expenses, variable income, substantial debt, or who lack financial discipline, alternative budgeting approaches may be more appropriate until these challenges are addressed. This budgeting method is ideal for Corporate Queens who are committed to building their savings and investments, ensuring their financial future is secure while maintaining discipline in their spending habits. It promotes financial stability and resilience by establishing a consistent savings habit that supports both short-term financial goals and long-term wealth accumulation.

The "No Budget" Budget

The "No Budget" Budget is a simplified approach to managing finances that eschews detailed expense-tracking in favor of automating financial processes and adhering to general spending guidelines. This method relies on setting up automatic transfers to savings and investment accounts, as well as automated bill payments, to ensure that financial goals are met without the need for meticulous budgeting. The primary advantage of the "No Budget" Budget is that it is less time-consuming and stress-inducing, making it a great fit for Corporate Queens who find traditional budgeting methods overwhelming. By automating financial tasks and adhering to predetermined spending guidelines, Corporate Queens can achieve their savings and investment goals efficiently. It promotes financial mindfulness and goal-oriented behavior without the need for detailed tracking, allowing Corporate Queens to focus on enjoying life while securing their financial future. However, the "No Budget" Budget may not be suitable for Corporate Queens who struggle with impulsive purchases or have difficulty staying within their spending limits. It requires discipline to adhere to the predetermined guidelines and ensure that financial goals are prioritized over discretionary spending.

Now that you've identified your Prosperity Plan approach to budgeting and you know a bit more about it, how are you feeling? Seriously, take a moment. For some of you, it might feel like a light has shined on why budgeting has been a struggle in the past. Perhaps the method you were using simply didn't align with what works best for you.

Personally, I started out in the Zero-Based Budgeting camp. At that time, I was laser-focused on building my emergency fund and paying off debt. Every dollar had to be meticulously allocated; I remember my biweekly eating out budget was a strict $40, and going over meant peanut butter and jelly sandwiches at home. As my financial situation evolved—becoming debt-free, increasing my income, and stabilizing my monthly spending habits—I transitioned to the "Pay Yourself First" Budget. This method aligns with my current financial goals, automating savings toward specific targets, giving me the freedom to spend within a consistent lifestyle without worry.

Now, as you delve deeper into your own approach, it's crucial to address unexpected challenges and how you'll make adjustments in your Prosperity Plan. Let's explore these key areas that impact what your Abundance Accelerator should focus on first. In the next Track, we'll dive into understanding and managing these challenges effectively, ensuring your path to financial abundance remains clear!

tFab in Action:
Your Prosperity Plan

This Track's tFab in Action moment has focused on your Prosperity Plan and on gaining a clear understanding of your current financial position, balancing income versus expenses, and choosing the optimal method to achieve your financial goals. Here are your action items:

Create Your Prosperity Plan: Calculate your total monthly income and understand your monthly lifestyle expenses to ultimately identify your Abundance Accelerator.

Complete the Prosperity Plan Quiz: Determine which budgeting approach aligns best with your financial habits and goals.

Build Your Prosperity Plan Toolkit: Select the apps, tools, and resources to effectively manage your finances.

Put Your Prosperity Plan into Action: Establish monthly or quarterly reviews to monitor your budget, track your net worth, and evaluate financial progress. Adjust as necessary based on your financial circumstances.

BYE-BYE DEBT, HELLO SAVINGS

All right, Corporate Queens, we've discussed identifying your abundance accelerator, but now let's explore how it can help you accelerate savings and tackle debts head-on. Your Abundance Accelerator represents the additional funds beyond your essential living expenses that can empower you to prioritize both savings and debt repayment. These funds can serve as a powerful tool in your journey toward financial freedom by allowing you to allocate them strategically. Let's dive into how your Abundance Accelerator can be leveraged to build savings and eliminate debt, setting the stage for a more secure and prosperous financial future.

We've already covered Your Prosperity Plan as part of the foundation of the 9-to-5er's Wealth Pyramid. However, two other components are equally integral to your Prosperity Plan: savings and a debt repayment plan (if applicable). Both are directly influenced by your Abundance Accelerator and are essential to establish before we can ascend the Wealth Pyramid. But before we delve into strategies for building savings and navigating debt, let's gain insight into the financial habits and debt landscape of the US population to understand why it's warranted we spend some time solving for this.

According to Northwestern Mutual's Planning & Progress Study 2024, personal debt in the US remains a significant concern for many young adults. The study, which examines attitudes and behaviors regarding money, reveals a slight increase in Americans' personal debt (excluding mortgages) from 2023 to 2024. Presently, 66 percent of Americans carry some form of personal debt, with an average debt amount of $22,713. Credit card debt takes the lead, surpassing both car loans and education loans in terms of amount owed.[2]

THE 9-TO-5er's WEALTH PYRAMID

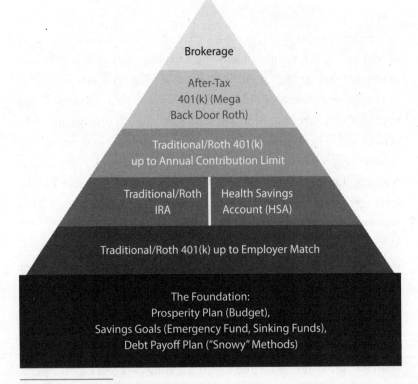

Brokerage

After-Tax
401(k) (Mega
Back Door Roth)

Traditional/Roth 401(k)
up to Annual Contribution Limit

Traditional/Roth
IRA

Health Savings
Account (HSA)

Traditional/Roth 401(k) up to Employer Match

The Foundation:
Prosperity Plan (Budget),
Savings Goals (Emergency Fund, Sinking Funds),
Debt Payoff Plan ("Snowy" Methods)

---

2 The information in this paragraph is from Northwestern Mutual 2024; see under References at the back of this book.

The Financial Abundance Blueprint

For individuals grappling with debt, nearly 29 percent of their monthly income is allocated to debt repayment. This substantial financial burden explains why 64 percent of adults prioritize debt repayment over saving, a trend that has been on the rise for two years. Despite this focus, fewer people have specific debt-repayment plans, dropping from 64 percent in 2022 to 59 percent today. Additionally, while 60 percent of Americans have an emergency fund, 40 percent do not. Among those with savings, the average emergency fund amounts to $25,500, yet only 53 percent believe it would cover more than six months of expenses. These statistics underscore the delicate balancing act young adults face in managing debt while striving to build a secure financial future.[3]

Why do I start with these statistics? Because it's time to break the taboo around debt and insufficient savings. Debt has become normalized in our society, but I envision a future in which society is free from its burden. Until then, I'm here to empower you to improve your financial standing today!

Navigating Debt: Reclaim 100% Control of Your Money One Payment at a Time

All right, if you're debt-free reading this, let's give you a round of applause! Being debt-free in today's economy, with bills piling up and life throwing curveballs, is a remarkable achievement! However, for the majority of Americans, debt remains a reality. For those of you grappling with debt, this section is crucial as we explore methods to free yourself from debt while still enjoying life along the way. We'll delve into two traditional and well-known methods in the financial community (called "Debt Snowball" and "Debt Avalanche") and a

---

3   The figures in this paragraph are from Northwestern Mutual 2024.

hybrid method ("Debt Blizzard") that I personally endorse based on my own experiences; shoutout to my Buffalo roots because we don't mind working through a little snow.

To bring these concepts to life, let's consider our friend Lila, who faces $48,000 in debt spread across student loans, credit cards, and a car loan. Table 5 shows us a snapshot of Lila's debt. As we explore each debt repayment method, we'll see how Lila can prioritize her loans effectively.

TABLE 5: LILA'S DEBT

Debt Type	Total Balance	Interest Rate	Minimum Due
Student Loan 1	$10,000	5%	$150
Student Loan 2	$15,000	4%	$200
Student Loan 3	$10,000	6%	$180
Credit Card	$5,000	18%	$100
Car Loan	$8,000	7%	$250
Total Debt	$48,000	-	$880 per month

Debt Snowball Method

The Debt Snowball Method is a debt repayment strategy that focuses on paying off debts from the smallest to the largest balance, regardless of interest rates. The primary advantage of this method is the psychological boost it provides; by quickly eliminating smaller debts, individuals gain a sense of accomplishment and motivation to continue tackling their remaining debts. However, a significant drawback is that it may result in higher overall interest costs since high-interest debts are not prioritized. This method is particularly effective for individuals who need quick wins to stay motivated and are more driven by the emotional satisfaction of seeing debts disappear rather than by minimizing interest payments. It's ideal for those who struggle with maintaining momentum in their debt repayment journey and benefit from seeing tangible progress. Here's how you can implement the Debt Snowball Method for yourself:

➥ List your debts from the smallest to the largest balance.

➥ Make minimum payments on all debts.

➥ Put any extra money toward the smallest debt until it's paid off.

Once the smallest debt is paid, move to the next smallest, and repeat.

TABLE 6: LILA'S DEBT PRIORITIZATION USING THE DEBT SNOWBALL METHOD

Debt Type	Total Balance	Interest Rate	Minimum Monthly Payment	Cumulative Minimum Monthly Payment
Credit Card	$5,000	18%	$100	$100
Car Loan	$8,000	7%	$250	$350
Student Loan 1	$10,000	5%	$150	$500
Student Loan 3	$10,000	6%	$180	$680
Student Loan 2	$15,000	4%	$200	$880

Explanation of Table 6:

➥ **Row 1 (Credit Card):** Starts with a minimum payment of $100 (hypothetical amount), which remains consistent until paid off.

➥ **Row 2 (Car Loan):** After paying off the credit card, Lila adds its $100 minimum payment to the car loan's $250 minimum payment, totaling $350 per month.

➥ **Row 3 (Student Loan 1):** After the car loan is paid off, Lila adds its $350 to Student Loan 1's $150 minimum payment, totaling $500 per month.

- **Row 4 (Student Loan 3):** After paying off Student Loan 1, Lila adds its $500 to Student Loan 3's $180 minimum payment, totaling $680 per month.
- **Row 5 (Student Loan 2):** Finally, after paying off Student Loan 3, Lila adds its $680 to Student Loan 2's $200 minimum payment, totaling $880 per month until all debts are paid off.

Debt Avalanche Method

The Debt Avalanche Method is a debt repayment strategy that prioritizes paying off debts with the highest interest rates first, regardless of the balance. The main advantage of this approach is its cost efficiency; by focusing on high-interest debts, individuals can save more money on interest over time and potentially pay off their total debt faster. However, the downside is that it may take longer to see significant progress, which can be discouraging for some people. This method is best suited for those who are disciplined, financially savvy, and motivated by long-term savings rather than immediate gratification. It's ideal for individuals who can stay committed to the plan without needing the psychological boost of quick wins. Here's how you can implement the Debt Avalanche Method for yourself:

1. List your debts from the highest to the lowest interest rate.

2. Make minimum payments on all debts.

3. Put any extra money toward the highest interest rate debt until it's paid off.

4. Once the highest interest rate debt is paid, move to the next highest, and repeat.

TABLE 7: LILA'S DEBT PRIORITIZATION USING THE DEBT AVALANCHE METHOD

Debt Type	Total Balance	Interest Rate	Minimum Monthly Payment	Cumulative Minimum Payment
Credit Card	$5,000	18%	$100	$100
Car Loan	$8,000	7%	$250	$350
Student Loan 3	$10,000	6%	$180	$530
Student Loan 1	$10,000	5%	$150	$680
Student Loan 2	$15,000	4%	$200	$880

Explanation of Table 7:

➦ **Row 1 (Credit Card):** Starts with a minimum payment of $100 (hypothetical amount), which remains consistent until paid off.

➦ **Row 2 (Car Loan):** After paying off the credit card, Lila adds its $100 minimum payment to the car loan's $250 minimum payment, totaling $350 per month.

➦ **Row 3 (Student Loan 3):** After the car loan is paid off, Lila adds its $350 to Student Loan 3's $180 minimum payment, totaling $530 per month.

➦ **Row 4 (Student Loan 1):** After paying off Student Loan 3, Lila adds its $530 to Student Loan 1's $150 minimum payment, totaling $680 per month.

➦ **Row 5 (Student Loan 2):** Finally, after paying off Student Loan 1, Lila adds its $680 to Student Loan 2's $200 minimum payment, totaling $880 per month until all debts are paid off.

Debt Blizzard Method

The Debt Blizzard Method is a hybrid debt-repayment strategy that combines elements of both the Debt Snowball and Debt Avalanche methods. It alternates between paying off the smallest balance debt (for quick wins) and the highest interest debt (for cost savings). The advantage of this method is that it provides the psychological motivation of eliminating small debts while also reducing overall interest costs. However, its complexity can make it harder to manage, as it requires careful tracking and alternating strategies. This method is ideal for individuals who need the motivational boost of seeing debts disappear but also want to minimize the total interest paid. It's best for those who can handle a more dynamic approach to debt repayment and want a balanced strategy that combines immediate rewards with long-term financial benefits. Here's how you can implement the Debt Blizzard Method for yourself:

1. List All Debts: include balance, interest rate, and minimum payment for each debt.

2. Categorize Debts: separate into high-interest debts and low-balance debts.

3. Choose Initial Focus:

➥ a. Start with the smallest balance debt (Debt Snowball) or

➥ b. Start with the highest interest debt (Debt Avalanche).

4. Pay Off Focus Debt: Make minimum payments on all debts except the chosen focus debt. Pay off the focus debt aggressively.

5. Switch Focus: After the first debt is paid off, switch to the other category (smallest balance if you started with highest interest, and vice versa).

6. Alternate Focus: Continue alternating between the smallest balance debt and the highest interest debt.

7. Repeat and keep alternating categories until all debts are eliminated.

Given how personal the decision is when it comes to the Debt Blizzard method, instead of illustrating with Lila, I'll simply include an overview of the process (see Table 8). The method involves applying the previous debt's minimum payment to the next debt, alternating between paying off the smallest balance debt and the highest interest debt. Regardless of which method you choose—Snowball, Avalanche, or Blizzard—the important takeaway is the motivation to get started. With each debt you eliminate, you free up more money to go toward your financial goals and accelerate your journey to becoming debt-free!

TABLE 8: EXAMPLE OF DEBT PRIORITIZATION USING THE DEBT BLIZZARD METHOD

Debt Type	Total Balance	Interest Rate	Monthly Minimum Payment	Cumulative Minimum Payment
Debt 1	$XXXXX	XX%	Min. Payment 1	Min. Payment 1
Debt 2	$XXXXX	XX%	Min. Payment 2	Min. Payment 1 + Min. Payment 2
Debt 3	$XXXXX	XX%	Min. Payment 3	Min. Payment 1 + Min. Payment 2 + Min. Payment 3

TABLE 8: EXAMPLE OF DEBT PRIORITIZATION USING THE DEBT BLIZZARD METHOD

Debt Type	Total Balance	Interest Rate	Monthly Minimum Payment	Cumulative Minimum Payment
Debt 4	$XXXXX	XX%	Min. Payment 4	Min. Payment 1 + Min. Payment 2 + Min. Payment 3 + Min. Payment 4
Debt 5	$XXXXX	XX%	Min. Payment 5	Min. Payment 1 + Min. Payment 2 + Min. Payment 3 + Min. Payment 4 + Min. Payment 5

Now, there's one more crucial element to highlight about these debt repayment methods, regardless of which one you choose: Your Abundance Accelerator! Remember those extra funds we identified in your Prosperity Plan? This is where they come into play. In all these methods, the strategy involves making minimum payments on all debts and then allocating any additional available funds toward the debt you're currently focusing on. That additional money is what we call Your Abundance Accelerator! How much of this accelerator goes toward debt repayment will depend on your other financial goals, such as establishing an emergency fund or saving for other priorities, as we'll discuss in a moment. The key takeaway here is the power of consistent, deliberate actions over time, whether it's building up savings, paying down debt, or investing in your future!

||||||||||||||||||||||||||||||||||||||||||||||||||||||||||||||||||||||||||||||||||||||||||||||||||||||||||||||||||||||||||||||||||||||||||||||||

Abundant Wealth Chronicle:
My Debt-Free Journey

All right, my Corporate Queens, let's dive into the numbers: $818. That's what I was shelling out monthly toward my debts back in

2014. Fresh out of college, I was staring down the barrel of student loans and a car payment that felt like they were holding me back from truly enjoying my hard-earned paycheck. No credit card debt, thankfully, but those loans were eating up nearly a quarter of my monthly coins. It was a wake-up call, to say the least.

In hindsight, it's what they call the false American dream—work hard in high school, get into college, land a decent job, and everything else will fall into place—except when it doesn't. But the reality hit hard: I was drowning in debt, with my income split between paying bills and barely scraping by.

Enter Ms. Arriaza, my office buddy who introduced me to Dave Ramsey's "Baby Steps," from the book mentioned earlier. Now, I'm not endorsing Dave Ramsey these days, but his strict approach to dealing with personal finances hit differently. Listening to his podcasts opened my eyes to financial literacy in a way that school never did. As a result, I found myself debt-free in just a few years. Since then, I've been influenced by more inclusive personal finance mentors and community members, who like me, make money guidance accessible to all without the guilt!

TABLE 9: MY STUDENT LOAN JOURNEY

#	Debt Details	Original Balance	Current Balance	Interest Rate	Minimum Payment
1	Private Student Loan	$1,500	$0	6.00%	$30
2	Private Student Loan	$2,750	$0	5.00%	$40
3	Car Loan	$18,158	$0	5.50%	$289

TABLE 9: MY STUDENT LOAN JOURNEY

#	Debt Details	Original Balance	Current Balance	Interest Rate	Minimum Payment
4	Other Student Loan	$426	$0	6.80%	
5	Other Student Loan	$1,456	$0	6.80%	
6	Other Student Loan	$2,750	$2,763	3.86%	
7	Other Student Loan	$2,750	$2,632	3.86%	
8	Other Student Loan	$3,044	$2,860	3.40%	
9	Other Student Loan	$3,378	$2,632	3.86%	$459
10	Other Student Loan	$3,500	$3,442	3.86%	
11	Other Student Loan	$3,566	$3,389	3.40%	
12	Other Student Loan	$4,000	$0	6.80%	
13	Other Student Loan	$5,500	$0	6.80%	
14	Other Student Loan	$6,000	$5,555	6.80%	
15	Other Student Loan	$6,934	$3,225	6.80%	
	Totals	**$65,712**	$26,498	-	$818

Just see for yourself, in Table 9. Debt #4 was a measly $426?! Meanwhile, my $459 in student loan payments toward the company owning my Other Student Loans in totality felt like dropping coins into a deep well, barely making a dent. That's when it hit me: something had to change. I flipped the switch to the Debt Snowball Method and started chipping away at those smaller debts first. Each one I paid off felt like a victory lap.

As I gained momentum, knocking out those smaller debts with the Debt Snowball Method, I felt unstoppable. Each paid-off loan fueled my determination. It wasn't all smooth sailing, though; I

The Financial Abundance Blueprint

switched jobs, tightened my belt, and even bunked up with roomies to cut costs. Sacrifices, yes, but they paid off big time. As my income grew and expenses decreased, harnessing my own Abundance Accelerator, I saw an opportunity to level up. That's when I switched gears to the Debt Blizzard method.

Fast forward to early 2018, and I made it; I was debt-free! Now, every dollar I earn is mine to allocate vs. owing to some lenders.

And those old minimum payments? They now fund my Travel Fund, because why not treat myself after all that hustle? Financial freedom tastes sweeter with each vacation booked, knowing I've reclaimed my income and my future. So, queens, remember: find a strategy that works for you and hustle hard. Whether it's the Snowball method, Avalanche method, or your own twist, the goal is the same: freedom to live your best life, debt-free and on your terms.

Establishing Savings: Stay Ready So You Never Have to Get Ready

Saving isn't just about being financially savvy; it's a powerful habit that empowers you to tackle unexpected expenses and pursue your dreams without relying on debt. At its core, saving for a rainy day means setting aside money for emergencies, ensuring you have a financial safety net when life throws curveballs your way. Emergency funds, typically equivalent to three to six months' living expenses, provide peace of mind during job loss, medical emergencies, or unforeseen large expenses. However, you should consider your own job security, potential healthcare costs, others dependent on you, etc., to determine the right amount to have in your emergency fund. These funds are your shield, allowing you to navigate financial storms without jeopardizing your long-term goals.

Recently, I faced unexpected bills totaling $1,100. First, my toddler misplaced my keys, costing nearly $700 to replace. Then, new parking rules around our residence added another $400 in fees when my car got towed :(. Despite these surprises, I handled them calmly because I was prepared. I want you to feel the same security and resilience.

Beyond emergencies, savings are key to achieving short- and long-term goals. "Sinking funds" are for anticipated expenses such as vacations or home repairs. Calculate the total anticipated cost and divide it by the number of months before you will need the funds, in order to set your monthly savings goal. Regular contributions to sinking funds ensures you're prepared, preserving your emergency funds for true emergencies.

Let's look at the example in Table 10 from our friend Lila, who has some incredible Savings Goals she wants to get a head start on. Let's assume she were to start working toward these goals in June 2025. Now, what you'll notice here is that depending on the total amount needed versus the number of months or the time Lila has to save toward it, her monthly contribution is either really high or really low. And if you did the math and added up all of the savings buckets, we'd be looking at setting aside $4,081 per month (at least during the initial months until she accomplishes other goals, say reducing debt, thus freeing up funds for her Savings Goals).

It's not to say Lila hasn't been doing this, but let's just assume not, which means we would have to prioritize and then move through the goals accordingly. I understand that might not be the best feeling, and you might think, "Oh, I can't work toward everything at once?" But honestly, that's a lot more realistic about what happens in life, especially when it comes to finances. You set goals, prioritize them accordingly, and have to make adjustments or tradeoffs in whatever you're balancing. And as you recall above, Lila is also paying off debt. Her minimum payments are $880 a month, and right now she's focused on eliminating that debt as soon as possible.

TABLE 10: LILA'S ORIGINAL SAVINGS PLAN

Lila's ORIGINAL Savings Plan	Total Amount Needed	Monthly Savings Set Aside	Goal Deadline	# of Months Needed to Save
Emergency Fund	$10,000	$2,000	October 2025	5
Shopping Spree	$1,000	$200	October 2025	5
Vacation	$5,000	$715	December 2025	7
New Car	$30,000	$833	June 2028	36
Wedding	$20,000	$333	June 2030	60

So what does the chart mean? Well, Lila likely won't be able to contribute to all of these savings goals at once, and that's completely okay. Similar to how she focuses on her debts and sees the compounding effects of eliminating one to increase her contributions to another, we can do the same thing here. Let's say Lila's Abundance Accelerator is at least $3,000 for the moment. She's getting really focused on her finances, has cut out a lot of unnecessary expenses, and has increased her monthly income from a dependable side hustle. This temporary adjustment will allow her to live more freely for years to come and beyond.

In this new reality, Lila is going to focus on leveraging her Abundance Accelerator to help her both build up her savings and eliminate debt. Let's just assume she is going to put $1,000 toward her student loans to cover her minimum payments plus adding a couple extra hundred dollars toward it to pay it off faster (building up her snowballs!). This leaves her with $2,000 to put toward her savings goals. Because Lila understands the importance of having an emergency fund first and foremost, and having that in a high-yield savings account, Table 11 shows what her updated savings goal timeline would look like. As you'll see here, that initial $2,000 per month would be going strictly toward the emergency fund, and she would achieve this by October 2025, assuming she starts in June 2025.

TABLE 11: LILA'S NEW SAVINGS PLAN

Lila's NEW Savings Plan	Total Amount Needed	Monthly Savings Set Aside	Goal Deadline	# of Months Needed to Save
Emergency Fund	$10,000	$2,000	October 2025	5
Shopping Spree	$1,000	$200	March 2026	5
Vacation	$5,000	$715	May 2026	7
New Car	$30,000	$833	November 2028	36
Wedding	$20,000	$333	November 2030	60

Here's the beautiful thing: similar to the debt elimination process, when it comes to savings goals, once she's reached one goal, it frees up that money to go toward the rest. Ironically, once Lila has her fully funded emergency fund, the freed-up $2,000 is almost enough to cover and start contributing to her remaining savings goals in November. She'll be short by $81, but by then, she'll likely have freed up debt she can then redistribute. Alternatively, focusing on increasing her income can help cover all her financial aspirations in a shorter timeframe (we'll explore this in Track 16). In the meantime, planning and prioritizing her financial goals will enable her to make steady progress.

Maximizing Your Savings: The Power of High-Yield Savings Accounts

Unlike traditional savings accounts that offer minimal interest rates, high-yield savings accounts (HYSAs) provide higher returns on your savings balance, allowing your savings to also generate additional income for you too! They are particularly advantageous for emergency funds, sinking funds, and other short-term savings goals where liquidity and safety are paramount.

Platforms like Marcus by Goldman Sachs, Ally Bank, or Discover Bank as examples offer not only competitive interest rates and no monthly fees but also the ability to categorize accounts for different savings goals. This feature allows you to designate separate accounts for each goal, giving them distinct names and tracking their progress individually. It's a convenient way to manage multiple financial objectives efficiently.

These accounts are FDIC-insured, ensuring your savings are protected up to the maximum limit. By utilizing HYSAs with goal categorization, you can optimize your savings strategy, earn more on your money, and maintain easy access to funds when needed. It's a smart approach to building a robust financial foundation and achieving your financial goals faster.

Achieving Financial Goals with SMART Planning

In true corporate fashion it's time to circle back to element number four of our Prosperity Plan: When do you want to work it? (What are your SMART Financial Goals?) SMART goals—Specific, Measurable, Achievable, Relevant, and Time-bound—serve as a powerful framework for setting clear financial objectives tailored to ambitious Corporate Queens! These structured goals provide a roadmap by defining precise targets that align with your financial goals. By setting SMART goals, Corporate Queens can prioritize financial efforts effectively and maintain focus amidst their dynamic careers. Here are examples of SMART Goals, tailored to each of Lila's savings goals mentioned earlier:

➥ Lila will save $10,000 in a High-Yield Savings Account by October 2025. She plans to allocate $2,000 per month starting in June 2025 to ensure financial security and preparedness within five months.

➥ By March 2026, Lila aims to save $1,000 for a discretionary spending spree. She will set aside $200 per month starting in November 2025 to achieve this goal within five months.

➥ Lila plans to save $5,000 for a vacation by May 2026. She will contribute $715 per month starting in November 2025, aiming to accumulate the funds within seven months.

➥ By November 2028, Lila intends to save $30,000 for a new car purchase. She plans to allocate $833 per month starting in November 2025, ensuring she meets her goal within 36 months.

➥ Lila will save $20,000 for her wedding by November 2030. She plans to set aside $333 per month starting in November 2025, aiming to accumulate the funds within 60 months.

Well, there we have it! Your Prosperity Plan is nearly complete, and I'm so proud of you for literally "working it" to get to this moment! At this point, you have grasped the essentials:

1. What are you working with? (What is your Income?)

2. Where do you want and need to work it? (What are your Lifestyle Expenses?)

3. How do you want to work it going forward? (What is your Abundance Accelerator and how will you allocate it?)

- Establishing an Emergency Fund
- Defining Short-Term vs. Long-Term Savings Buckets
- Reclaiming Your Income through a Debt Payment Plan

4. When do you want to work it? (What are your SMART Financial Goals?)

5. How you're going to keep working it because it's worth it? (How are you going to invest to achieve Financial Freedom?) → *Coming up next!*

In the next Track, we'll focus on the final aspect: building your 9-to-5er's Wealth Pyramid (9-to-5er's WP). This step is crucial, and it wouldn't be possible without first laying the groundwork with the four elements of Your Prosperity Plan. This is why we've spent time discussing navigating the workplace, because I'm committed to helping all my "Future Financially Free Corporate Queens" achieve that corporate success with ease and speed. As Biggie might say, "Mo' Money can actually lead to No Problems!" By increasing our income, our Abundance Accelerator grows, making it easier to balance our financial goals and live our Abundant Lives ASAP! Spoiler alert: this same Abundance Accelerator will also fund your 9-to-5er's WP for investing toward financial freedom, underscoring why it's essential to prioritize laying a solid foundation first!

tFab in Action: Establishing a Strong Financial Foundation

This tFab in Action moment has focused on laying a robust financial foundation for your Prosperity Plan, allowing you to prioritize building wealth toward financial freedom. In your journey toward financial stability and freedom, effectively managing savings and tackling debt are crucial steps. Here are you action items:

Build an Emergency Fund: Decide on the size of your emergency fund and set up regular transfers to a High-Yield Savings Account until your target is met.

Define Savings Goals (Short- vs. Long-Term): Categorize financial aspirations by timeframe and importance. Allocate funds based on your Abundance Accelerator, considering tradeoffs with other goals or expenses.

Set Up a Debt-Repayment Plan: List debts by balances, interest rates, and minimum payments. Choose a "Snowball" repayment strategy and allocate extra funds from your Abundance Accelerator toward your primary debt while meeting minimum payments on others.

Craft SMART Financial Goals: Create Specific, Measurable, Achievable, Relevant, Time-bound goals to bring clarity and accountability to your financial plan.

BUILDING γPIP WITH THE 9-TO-5ER'S WEALTH PYRAMID

You've come so far on this Financial Abundance Blueprint journey, committing yourself to the process and reaching this pivotal point. That is no small feat. According to CNBC, only 44 percent of Americans say they could cover a $1,000 emergency from their savings[4]. If you're here, it means you've defined your Prosperity Plan, set savings goals, and created a debt-payoff plan if needed. You're ahead of the game, and that makes you a winner in my book because none of this is easy! When life happens and perhaps a $1,000 emergency were to come your way, you're going to be in a position of power to navigate through it without the stress because you've created a safety net. You've established your financial foundation, which is crucial. Trying to build wealth without a solid foundation is like building a house on sand and we know that ain't gonna go well.

---

4   Konish 2024.

As we dive into investing, you'll see how vital it is to let your invested money grow undisturbed. This isn't possible if you constantly have to dip into it. So, again, congratulations on doing the hard work to give yourself the ability and option to build wealth. Many people have the potential to build wealth, but not everyone is willing to do what it takes. I'm glad to know that's not you!

Now, I'm going to share something that might sound surprising: investing can be boiled down to three simple steps. Yes, you read that correctly. It doesn't have to be complicated. Here they are:

1. Decide How Much You Want to Invest: This is where your Abundance Accelerator comes in. These are the funds you have available to invest. As we discussed in earlier Tracks, this number can change over time based on shifts in your income, checking off financial goals, and life's changing priorities. Remember, this isn't just your income minus expenses from your consistent paychecks. It also includes bonuses, tax returns, and side hustle income. It's about maximizing your Abundance Accelerator by planning for all your income over the year to work toward your Abundant Life.

2. Choose What to Invest In and How to Invest: It's not enough to set money aside; you need to invest it so it can grow. I'm excited to introduce you to your Prosperity Investing Playlists yPIP. We're reclaiming the acronym PIP, typically dreaded in corporate circles (see our discussion of "Performance Improvement Plans [PIPs]" in an earlier section of this book), for something positive. The yPIP approach will break down investing into easy-to-understand steps, making it feel as simple as building your favorite musical playlist. Traditional financial language can be off-putting, so we're going to speak *our* language. Music is universal and connects us all. I'm thrilled to guide you through the yPIP approach!

3. Select Where to Park Your Money So It Can Grow: This is where my 9-to-5er's Wealth Pyramid (9-to-5 WP) Framework comes in and brings it all together. The 9-to-5er's WP will help you:

- Understand what's available to you as a corporate professional
- Grasp the general pros and cons of each option based on your circumstances
- Create a visual plan to start your wealth-building journey today.

The beauty of the 9-to-5er's Wealth Pyramid is its ability to evolve as your situation and Abundance Accelerator change. My 9-to-5er's WP looks very different today, ten years into my corporate career, compared to when I was just starting out and paying off student loans. This framework was designed with flexibility and personal financial nuance in mind. Our individual wealth pyramids may look different but will enable each of us to achieve success in our own unique ways.

Maximizing Your Abundance Accelerator for Financial Independence

Before we dive into the intricacies of investing, account types, and the buzzwords that often surround them, let's take a step back. Depending on your background and experiences, the idea of building wealth might have seemed out of reach or overly complicated. My goal over the next several pages is to demystify investing and make it feel like a second language, something you're at least fluent enough in to pass the 101 class. I've enjoyed presenting this content to young professionals at top companies and tech conferences, leaving them empowered with the belief that they too can invest and build financial abundance for their families and leave a legacy. I'm so excited for you to experience that "Ah-ha!" moment too!

As with all things relating to personal finance, we must begin with a goal, and investing is no different. This goal is your Financial Independence goal. Often, if you ask people how much money they need to feel wealthy, they might say 5 or 10 million dollars. Sure, that's great, but what if your goal is even more within reach? What if your goal is just 2 million dollars? If you're single with no kids, your goal could be even less, allowing you to go from working 40 hours a week to part-time. Depending on how you go about this, you might be closer to hitting that goal than you realize. You don't necessarily have to work until age 65—maybe you can hit your goal at age 50 if you start today. Or, if you're in a solid place, your goal could be within reach in the next five to seven years. There's something empowering about knowing where you're going, having a plan, and seeing progress over time.

Let's get back to this goal, your Financial Independence Number, coined from the FIRE movement (Financially Independent, Retire Early). The simplest way to calculate this is to take your average annual expenses and multiply by 25. Essentially, when you have this figure set aside and invested in the stock market, you can retire early. If you only withdraw roughly 4 percent of that total number each year, that should be enough for you to live off, assuming your annual expenses stay constant. The remaining money would continue to grow through compound interest, dividends, and other returns, ensuring you're unlikely to run out of money in your lifetime. Of course, your original FIRE goal may shift due to a variety of changes in your life; I know mine sure did! That's why there are different levels of financial independence and specifically the levels of FIRE that can be pursued:

→ **Lean FIRE:** Lean FIRE focuses on achieving financial independence by maintaining a frugal lifestyle with minimal expenses. Followers of this approach optimize their spending to include mainly essential needs, allowing them to retire early on a smaller size portfolio. Typically, this number is a fraction of their calculated FI goal.

→ **Fat FIRE:** Fat FIRE aims for financial independence with a comfortable and luxurious lifestyle. This approach involves accumulating a larger portfolio to support higher spending levels, enabling more flexibility and indulgence in discretionary expenses like frequent travel and more costly hobbies. Typically, this number is at least twice as much as their calculated FI goal.

→ **Barista FIRE:** Barista FIRE seeks partial financial independence, allowing individuals to semi-retire or work in less demanding jobs while pursuing personal interests. This approach combines passive income and part-time work to cover living expenses, balancing financial freedom with meaningful activities. In this scenario, the nest egg required is quite smaller, given that the person will still actively bring in income in parallel with their investment portfolio.

→ **Coast FIRE:** Coast FIRE involves accumulating enough invested capital early on so that returns alone can sustain future retirement needs. Followers of this approach rely on compound growth over time to continue growing their portfolio to their FI goal by age 65, without them having to personally contribute any more funds to the portfolio. This essentially allows them to reduce savings rates or career intensity to enjoy more in the present, knowing their future is taken care of.

→ **House-Hacking FIRE:** House-Hacking FIRE leverages real-estate investments to achieve financial independence. This strategy includes renting out portions of one's primary residence or owning rental properties to generate passive income, accelerating wealth accumulation through property income.

→ **Geoarbitrage FIRE:** Geoarbitrage FIRE leans on location selection to optimize living expenses and accelerate wealth accumulation. By living in lower-cost areas or countries with favorable tax environments, followers of this approach can stretch their savings further and achieve financial independence more quickly.

Let me also acknowledge a new spin on this approach that is moderately known as FINE (Financially Independent, Next Endeavor)! FINE is like embracing that "FAT Barista FIRE" vibe. It's all about hitting that financial independence sweet spot, but instead of grinding to never work again, it's about having the freedom to chase passions that light you up without stressing over cash flow. You get to live your life on your terms, diving into what you love while still having a solid financial cushion to back you up.

To calculate your Financial Independence Number, we need to first determine your monthly lifestyle expenses. These expenses include everything necessary to maintain your desired standard of living, such as housing, utilities, food, transportation, healthcare, entertainment, and any other discretionary spending. Once we have your monthly lifestyle expense number, we'll multiply it by 12 to get your annual lifestyle costs. Then, we'll multiply that by 25 to determine your starting point for financial independence. Feel free to adjust this number up for Fat FIRE, allowing you to enjoy more lifestyle pleasures and luxuries. Alternatively, you can bring it down if you plan on Geoarbitrage, moving to a lower cost of living area, or cutting back on expenses to achieve your freedom sooner. Personal finance is personal so the choice is entirely yours.

> **Financial Independence =**
> **Annual Lifestyle Expenses x 25**

After identifying your Financial Independence Number, we'll allocate funds within your Prosperity Plan to your Abundance Accelerator. This accelerator will help you achieve your financial goals, including reaching financial independence. It's essential to ensure that your plan accounts for any irregular income streams, such as bonuses, in addition to your regular 9-to-5 income, which can be directed toward investing for financial independence.

Abundant Wealth Chronicle: My Financial Independence Goals

Let's rewind to April 2021, a moment that feels like a distant memory in 2024. At that time, I had already calculated my FIRE number, but life has a way of evolving, in this case prompting me to revise it upward. By then, I had been married for five years, although I calculated my FIRE number based on sustaining my lifestyle independently in California. This decision was rooted in practicality, ensuring that regardless of circumstances, I would be financially prepared. As a woman navigating society, preparedness is essential, even within the safety net of marriage.

Financial independence represents the freedom to live without the necessity of a job. For someone like me, a recovering perfectionist and workaholic, work was never the issue; it was the choice that financial independence afforded me. It was the liberation to quit with peace of mind, knowing my bills were covered for years or potentially a lifetime—a level of freedom and peace unparalleled in life.

Here's how I calculated my own path to financial independence on that distant day in 2021. First, I determined my monthly expenses, which totaled $3,600 at the time. This figure included future lifestyle activities like increased travel and personal indulgences, once part of my previous student loan payments, now redirected into my Abundance Accelerator. Furthermore, the number was based on my California rent costs in which I knew geoarbitrage would be an influencing factor as well, because retiring in California was certainly not in the plan and my belief was my housing costs would not be higher than that number. Multiplying this by 12 for annual expenses gave me $43,200. Applying the 25x rule, my initial financial independence goal was $1,080,000.

Since then, life has evolved, prompting me to adjust my goal upwards significantly, considering lifestyle changes and the arrival of our child. Revisiting this number is crucial as circumstances change; raising it may mean adjusting my investment strategy (i.e., investing $XX,000 annually consistently) to meet my original timeline or maintaining the plan and extending the journey by a few years.

Achieving this goal seemed daunting initially but breaking it down into manageable steps made it feasible. Tools like net-worth trackers and investing calculators, available online, are invaluable for projecting how my annual investments with modest returns can accelerate reaching financial independence. I truly realize what that quote meant around how "you can't save your way to wealth; you have to invest." For instance, this approach showed me I could achieve my goal within 12 years, a revelation that stunned me. This projection didn't even include other potential income streams such as company equity, a topic we'll delve into later in our discussion of maximizing corporate benefits.

Knowing my financial independence goal and understanding my own Abundance Accelerator were pivotal, especially once I became debt free and reclaimed more than $800 per month that used to go into someone else's pocket. My own Abundant Life was more in reach than I realized, but it was up to me to make decisions in alignment with that vision to bring it to pass. Remember, there's a tradeoff to everything. Saying yes to FIRE meant saying no to other, less important things to me, at least temporarily. However, once I knew financial independence was truly possible, it was hard to turn back; I had to go all in!

Now that we've laid the groundwork for achieving financial independence and explored the fundamentals of FIRE (Financial Independence, Retire Early), let's transition into the world of investing. Investing is the strategic allocation of your resources (i.e., your time and money) into assets with the expectation of generating a return or profit over time. It's not just about growing wealth; it's about making your money work for you to achieve your financial goals faster and more efficiently.

Redefining Investing for Corporate Queens

Think of building wealth like curating your ultimate financial freedom playlist. You know how every epic moment has a song that takes you right back to it? Music speaks to everyone, no matter your background or bank account. We all have our favorite jams like Usher's "Confessions" on repeat, blasting Chris Brown's debut album to get hyped, and of course, any Keith Sweat song for that smooth, timeless feel. I could keep going all day!

Imagine if investing were as easy as building a fire playlist on Spotify? Well, buckle up, Queen, because that's exactly what we're going to do! It's all about how many playlists you want to create, what goes in each one, and how often you update them. Trust me, it'll all come together. We'll revisit these playlists later, but first, let's talk about building a solid financial foundation.

Just as your favorite high school playlist keeps growing with new bops, your investment accounts should too. Treat your money like those bomb playlists you keep adding to and revisiting. That's the magic of compound interest. It's like your money on repeat, growing and multiplying without you even lifting a finger. Just sit back, listen to that financial freedom flow, and watch your money work!

Your Prosperity Investing Playlists (yPIP)

Remember, there are three simple steps to investing:
1. Decide How Much You Want to Invest (FI Goal)

2. Choose What to Invest In and How You'll Invest It (yPIP)

3. Select Where to Park Your Money So It Can Grow (9-to-5er's WP)

We've just covered the first step to investing, and as a result, you now have a baseline financial independence goal! Now, let's talk about the essence of investing itself and the specific assets that grow over time, accumulating compound interest and gains. Enter yPIP: your Prosperity Investing Playlists! Yes, it's a play on PIPs, typically associated with corporate performance plans. But here, we're reclaiming it to make it a positive for my Corporate Queens.

Just as your Spotify playlist holds the music of your choice, your Prosperity Investing Playlists will hold investments intentionally chosen and curated by you. Over time, these playlists grow as you add new investments or simply by using them. I want investing to be as enjoyable and simple for my Corporate Queens as curating different playlists, each with its own unique theme. Whether it's capturing a specific vibe, exploring an artist's entire discography, or blending diverse genres, the choice is entirely yours. The art of investing lies in crafting these playlists and letting them evolve over time.

To make the technical aspects more relatable, I'll draw parallels with music. When you invest, you're not just putting money aside; you're acquiring assets that grow and yield returns over time; similar to how your favorite playlist sounds better with each play! But first, let's kick things off with a fun activity: Think about your favorite artists, albums, songs, and genres. I've even shared mine below in Table 12 (don't judge me, judge ya mama!). Keep these in mind as we explore the world of investing and all that goes into building your playlists for prosperity!

TABLE 12: MY TOP 5 MUSICAL HIGHLIGHTS

Top 5 Albums	Top 5 Songs	Top 5 Genres	Top 5 Artists
"Confessions," by Usher	"Twisted," by Keith Sweat	90's R&B	Keith Sweat
"The Good, the Bad, the Sexy," by Joe	"Lights Out, Candles Lit," by Quiet Storm	Hip Hop	Usher
"Indigo," by Chris Brown	"My Heart Belongs to You," by Jodeci	Gospel	Chris Brown
"Blue Stars," by Pretty Ricky	"Work It Out," by Usher	Oldies	Tank
"Day Ones," by Day26	"Nobody," by Keith Sweat	00's Pop	Joe

Let's groove into our investing adventure by jazzing up some essential terms with a musical twist! Drawing inspiration from your musical preferences, customize these definitions to make them resonate with you—put the terms in your musical references you can relate to!

Individual Stocks: A stock is a security that represents ownership in a company. These are like your favorite single songs by your favorite artists (e.g., for me that might be "Twisted," by Keith Sweat). You can pick and choose exactly which songs (stocks) you want on your playlist (investment account). But remember, just like a playlist with only one artist, this can be risky if that artist falls out of favor (the company's stock price goes down). That's why it's important to select a variety of songs (or stocks) from different artists (or companies) to ensure that your playlist (investment account) still has some diversification to help mitigate risk. In other words, don't put all your eggs in one basket—a.k.a. a one-hit wonder!

Bonds: A bond is a debt security issued by a company or government. When you purchase a bond, you are essentially loaning money to the issuer (the company or government) for a specific period of time, at a fixed interest rate. Bonds are more like singing along to your favorite artist's song live! Instead of owning a piece of the artist (company stock), you're basically lending them money to perform that song (run their business), and they pay you back with interest (think of it as getting VIP access for supporting them!). These are generally considered safer investments than stocks because you are guaranteed to get your money back (the principal amount you loaned) if the issuer is solvent (able to repay its debts). However, the interest rate (return) on bonds is typically lower than the potential return on stocks. I compare this to attending a concert live—I know I'm going to enjoy myself in the moment, but I get a better return listening to my curated playlist at home.

Index Funds/Mutual Funds/ETFs: Mutual funds and exchange-traded funds (ETFs) are collections of investments (stocks and bonds) owned by a group of investors. An index fund is a type of mutual fund that tracks a specific market index (such as the S&P 500). Think of these as full albums or epic mixtapes. An index fund might be like a greatest hits album from the most popular artists (think S&P 500 companies). A mutual fund could be a mixtape by a DJ (fund manager) who mixes songs (stocks) from different artists (companies) following a specific theme, like "Hip-Hop Legends" or "Rock Anthems." An ETF is similar to a mutual fund mixtape, but it trades throughout the day like individual stocks. The beauty of these albums (Funds/ETFs) is the variety! You get exposure to a bunch of different artists and songs (companies and stocks) without having to pick each one yourself. Ultimately, you get more diversification to spread out risk while still being aggressive enough to see solid returns (as one artist's or one "company's" poor performance won't bring down the entire portfolio)!

Target Date Funds: A target date fund is a type of investment that automatically adjusts its holdings (investment choices) over time based on a target date (such as your retirement date). Imagine a "Best of the '90s" or a "Chris Brown Radio" playlist put together by Spotify, but for investing! These premade playlists (funds) focus on a specific time horizon and automatically adjust the music (investments) over time. You set it and forget it, letting the DJ (fund manager) handle the song selection (investment choices).

Real Estate Investment Trusts (REITs): A real estate investment trust (REIT) is a company that owns, operates, or finances income-producing real estate. REITs are like owning the concert venue or recording studio where all your favorite artists perform (businesses operate). You don't own the artists themselves (individual companies), but you get a share of the profits (rent) they generate when they perform (when businesses operate there). It's a way to get involved in the real estate game without having to be a landlord yourself! Put otherwise, you'd actually be the one receiving a check\ for every tour stop Pretty Ricky makes to serenade the ladies while singing "On the Hotline."

Cryptocurrency (Crypto): A cryptocurrency is a digital asset designed to work as a medium of exchange that uses cryptography for security. Imagine a whole new genre of music emerging from the internet, with its own artists and songs (cryptocurrency networks and specific cryptocurrencies). This genre is still relatively new and can be quite volatile (like some underground music scenes), but some believe it has the potential to revolutionize the financial system the way hip-hop did in the mainstream. Just keep in mind that crypto is like a new, risky musical choice so you should start small and learn more before making it a playlist favorite.

Choosing Your Genre: Exploring Investment Styles

Now that you've established a musical understanding of the types of things you can invest in, it's time to uncover the different types of approaches for how you can choose to do this. We'll frame these investment styles through the lens of your preferred genres to listen to. As you've learned through this book, I have a strong affinity toward '90s R&B, so I've renamed my investing style in alignment with what you'll find later in this section ("'90s R&B," "Oldies," "Pop," etc.). As we explore these terms, I challenge you to put this into your own language and musical analogies. Our goal again is to gain a simple, foundational understanding of the world of investing, just enough to be empowered to create a financial legacy. It doesn't take much to get started, and we're almost halfway there!

Dollar-Cost Averaging

Dollar-cost averaging is an investment strategy ideal for busy corporate professionals. Picture building your playlist one song at a time, on the same day each week, regardless of price fluctuations. Some weeks, your favorite artist may release a hit (stock price is high), while other times, classic songs go on sale (stock price is low). By consistently investing at regular intervals, you average out the cost per song (share) over time. This method helps smooth out market ups and downs, creating a consistent vibe in your playlist despite individual song prices.

Buy and Hold

For those preferring a hands-off approach, buy and hold is like curating a timeless playlist of your all-time favorite artist's albums. You believe these investments will hold or grow in value over time, like listening on repeat to Usher's "Confessions," his best album ever even 20 years later standing the test of time. By investing in the same stocks/bonds/funds, etc., without chasing short-term trends or fads, this strategy focuses on long-term wealth creation without constant portfolio adjustments. This method prioritizes consistency and conviction in the chosen investments, aiming to capitalize on their enduring value.

Value Investing

Value investing appeals to those who enjoy uncovering hidden gems. It involves finding undervalued companies trading below their intrinsic worth. Imagine stumbling upon a rare gem in a dusty record store like a legendary album at a bargain price! Value investors seek out companies with strong fundamentals but overlooked by the market, aiming for significant future appreciation.

Growth Investing

If you enjoy discovering promising new artists before they hit the mainstream, growth investing may resonate with you. This strategy targets companies with high growth potential, often reinvesting profits rather than paying dividends. Like discovering a rising star, growth investors seek companies poised for rapid expansion and potential stock price appreciation, despite higher risks.

Dividend Investing

For those seeking stable income streams from investments, dividend investing focuses on companies that distribute profits to shareholders regularly. Dividend investors prioritize steady income, similar to earning royalties from songs getting played on the radio, making it an advantageous strategy for those seeking another income stream in retirement. Keep in mind that dividend investing should be seen as a secondary strategy that compliments some of the others.

Index Investing

Index investing involves buying a collection of securities that mirror a specific market index, such as the S&P 500. It's like creating a playlist featuring all the top hits on the charts. Index investors benefit from diversification and lower costs while tracking overall market performance passively.

Socially Responsible Investing (SRI)

Socially responsible investing aligns investments with personal values, supporting companies that prioritize social and environmental causes. It's comparable to curating a playlist that not only reflects musical taste but also includes non-problematic artists. SRI resonates with professionals aiming to make a positive impact alongside financial returns.

Here's how I'd summarize our Investing Strategies by Genre based on my own personal musical preferences; however, you should feel empowered to define them in whatever way resonates. These strategies can be combined to create a diversified investment portfolio tailored to your financial goals and risk tolerance. Note that I'm a predominantly Buy and Hold, Index Investing Investor, with a side of Dividend Investing.

➥ **Index Investing:** '90s R&B (following the established hits and trends of the market)

➥ **Buy and Hold:** Oldies (classic and timeless, meant to be enjoyed over the long term)

➥ **Dollar-Cost Averaging:** Pop (reflecting its broad appeal and steady accumulation)

➥ **Dividend Investing:** Gospel (providing steady, reliable returns)

➥ **Growth Investing:** Hip-hop (focusing on the next big thing and rapid growth potential)

➥ **Value Investing:** Blues (digging deep for undervalued gems)

➥ **Socially Responsible Investing (SRI):** Folk (focused on community and ethical values)

Beyond the Playlist: Mastering the Financial Instruments

Choosing your investment strategies is like curating your playlist, but the financial world has a few extra musical elements to learn about. Here's a breakdown of some additional key concepts to help you master your financial soundtrack.

Diversification Is Key: Imagine spreading your favorite songs across different playlists to avoid losing them all if one playlist falls out of favor. Diversification in investing works the same way. Instead of putting all your money into one investment, spread it across different types (stocks, bonds, real estate, etc.) to reduce risk. Asset allocation refers to the specific mix of investments in your portfolio, tailored to your risk tolerance and financial goals, whether it's retirement savings or buying a home.

Stock Performance, Yield, and Dividends: Stocks, like songs, can rise and fall in popularity over time. Historical performance can offer insights, but it doesn't predict future outcomes. Yield is the return an investment generates, often shown as a percentage. Dividends are a type of yield where companies pay shareholders a portion of their profits. Although you could withdraw those dividends, reinvesting them allows your earnings to continue to grow in value in addition to your original holdings. Reinvested dividends are the literal personification of your money making you more money!

Capital Gains and Losses: Selling an investment for more than you paid results in a capital gain; selling for less means a capital loss. Understanding these concepts helps shape your investment strategy, especially regarding taxes and long-term growth.

Understanding Your Risk Tolerance: Investments come with varying degrees of risk, just as some musical activities are riskier than others (for example, singing live karaoke in front of your coworkers). It's crucial to understand your risk tolerance and how comfortable you are with potential losses. If you find yourself preferring less risk, you might lean toward more conservative investments such as index funds rather than single stocks. The market itself can also be volatile, with periods of strong growth (bull markets) and decline (bear markets). Knowing these cycles can help you manage your risk tolerance over time.

Abundant Wealth Chronicle: Risk Tolerance Quiz

This quick quiz will help you understand your risk tolerance and suggest an investment strategy that aligns with your comfort level. Answer honestly and choose the option that best reflects your feelings.

1. How comfortable are you with the idea of your investments losing value in the short term?

A) I'm very uncomfortable; I prefer stability.

B) It would make me nervous, but I understand it can happen.

C) I'm somewhat comfortable with it, as long as there's potential for long-term growth.

D) I'm comfortable with some short-term losses if the potential for high returns is there.

2. Imagine you have $1,000 to invest. How would you react if its value dropped by 10% in a month?

A) I would want to sell everything immediately to avoid further losses.

B) I would be concerned but wouldn't take any drastic action.

C) I would be curious to see if the market rebounds.

D) I wouldn't be surprised and might even consider buying more at a discount.

3. When researching investments, what information do you prioritize?

A) Safety and security of the principal amount

B) Consistent returns with low risk

C) Balance between risk and reward potential

D) High growth potential, even if it means higher risk

4. How long is your investment time horizon? (The amount of time you plan to hold your investments.)

A) Less than 5 years (short-term goals)

The Financial Abundance Blueprint

B) 5–10 years (medium-term goals)

C) 10–20 years (long-term goals)

D) 20+ years (retirement or long-term wealth building)

5. How much time are you willing to dedicate to researching and managing your investments?

A) I prefer a hands-off approach with minimal effort.

B) I'm comfortable with some research but would like guidance.

C) I'm willing to put in moderate time to learn and manage my portfolio.

D) I enjoy actively researching and managing my investments.

Mostly Checked A's: You have a conservative risk tolerance. This means you prioritize the safety and security of your principal investment. Your investment strategy should focus on preserving your capital, even if it means sacrificing some potential for growth. Bonds, certificates of deposit (CDs), and target-date funds with a conservative asset allocation are all good options to consider. These investments typically offer lower volatility and steadier returns, making them suitable for those approaching retirement or with a short-term investment horizon.

Mostly Checked B's: Your risk tolerance leans toward moderate. You value stability with the potential for some growth. A diversified portfolio that balances income and capital appreciation could be a good fit for you. Explore a mix of investment-grade bonds that provide regular interest payments and stocks that offer the potential for long-term growth through capital appreciation. Target-date funds with a moderate asset allocation can also be a great option, as they automatically adjust their asset mix over time to become more conservative as you near your retirement date.

Mostly Checked C's: You have a balanced risk tolerance. You're comfortable with some risk in exchange for the potential of higher returns. A diversified portfolio with a mix of stocks, bonds, and potentially some alternative investments could be suitable. Stocks can provide significant growth potential, but also come with inherent volatility. Bonds can help offset some of this volatility by providing steadier income and capital preservation. Alternative investments such as real estate investment trusts (REITs) or commodities can add diversification and potentially higher returns to your portfolio, but also come with their own set of risks. It's important to carefully research these options before investing.

Mostly Checked D's: You have an aggressive risk tolerance. While you're comfortable with significant risk in pursuit of high potential returns, it's important to build a secure foundation for your portfolio. Consider a buy-and-hold strategy with a core allocation to foundational assets such as stock index funds and low-cost ETFs. This will provide stability and long-term growth, while also leaving you with some liberties to explore growth stocks or alternative investments that align with your risk tolerance. Remember, diversification is key, even for aggressive investors.

Disclaimer: This quiz is a simplified tool and should not be taken as financial advice. Always consult with a qualified financial professional before making any investment decisions.

Prioritizing Your Prosperity Investing Playlists with the 9-to-5er's Wealth Pyramid

Now that we've established the foundational aspects such as budgeting, emergency funds, and debt payoff plans, and you've gained a solid understanding of key investing terminology, we're prepared to embark on the journey of constructing your 9-to-5er's Wealth Pyramid (or 9-to-5er's WP, for short). Let's set clear expectations: while this may seem like a lot of information, my aim is to simplify investing in a manner that empowers you without inundating you with unnecessary complications.

Without jumping too far ahead, I want you to think of your Wealth Pyramid as a collection of all of your Prosperity Investing Playlists. Over time, these playlists grow as you add new investments or simply by holding on to the ones you already have. The 9-to-5er's Wealth Pyramid is a visual representation of the primary playlists you could potentially build, each with its own theme and also its own pros and cons. Which playlists you'll choose to prioritize comes down to your own Financial Independence goals and the size of your Abundance Accelerator based on any other financial goals you're juggling. Remember, the 9-to-5er's WP was crafted with flexibility in mind. Your 9-to-5er's WP should evolve over time as your life, priorities, and income evolves too.

Just as you can create countless playlists, you likely have specific reasons behind which ones you prioritize, when, and why. It's time to unveil the different layers of the 9-to-5er's WP, which represent the pivotal prosperity playlists you'll want to curate; each ordered based on your unique circumstances as a Corporate Queen.

THE 9-TO-5er's WEALTH PYRAMID
(UP TO LAYER 1)

Traditional/Roth 401(k) up to Employer Match

The Foundation:
Prosperity Plan (Budget),
Savings Goals (Emergency Fund, Sinking Funds),
Debt Payoff Plan ("Snowy" Methods)

Layer 1: Investing in Your 401(k) up to the Employer Match

Let's start building your 9-to-5er's Wealth Pyramid with your 401(k). This retirement account is like the Beyoncé of all the "playlists" you could build and should prioritize accordingly; it's where you stash money for the future, and your employer might even match what you put in.

What's a 401(k)? It's a retirement plan sponsored by your employer. In 2024, you can set aside up to $23,000 annually (with an extra $7,500 if you're 50+).

Types of 401(k)

Traditional: Your contributions come out of your paycheck before taxes, so you pay taxes when you withdraw the money later.

Roth: You pay taxes up-front on what you contribute, but you won't owe taxes when you take the money out in retirement.

Why It Matters

Contributing to your 401(k) is smart because:

➥ **Free Money:** Your employer may match your contributions, which is basically free money toward your retirement.

➥ **Tax Benefits:** Traditional 401(k) contributions lower your taxable income now, and a Roth 401(k) lets your investments grow tax-free.

Key Details to Know

➥ **Vesting:** Some companies require you to work there a certain amount of time before their contributions are fully yours.

➥ **Investment Options:** You'll have a set of investment choices in your plan to grow your money over time.

The Financial Abundance Blueprint

➥ **Withdrawal Rules:** Typically, you can't touch the money penalty-free until age 59½, but there are exceptions.

➥ **Required Minimum Distributions:** Once you turn 73, you'll need to start taking money out of your 401(k).

TABLE 13: COMPARING 401(K) SUB-ACCOUNT TYPES[5]

	Traditional 401(k)	Roth 401(k)
Contributions	Before-tax dollars	After-tax dollars
Tax on Contributions	Reduces taxable income in the year contributed	No tax benefit on contributions
Tax on Withdrawals	Taxed as ordinary income in retirement	Tax-free withdrawals (including earnings) if qualified
Investment Growth	Grows tax-deferred	Grows tax-free
Employer Match	Employer matches are pre-tax	Employer matches are pre-tax
Required Minimum Distributions (RMDs)	Yes, starting at age 73	No RMDs while owner is alive
Ideal For	Those in a higher tax bracket now and expect to be in a lower tax bracket in retirement	Those in a lower tax bracket now and expect to be in a higher tax bracket in retirement
Contribution Limit	$23,000 for 2024 (+$7,000 catch-up for those over 50)	Same as Traditional 401k

---

5   Warren 2024.

Abundant Wealth Chronicle: From 401(k) to Millionaire

Meet Alisha, a registered nurse in Atlanta, Georgia, who currently has a $100,000 salary. She has a meeting with the benefits team to confirm her employer's match but has asked us to run a few scenarios to help her understand the possibilities and explain the whole employer match-401(k) lingo. In all three scenarios as shown in Table 14, the company is willing to match a percentage of her contribution up to 6 percent of her salary, which in this case would be $6,000 ($100,000 x 0.06 = $6,000). The difference here is exploring how much Alisha would need to contribute to obtain that full $6,000 from her employer, depending on their matching plan percentage. As you'll see, due to the 401(k) contribution limit, Alisha can't even receive the full $6,000 if her Employer Match Plan is 25 percent because that would require a $24,000 contribution, but she can still get pretty close!

TABLE 14: SCENARIO #1: EMPLOYEE INVESTS ENOUGH TO MAXIMIZE EMPLOYER MATCH

Company Match Plan	Maximum Employer Match Amount ($)	Alisha's Contribution	Employer Contribution	Total Contribution
100% ($1:$1)		$6,000	$6,000	$12,000
50% ($0.50:$1)	$6,000	$12,000	$6,000	$18,000
25% ($0.25:$1)		$23,000	$5,750	$28,750

Let's explore an alternative in which Alisha simply sets a personal annual contribution goal of $10,000. In Table 15, you'll see how that amount translates when combined with the employer's matching contribution, again, based on her employer's plan. As illustrated in the table, Alisha's $10,000 contribution would yield a range of

potential employer contributions depending on the company's
match plan.

TABLE 15: SCENARIO #2:
EMPLOYEE INVESTS $10,000 ANNUALLY

Company Match Plan	Maximum Employer Match Amount ($)	Alisha's Contribution	Employer Contribution	Total Contribution
100% ($1:$1)			$6,000	$16,000
50% ($0.50:$1)	$6,000	$10,000	$5,000	$15,000
25% ($0.25:$1)			$2,500	$12,500

In Scenario 3 (Table 16), in which Alisha contributes the maximum
amount of $23,000 into her 401(k), she receives the full employer
match in two of the three scenarios based on the plan type.

TABLE 16: SCENARIO #3:
EMPLOYEE INVESTS UP TO 401(K) LIMIT

Company Match Plan	Maximum Employer Match Amount ($)	Alisha's Contribution	Employer Contribution	Total Contribution
100% ($1:$1)			$6,000	$29,000
50% ($0.50:$1)	$6,000	$23,000	$6,000	$29,000
25% ($0.25:$1)			$5,750	$28,750

Key Takeaway: The amount of money Alisha needs to contribute to
obtain the full employer match is a direct function of the employer's
matching policy. Her goal is to obtain the entire $6,000; however,
in this example, depending on whether her employer match is
100 percent ($1:$1) vs. 25 percent ($0.25:$1), there's an $18,000
difference ($24,000 – $6,000) in how much she needs to contribute

to get that $6,000 in free money. However, something is better than nothing!

Let's say Alisha gets confirmation that her employer match plan is at the 50 percent threshold, and she can commit to contributing that $10,000 per year, capturing that $5,000 contribution match from her employer. The following graphs shows what that could mean for her after 25 years of consistently doing that, assuming a 7 percent annual return on her investment.[6]

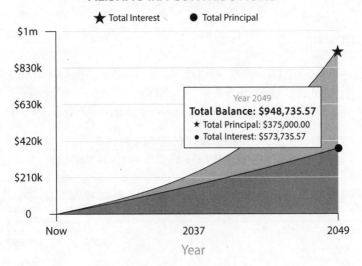

ALISHA'S IRA CONTRIBUTIONS

★ Total Interest   ● Total Principal

Year 2049
Total Balance: $948,735.57
★ Total Principal: $375,000.00
● Total Interest: $573,735.57

INVESTMENT DETAILS

Initial Investment	$0
Additional Investment Contributions	$15,000
Frequency of Investment Contributions	Annual
Years to Grow	25
Expected Rate of Return	7%
Compound Frequency	Annual

---

6   Davis 2024; see under References at the back of the book.

It's incredible to see how consistent investing in one's 401(k) can set you up for financial security down the road. Alisha would be on the cusp of 1 million dollars just through her 401(k)! That is huge because let's be real, just setting aside $10,000 per year is a stretch for the average American balancing finances with life's other priorities. However, if you are able to carve out enough space in your Abundance Accelerator to do so, to invest as close to your Employer Match potential as possible, that is enough to put you in a solid position. Yes, I understand $1 million today will not be worth $1 million twenty-five years from now, but trust me, you'll be happier having quite a few hundreds of thousands invested for retirement rather than nothing at all.

Societal mindsets often push for quick gains, but balancing immediate needs with long-term goals is key. Layer 1 of the 9-to-5er's WP emphasizes investing in your 401(k) up to the employer match as it's essentially free money and part of your total compensation. Missing out means leaving thousands on the table, potentially leading to significant losses in compound interest over time, as shown earlier in our calculations.

As we delve deeper into the 401(k) limit later on, some may find themselves investing up to the full $23,000 and beyond, especially as salaries rise and contribution limits increase. Automating contributions can streamline this process, ensuring you always maximize your investment potential. Lastly, people often debate whether to invest in a Traditional 401(k) or a Roth 401(k). Table 17 provides a few guiding questions and things to consider when answering them, to help you navigate this decision.

TABLE 17: 401(K) SUB-TYPE GUIDING QUESTIONS

Guiding Question	If Yes, Consider	If No, Consider
1. What is my current tax bracket compared to my expected tax bracket when I retire?	**Traditional 401(k):** If you expect to be in a lower tax bracket in retirement, the immediate tax deduction can be beneficial.	**Roth 401(k):** If you expect to be in a higher tax bracket in retirement, paying taxes now at a lower rate can be advantageous.
2. Do I prefer to lower my taxable income now?	**Traditional 401(k):** Immediate tax deduction lowers your taxable income for the current year.	**Roth 401(k):** No immediate tax benefit, as contributions are made with after-tax dollars.
3. Do I prefer tax-free withdrawals when I retire?	**Roth 401(k):** Contributions grow tax-free, and qualified withdrawals in retirement are tax-free.	**Traditional 401(k):** Withdrawals in retirement will be subject to income tax.
4. Do I expect my income to increase significantly in the future?	**Roth 401(k):** If your income will increase, locking in the current lower tax rate by paying taxes now is beneficial.	**Traditional 401(k):** If you don't expect a significant income increase, the immediate tax deduction can be more beneficial.
5. Do I want to avoid Required Minimum Distributions (RMDs) when I retire?	**Roth 401(k):** RMDs can be avoided by rolling into a Roth IRA, which has no RMDs during your lifetime.	**Traditional 401(k):** RMDs are required starting at age 73, increasing taxable income in retirement.
6. Will I need to access my contributions before I retire?	**Roth 401(k):** Contributions can be withdrawn anytime without penalties, providing flexibility.	**Traditional 401(k):** Early withdrawals typically incur a 10% penalty and are subject to ordinary income tax.

For most individuals, contributing to a Roth 401(k) is often the optimal choice. All contributions and withdrawals grow tax-free, offering flexibility in accessing funds early or letting them accumulate if not immediately needed. However, high-income earners

The Financial Abundance Blueprint

leveraging multiple layers of our 9-to-5er's Wealth Pyramid may find the Traditional 401(k) more advantageous initially, because they benefit from up-front tax breaks. As we explore higher levels of the pyramid, additional opportunities to contribute to a Roth 401(k) will become clearer (more on that later in this Track). The key is to start contributing; choose one and begin growing your money. You can always adjust your strategy over time; in my early years, I switched back and forth between the two, which is perfectly okay! As your income grows and circumstances evolve, so too will your financial decisions. Remember, personal finance is personal!

A Brief Mention of 403(b) Plans

For those who work in nonprofit sectors, such as public schools or universities, a 403(b) plan serves as the counterpart to the 401(k). Similar to its corporate sibling, a 403(b) allows employees to defer salary into an individual account. Options include traditional pre-tax contributions or Roth accounts, balancing tax advantages based on immediate versus future needs. The 2024 elective deferral limit is $23,000, with a +$7,500 catch-up for ages 50+. While offering flexibility in contributions and potential for loans or hardship withdrawals, 403(b) plans may feature limited investment choices and higher administrative costs. Early withdrawals before age 59½ could incur penalties, emphasizing the plan's focus on long-term retirement savings.

In the 9-to-5er's Wealth Pyramid Framework, the next layer offers two options, often causing analysis paralysis among Corporate Queens unsure of where to allocate their funds next. The truth is, any choice is better than none, so it's crucial to simply take action. For those seeking a deeper understanding, I will categorize these as Layer 2A and Layer 2B. Your decision on which to prioritize will boil down to personal preferences regarding investment choices versus such considerations as medical circumstances. Let's delve into the details.

THE 9-TO-5er's WEALTH PYRAMID
(UP TO LAYER 2)

Traditional/Roth IRA	Health Savings Account (HSA)

Traditional/Roth 401(k) up to Employer Match

The Foundation:
Prosperity Plan, Savings Goals, Debt Payoff Plan

Layer 2A: Individual Retirement Account

What's an IRA? IRAs are special accounts designed for retirement savings. For 2024, you can contribute up to $7,000 annually ($8,000 if you're 50 or older). There are two main types: Traditional and Roth IRAs.

Traditional IRA:

⇥ Contributions are usually tax-deductible, reducing your taxable income for the year.

⇥ Investments grow tax-deferred until withdrawal, when they're taxed as regular income.

Roth IRA:

⇥ Contributions are made with after-tax dollars, so they don't lower your current taxable income.

⇥ Earnings grow tax-free, and qualified withdrawals in retirement are also tax-free.

Why It Matters

IRAs offer flexibility and broader investment options compared to employer-sponsored 401(k) plans:

→ You can choose from stocks, bonds, mutual funds, and ETFs to tailor your investments.

→ Contributions can be made up to the tax filing deadline, giving you more time to save for retirement each year.

→ IRAs are also beneficial for estate planning, allowing efficient wealth transfer with potential tax advantages.

Key Details to Know

→ **Income Limits:** Roth IRAs have income restrictions for contributions. For 2024, full contributions phase out for single filers earning over $146,000 (partial up to $161,000) and for married couples filing jointly earning over $230,000 (partial up to $240,000). Traditional IRAs have no income limits for contributions, but deductibility can be affected.

→ **Withdrawal Rules:** Early withdrawals from Traditional IRAs before age 59½ may incur a 10 percent penalty, plus taxes. Roth IRA contributions can be withdrawn anytime penalty-free, but earnings withdrawals before age 59½ and before the account is five years old may have taxes and penalties.

→ **Conversion:** You can convert Traditional IRAs to Roth IRAs, paying taxes on the converted amount up-front for tax-free withdrawals in retirement.

→ **Required Minimum Distributions (RMDs):** Traditional IRAs require RMDs starting at age 73, but Roth IRAs do not during your lifetime.

→ **Beneficiary Designations:** You can select beneficiaries to ensure your assets pass efficiently, potentially avoiding probate and providing tax benefits to heirs.

TABLE 18: TRADITIONAL IRA VS. ROTH IRA[7]

	Traditional IRA	Roth IRA
Contributions	Before-tax dollars (may be tax-deductible)	After-tax dollars
Tax on Contributions	May be tax-deductible depending on income and coverage by a retirement plan at work	No tax benefit on contributions
Tax on Withdrawals	Taxed as ordinary income in retirement	Tax-free withdrawals (including earnings) if qualified
Investment Growth	Grows tax-deferred	Grows tax-free
Required Minimum Distributions (RMDs)	Yes, starting at age 73	No RMDs while owner is alive
Income Eligibility Limits	None for contribution, but tax-deductibility may be phased out for higher earners	The Roth IRA income limits are less than $161,000 for single tax filers and less than $240,000 for those married filing jointly
Contribution Limit	$7,000 for 2024 (+$1,000 catch-up for those over 50)	Same as Traditional IRA

The Backdoor Roth IRA Method for High-Income Earners

Believe it or not, some individuals earn too much to contribute directly to a Roth IRA. Again, if a single person's gross income is $161,000 or more, or if a married couple filing jointly has a gross income of $240,000 or more, they aren't allowed to contribute to a Roth IRA

---

7   Investopedia Team 2024.

directly. However, that shouldn't prevent them from enjoying the advantages of tax-free withdrawals and tax-free growth that a Roth IRA offers. The Backdoor Roth IRA Method is a straightforward strategy allowing high-income earners to circumvent income limits and benefit from a Roth IRA.

Here's how it works:

1. Open a Traditional IRA account.
2. Contribute directly to your Traditional IRA account.
3. Allow two to three days for the contribution to settle into the account.
4. Move the funds from your Traditional IRA account into a Roth IRA account.
5. Choose your investments and enjoy tax-free growth.
6. Repeat this process annually or whenever you contribute.

It's that simple! By utilizing this method, high-income earners can maximize the benefits of a Roth IRA regardless of income limitations!

THE BACKDOOR ROTH IRA PROCESS

 1. Open a Traditional IRA and a Roth IRA (if you don't already to have them).

 2. Contribute after-tax, net-income money to the Traditional IRA account.

 3. Wait a few days for the money to settle into the account.

4. Move that money from your Traditional IRA into your Roth IRA account.

5. Don't forget to buy assets so the money in the Roth IRA account is actually invested!

Abundant Wealth Chronicle: Leaning into Those Tax-Free Gains

Let's check in with Alisha again. She's now been diligently contributing $12,000 annually to her 401(k) to earn her full employer match of $6,000, thanks to her company's generous 50 percent matching policy. She spreads this contribution out through her biweekly paychecks over the year. Now, Alisha earns an annual bonus of $10,000, and she's decided to put this extra income toward her financial goals. We're so proud of her!

Alisha is considering contributing to a Roth IRA to benefit from tax-free growth, but first, she needs to verify if she meets the income limits for direct contributions. For single tax filers, the Roth IRA income limit is $141,000 (2024 limit). Since Alisha earns $100,000 annually, she comfortably falls below this threshold, making her eligible to contribute directly to a Roth IRA. In the following figure, we've illustrated what that could mean for her if she invests $7,000 of her new bonus into a Roth IRA and continues making consistent contributions annually for 25 years with a 7 percent annual return on her investment.

ALISHA'S IRA CONTRIBUTIONS

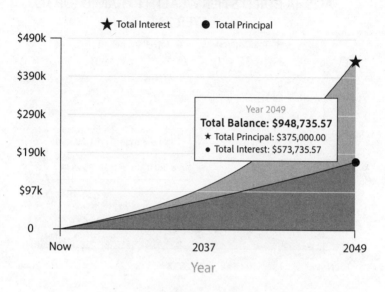

★ Total Interest   ● Total Principal

Year 2049
Total Balance: $948,735.57
★ Total Principal: $375,000.00
● Total Interest: $573,735.57

$490k
$390k
$290k
$190k
$97k
0

Now   2037   2049

Year

INVESTMENT DETAILS

Initial Investment	$0
Additional Investment Contributions	$7,000
Frequency of Investment Contributions	Annual
Years to Grow	25
Expected Rate of Return	7%
Compound Frequency	Annual

Now, in addition to her 401(k) contributions totaling $18,000 annually ($12,000 from her and $6,000 from her employer), Alisha plans to contribute $7,000 annually to her Roth IRA. That's a combined total of $25,000 annually ($18,000 + $7,000) working toward her financial future. Here's what that could mean for her after 25 years of consistent contributions, assuming a 7 percent annual return on her investment.[8]

---

8   Davis 2024; see under References at the back of the book.

ALISHA BUILD'S HER WEALTH PYRAMID (UP TO LAYER 2A)

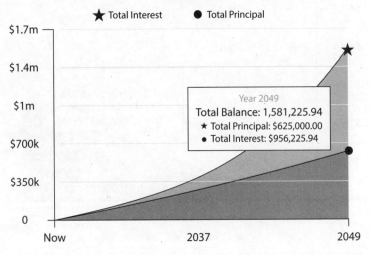

★ Total Interest   ● Total Principal

Year 2049
Total Balance: 1,581,225.94
★ Total Principal: $625,000.00
● Total Interest: $956,225.94

INVESTMENT DETAILS

Initial Investment	$0
Additional Investment Contributions	$25,000
Frequency of Investment Contributions	Annual
Years to Grow	25
Expected Rate of Return	7%
Compound Frequency	Annual

Now we're really starting to see the value of the 9-to-5er's Wealth Pyramid! Building wealth can be straightforward, even if you're just starting out on the first couple of layers. Alisha could stop right there, and she'd still be looking at a nearly 1.6 Million Dollar nest egg for retirement. There's this guiding principle that we should set aside 10 to 15% of our income toward financial goals to set ourselves up nicely in the future. As it currently stands, Alisha is investing ~17% ($19,000/$110,000) by tapping into these first two layers of the pyramid. I acknowledge this here because I don't want my Corporate Queens to feel that they may not have the financial means to build up each and every layer as we continue on. I know some of you might be thinking, "Well, Amanda, I don't have an extra $1,000 per month to contribute to my 401(k)," or "Amanda, I don't receive any annual bonuses." To you, I'd say, start where you are! Maybe your Abundance Accelerator is simply $100 a month. Even that $100 per month adds up to $1,200 a year, which can significantly improve your financial outlook over time compared to doing nothing.[9] Personal finance is personal. We're all balancing different life priorities and goals. The beauty in the 9-to-5er's WP is in its flexibility to help Corporate Queens secure all types of corporate bags to create a financial system that enables them to achieve their financial goals, their financial abundant life vision, as defined by them!

$1,200 IRA CONTRIBUTIONS

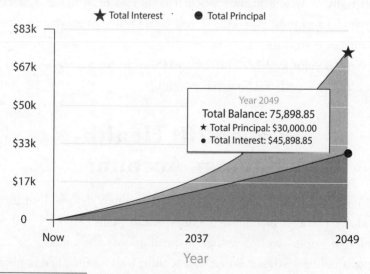

★ Total Interest   ● Total Principal

Year 2049
Total Balance: 75,898.85
★ Total Principal: $30,000.00
● Total Interest: $45,898.85

---

9   Davis 2024; see under References at the back of the book.

Initial Investment	$0
Additional Investment Contributions	$1,200
Frequency of Investment Contributions	Annual
Years to Grow	25
Expected Rate of Return	7%
Compound Frequency	Annual

Consider the example above: Investing $30,000 over 25 years at a modest return could potentially yield $45,000 in gains. I know some might say, "That's not a lot of money," but think about it—if someone handed you $45,000 right now, you'd likely see it as a significant blessing, like winning the lottery! Every dollar you invest starts working for your future, no matter how small it may seem at first. Don't forget the lessons in Side A to guide you in growing your income through navigating the workplace more effectively so you'll be able to invest more to accelerate your timeline to financial abundance.

Now, let's explore the other side of the second layer. Again, there's no right or wrong answer when it comes to prioritizing different financial accounts, especially if you have limited funds due to other financial obligations. Let's be real, if you're in a position to utilize the 401(k) plus an IRA, and/or an HSA (Health Savings Account), you're in a wonderful financial position.

Layer 2B: Health Savings Account

What's an HSA? HSAs are specialized accounts designed for individuals enrolled in high-deductible health plans (HDHPs). HSAs offer a triple tax advantage: contributions are made pre-tax, investment growth is tax-free, and withdrawals for qualified medical expenses are also tax-free. For 2024, contribution limits are $4,150 for self-only coverage and $8,300 for family coverage, with an additional $1,000 catch-up contribution for those 55 and older.

Why It Matters

HSAs are not just for immediate healthcare costs; they're strategic savings vehicles:

➥ You own the account, so funds roll over year after year, even if you change jobs or health plans.

➥ Use receipts to reimburse yourself tax-free for qualified medical expenses, including deductibles, prescriptions, and more.

➥ Contributions and growth are tax-free, allowing you to build savings for future medical needs or retirement.

Key Details to Know

➥ **Qualification:** You must have an HDHP and cannot be covered by other health plans, except for certain exceptions like dental or vision insurance.

➥ **Employer Contributions:** Employers can contribute to your HSA, which counts toward the annual limit.

➥ **Investment Options:** Some HSAs offer investment opportunities once a minimum balance is met, potentially increasing your savings beyond standard interest rates.

➥ **Withdrawal Rules:** Withdrawals for non-medical expenses before age 65 incur a 20 percent penalty plus income tax. After 65, withdrawals for non-medical expenses are taxed as income without penalty, akin to a Traditional IRA. Withdrawals for qualified medical expenses, on the other hand, are always tax-free.

Abundant Wealth Chronicle:
Health Is Wealth with an HSA

Imagine, it's been two years since we last connected with our girl Alisha. She now has a salary of $120,000 per year, which includes a $12,000 bonus (yay for her, she got a promotion!). Alisha continues to prioritize her financial future by maintaining her $12,000 contribution to her 401(k) and a $7,000 contribution to her Roth IRA. However, due to changes in her company's healthcare options, she's decided to switch from a preferred provider organization (PPO) health plan to a high-deductible health plan (HDHP), making her eligible for a Health Savings Account (HSA) for the first time ever.

Alisha is in relatively good health, and her typical medical expenses include co-pays for annual visits and approximately $550 per year for glasses and contacts. She prefers paying for these expenses out of pocket and plans to keep her receipts. Although recently engaged, Alisha maintains her single status on her HDHP, allowing her to contribute up to $4,150 annually to her HSA. Additionally, her employer contributes $650 per year toward her account for the singles coverage plan (versus $1,300 for the family coverage plan). This means Alisha can contribute an additional $3,500 to her HSA for investing purposes ($4,150 total contribution *minus* $650 employer contribution.) Because her plan requires maintaining a $500 minimum cash balance, out of the total $4,150 contributed she allocates $3,650 toward investing in selected mutual funds available in the account. Here's what that could mean for her after 25 years of consistently doing that, assuming a 7 percent annual return on her investment.[10]

---

10   Davis 2024; see under References at the back of the book.

The Financial Abundance Blueprint

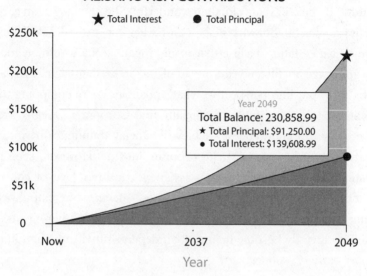

ALISHA'S HSA CONTRIBUTIONS

★ Total Interest ● Total Principal

Year 2049
Total Balance: 230,858.99
★ Total Principal: $91,250.00
● Total Interest: $139,608.99

INVESTMENT DETAILS

Initial Investment	$0
Additional Investment Contributions	$3,650
Frequency of Investment Contributions	Annual
Years to Grow	25
Expected Rate of Return	7%
Compound Frequency	Annual

Keep in mind, Alisha's retirement nest egg was already approaching $1.6 million dollars just by building her Wealth Pyramid through capturing her Employer's Match and using the Roth IRA. As we now see, adding an HSA into the mix could grow that nest egg by another ~$230,000, getting her very close to having $2 Million set aside for retirement.

Can we also take a moment to acknowledge we have no idea how old Alisha is?! We're forecasting growth that is 25 years into the future. If she's 35 years old, then wonderful! She's looking at an early retirement at 60. But what if she's 25, earlier in her career? Well, now we're just ecstatic, because that would mean Alisha would be good to go by age 50, fifteen years ahead of the "retirement age." I say all of this to put into perspective what's possible. We're equipping the next generation of future financially free Corporate Queens with the tools and knowledge to achieve financial abundance by maximizing the heck out of their corporate income. However, keep in mind again that these estimates assume a consistent level of contribution coming solely from Alisha's 9-to-5 income. She can always choose to grow her Abundance Accelerator through other means as well, to literally become financially independent with the option to retire early . . . sooner!

Layer 3: Maximize Your 401(k) Contribution (Elective Deferral)

Why It Matters: At this stage, you're likely already maximizing your employer match in your 401(k) and have prioritized contributions to your IRA and/or HSA. Now it's time to take your wealth building to the next level by contributing up to the full 401(k) elective deferral limit.

Key Details to Know:

➥ **Elective Deferral Limit:** For 2024, you can contribute up to $23,000 to your 401(k) ($32,500 if you're 50 or older).

➥ **Employer Match:** Depending on your employer's plan, it may take your contributing up to the elective deferral limit to receive the maximum match amount.

THE 9-TO-5er's WEALTH PYRAMID
(UP TO LAYER 3)

Traditional/Roth 401(k)
up to Annual Contribution Limit

| Traditional/Roth IRA | Health Savings Account (HSA) |

Traditional/Roth 401(k) up to Employer Match

The Foundation:
Prosperity Plan, Savings Goals, Debt Payoff Plan

TABLE 19: 9-TO-5ER's WEALTH PYRAMID
LAYERS 1–3 SUMMARY

401(k) Elective Deferral	$23,000
Employer Match ($EM)	TBD (Fill in for yourself)
IRA (Traditional or Roth)	$7,000
HSA	$4,150 (Single) / $8,300 (Family)
Total	$34,150 / $38,300 + $EM

|||||||||||||||||||||||||||||||||||||||||||||||||||||||||||||||||||||||||||||||||||||||||||||||||||||||||||||||||||||||||||||||||

Abundant Wealth Chronicle: Alisha Builds Up Her 9-to-5er's Wealth Pyramid

Let's take it up a notch and envision what this would look like if Alisha committed to contributing up to the full limit of $23,000 per year to her 401(k), while still capturing her employer's $6,000 match. Here's what that could mean for her after 25 years of consistently doing that, assuming a 7 percent annual return on her investment. In this example, we're assuming that everything (salary, contribution limit, and employer match) remains steady. However, in reality, we'd expect these factors to continue growing over time, potentially accelerating her wealth accumulation even further than what we're projecting below. Wow... $1.8 million just from consistently maxing out her 401(k) every year! That's truly incredible. But wait, there's more.

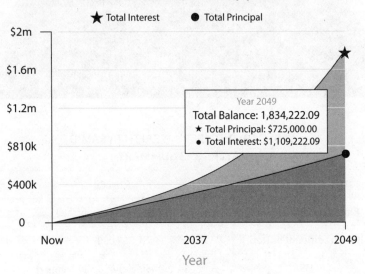

ALISHA MAXES OUT 401(K) ONLY

★ Total Interest   ● Total Principal

Year 2049
Total Balance: 1,834,222.09
★ Total Principal: $725,000.00
● Total Interest: $1,109,222.09

INVESTMENT DETAILS

Initial Investment	$0
Additional Investment Contributions	$29,000
Frequency of Investment Contributions	Annual
Years to Grow	25
Expected Rate of Return	7%
Compound Frequency	Annual

Let's fast forward five years since we first connected with her. Alisha is now married to an amazing life partner and has advanced into a leadership position at work by embracing the EMBODY Framework. Her new total compensation package stands at $165,000 per year (salary + bonus). With shared expenses with her partner, Alisha now has the capacity to allocate more toward her financial goals. She's maximizing contributions across layers 1 to 3 of the 9-to-5er's Wealth Pyramid. Note: She continues with a Single-Coverage High Deductible Health Plan because it's more cost-effective for her and her partner to maintain separate insurance. Plus, her Employer Match potential has increased to $9,000 with her newfound compensation growth! Let's review Alisha's annual contribution table (Table 20).

TABLE 20: ALISHA'S WEALTH PYRAMID (EXAMPLE)

401(k) Elective Deferral	$23,000
Employer Match ($EM)	$9,900 (up to 6% of salary, 50% contribution)
IRA (Traditional or Roth)	$7,000
HSA	$4,150 (Single)
Total	$44,050

Alisha is now contributing $44,050 per year toward her financial goal! Here's what that could mean for her after 25 years of consistently doing that, assuming a 7 percent annual return on her investment.

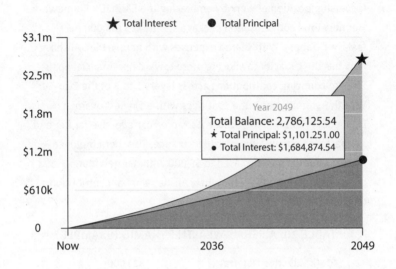

ALISHA INVESTS IN LAYERS 1–3

★ Total Interest   ● Total Principal

Year 2049
Total Balance: 2,786,125.54
★ Total Principal: $1,101.251.00
● Total Interest: $1,684,874.54

$3.1m
$2.5m
$1.8m
$1.2m
$610k
0

Now   2036   2049

INVESTMENT DETAILS

Initial Deposit	$0
Contribution Amount	$44,050
Contribution Frequency	Annual
Years of Growth	25
Estimated Rate of Return	7%
Compound Frequency	Annual

Here's where we'll pause on Alisha's incredible journey. Achieving this level is a remarkable accomplishment, especially considering that her annual investing contributions surpass the average median household income for some families in the US! Rather than being discouraging, Alisha's story should inspire and motivate my fellow Corporate Queens, the primary audience for this book. While we haven't delved into Alisha's specific budget or her Financial Independence, Retire Early (FIRE) number yet, crossing the $1 million threshold, let alone reaching ~$2.8 million in 25 years, positions her incredibly well for the future.

Let's seamlessly transition this section into the next layer, because they are closely related. I recommend that you all begin crafting your own Wealth Pyramid plan. The beauty of the Wealth Pyramid lies in its flexibility as you can add or remove layers as your personal circumstances change. As Alisha and her partner pursue other life goals, such as travel, homeownership, or starting a family, their pyramid will naturally adjust. Different life choices require varying financial resources, and this blueprint is designed to help outline what's possible and provide a plan to achieve it.

While this book targets Corporate Queens, the Financial Abundance Blueprint is universal. It serves as a guide for outlining your possibilities and crafting a plan to achieve them. Ultimately, defining your own life and what brings you joy is paramount. Everyone deserves financial freedom, whether you aim to maximize earnings or seek contentment with meeting basic needs and enjoying occasional vacations. Both paths deserve respect and the opportunity to achieve financial security on their own terms. Okay, back to the 9-to-5er's WP, we have two layers left to go!

Layer 4: After-Tax 401(k)s Contributions (a.k.a. Mega Backdoor Roth)

Yes, we're still talking about 401(k)s, but this is a whole new level. The Mega Backdoor Roth 401(k) allows high-income earners to supercharge their retirement savings beyond the traditional limits. If your employer offers this option and you're in the financial position to take advantage of it, you're in for some serious benefits.

What Exactly Is It?: The Mega Backdoor Roth strategy involves making after-tax contributions to your 401(k) plan above and beyond the regular limits and then converting those contributions into a Roth 401(k) or a Roth IRA. This means you're setting aside more money for retirement in a tax-efficient way, with all future growth and qualified withdrawals being completely tax-free.

Why It Matters

→ **Maximize Contributions:** You can contribute up to the total 401(k) plan limit, which is $69,000 for 2024 (or $76,500 if you're 50 or older). This is a significant increase from the standard contribution limits.

→ **Tax-Free Growth:** Since these contributions go into a Roth account, you're looking tax-free growth over the years, setting you up for a financially secure retirement.

THE 9-TO-5er's WEALTH PYRAMID (UP TO LAYER 4)

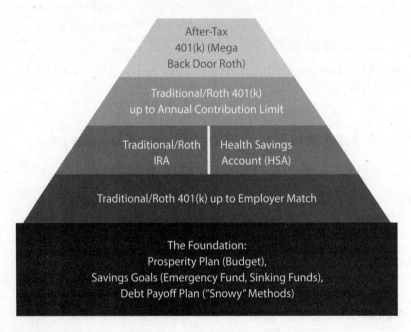

After-Tax 401(k) (Mega Back Door Roth)

Traditional/Roth 401(k) up to Annual Contribution Limit

Traditional/Roth IRA | Health Savings Account (HSA)

Traditional/Roth 401(k) up to Employer Match

The Foundation:
Prosperity Plan (Budget),
Savings Goals (Emergency Fund, Sinking Funds),
Debt Payoff Plan ("Snowy" Methods)

- **Flexibility:** You have the option to roll over these funds into a Roth IRA later on, giving you more investment choices and no required minimum distributions (RMDs), which adds flexibility to your retirement planning.

401(K) EMPLOYEE + EMPLOYER LIMIT

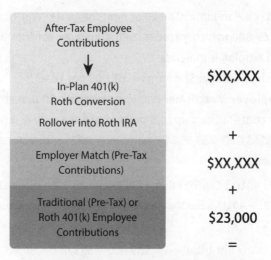

After-Tax Employee Contributions ↓ In-Plan 401(k) Roth Conversion Rollover into Roth IRA	**$XX,XXX**
	+
Employer Match (Pre-Tax Contributions)	**$XX,XXX**
	+
Traditional (Pre-Tax) or Roth 401(k) Employee Contributions	**$23,000**
	=

2024 401(K) CONTRIBUTION LIMIT: $69,000
For folks age 50+ with catch-up contributions: $76,500

Key Details to Know

- **Plan Specifics:** Not all 401(k) plans offer the option for after-tax contributions or in-plan Roth conversions, so check your plan details carefully.
- **Timing Is Key:** If you do utilize this strategy, make sure to convert your after-tax contributions promptly to avoid unnecessary taxes on any earnings.
- **Long-Term Benefits:** The Mega Backdoor Roth is particularly beneficial if you're aiming to maximize tax-free retirement income and have the financial capacity to save more aggressively.

Abundant Wealth Chronicle: Alisha's After-Tax 401(k) Contributions (Mega Backdoor Roth)

To calculate Alisha's potential for After-Tax Mega Backdoor contribution potential, we need to consider the 2024 401(k) plan limit and her current salary and employer match details:

➡ **401(k) Plan Limit:** The 2024 limit for 401(k) contributions is $69,000, which includes both employee contributions and employer matches.

➡ **Alisha's Salary:** She earns $165,000 per year.

➡ **Employer Match:** Her employer matches 50 percent of her contributions up to 6 percent of her salary → 6 percent of $165,000 = $9,900 (maximum employer match based on salary).

After-Tax 401(k) Contribution = IRS Employer & Employee Limit ($69,000) – 401(K) Elective Deferral Limit ($23,000) – Employer Match ($ TBD):

➡ After-Tax Contribution = $69,000 – $23,000 – $9,900
➡ After-Tax Contribution = $69,000 – $32,900
➡ After-Tax Contribution Potential = $36,100

Note: Changes made to her employer plan, or shifts in her own income, will cause this number to fluctuate.

Layer 5: Brokerage Accounts

What They Are: A Brokerage Account, also known as a taxable investment account, is where you can buy and sell a wide range of investments, such as stocks, bonds, mutual funds, and ETFs. It's all about flexibility and accessibility, allowing you to tailor your investment portfolio to your specific financial goals.

Why They Matter

➥ **Flexibility and Accessibility:** One of the standout benefits of a brokerage account is liquidity. You can access your funds at any time without penalties, which is ideal for both short-term needs and long-term investments.

➥ **No Income Limits:** Unlike retirement accounts, there are no income limits for contributing to a brokerage account. Anyone can open and contribute to one, regardless of their income level.

Key Points to Consider

➥ **Taxation:** Earnings in a brokerage account are subject to capital gains taxes. Short-term gains (on assets held for less than a year) are taxed at ordinary income rates, while long-term gains (on assets held for more than a year) benefit from lower capital gains tax rates.

➥ **Dividends and Interest:** Any dividends and interest earned in a brokerage account are taxable in the year they are received. Qualified dividends may qualify for lower tax rates.

➥ **Account Types:** You can choose between individual or joint brokerage accounts, depending on whether you want sole ownership or joint management with a spouse or partner.

➥ **No Required Minimum Distributions (RMDs):** Unlike retirement accounts, there are no RMDs for brokerage accounts. You have the flexibility to leave your investments untouched for as long as you prefer.

➥ **Estate Planning:** Brokerage account assets transfer easily to heirs and may benefit from a step-up in basis, which adjusts the asset's value to its market price at the time of death. This can reduce the capital gains tax liability when the heirs sell the asset.

Why They're Last on the Wealth Pyramid: Brokerage accounts are typically prioritized last because they lack the tax advantages of retirement accounts such as 401(k)s, HSAs, and IRAs. However, they offer unique advantages that might appeal to certain investors seeking liquidity, broader investment options, and no contribution limits.

When to Prioritize Brokerage Accounts Earlier in Your 9-5 WP:

→ **Liquidity:** Need flexible access to your funds? Brokerage accounts provide high liquidity without early withdrawal penalties, making them suitable for short-term financial goals.

→ **Investment Choices:** Enjoy a wider array of investment options compared to many retirement accounts, allowing for a more customized investment strategy.

→ **No Contribution Limits:** Invest as much as you want, beyond the limits of tax-advantaged accounts, which can be advantageous for high-income earners looking to maximize savings.

→ **No RMDs:** Avoid mandatory withdrawals, allowing your investments to grow tax-efficiently for as long as you choose.

Beyond Yourself: Investing for Others

This section delves into mini playlists (accounts), where your Abundance Accelerator involves setting aside funds for other household members—be it your children, spouse, or employees if you venture into entrepreneurship. While the applicability varies based on personal circumstances, it's crucial to recognize these additional wealth-building avenues because they begin with us but extend beyond us. Table 21 on page 238 shows other investing accounts (playlists) you can contribute to for yourself or other people.

Whew! I know Table 21 just covered a lot of ground, and now it's time to bring it all together. While it may have seemed like we pressed pause on the musical references, everything converges in this moment where we learn how to invest step by step. Surprised? You actually know more than you think. You're familiar with the basic terms of investing, have identified your initial strategies, and pinpointed what you want to invest in. Plus, we've just built your 9-to-5er's Wealth Pyramid, so you know which investment accounts to prioritize.

Here's the deal: We can finally curate your Prosperity Investing Playlists. Each layer of the Wealth Pyramid represents a playlist option for you to tap into. Depending on your current situation, you might focus on one playlist (account) right now, or if your finances allow, you can tackle multiple playlists. Remember, your Abundance Accelerator signifies the funds available for you to invest in these accounts while balancing your other financial goals.

How to Actually Invest Step by Step

1. Build Your Playlist (Open/Choose an Investment Account): Think of this as your home base for investments, similar to your favorite music streaming platform. Choose an account that suits your financial situation. The order you choose to prioritize these accounts depends on your specific goals; refer to our 9-to-5er's WP for guidance.

2. Contribute Money into the Designated Account: Fund your chosen investment account with the amount you're comfortable investing. This is like deciding how long of a listening session in minutes you're in the mood for.

3. Pick Your Playlist Vibe (Select Your Asset Classes): Now that we've defined the differences between stocks, bonds, funds, and more, it's time to choose which of these will make it onto your investment playlist. Remember that some accounts, like HSAs and 401(k)s, will limit your options, so consider how each asset class fits your financial goals and your personal risk tolerance.

TABLE 21: INVESTING FOR OTHER PEOPLE (ACCOUNT SUMMARY)

Account	Who It's For	Contribution Limits (2024)
Spousal IRA	Married couples with one spouse having earned income	Up to $7,000 ($8,000 if age 50+), shared with contributing spouse
SEP IRA	Self-employed individuals and small business owners	Contributions are generally capped at 25% of an employee's compensation, up to a maximum of $69,000 (whichever is less).
SIMPLE IRA	Small businesses with 100 or fewer employees	Up to $16,000 ($19,500 if age 50+)
Self-Directed IRA	Investors seeking alternative asset classes	Up to $7,000 ($8,000 if age 50+)
Custodial IRA or Minor's IRA	Parents for children with earned income	Up to child's earned income or $7,000
529 Education Savings Account	Parents saving for a child's education expenses	Up to $18,000 per beneficiary per year (married couples can contribute up to $36,000)
UTMA/ UGMA Custodial Brokerage Accounts	Parents or guardians wishing to transfer assets to minors	No contribution limits; gift-tax considerations apply

TABLE 21: INVESTING FOR OTHER PEOPLE (ACCOUNT SUMMARY)

Tax Treatment	Benefits	How It Works
Same as Traditional or Roth IRA, based on type	Provides retirement savings for non-working spouses	Contributions based on working spouse's income; non-working spouse must be married and file jointly.
Tax-deductible contributions; earnings tax-deferred; withdrawals taxed as ordinary income	High contribution limits; employer contributions	Contributions made by employer; flexible contribution amounts based on income
Contributions tax-deductible; earnings tax-deferred; withdrawals taxed as ordinary income	Easy administration; employer matching or non-elective contributions	Mandatory employer contributions; lower administrative costs than 401(k) plans
Same as Traditional or Roth IRA, based on type	Diverse investment options beyond traditional securities	Allows investment in alternative assets; requires a custodian that permits such investments
Contributions made with earned income; earnings grow tax-deferred or tax-free in Roth IRAs	Early start to retirement savings; potential for long-term growth	Contributions limited to child's earned income; can be Traditional or Roth IRA depending on eligibility
Tax-free growth for education; some states offer tax deductions for contributions	Used for qualified education expenses; beneficiary can be changed	While there's no federal cap, many states have set their own aggregate limits on the total amount you can contribute to a single beneficiary's 529 plan.
Investment income taxed at child's rate; may have favorable tax treatment	Flexible use for child's benefit; custodian management of assets until child reaches adulthood	Assets become child's property at adulthood; may impact financial aid eligibility

4. Choose Your Songs (Decide How Many Shares to Buy):
Once you've selected an asset class, determine how much of it you want to invest in. Just like picking songs for your playlist, the more shares you buy of a stock or fund, the greater your investment in that asset.

5. Set the Volume (Choose Your Order Type): Decide on the order type that suits your strategy. A Market Order buys at the current price, like purchasing a song immediately. A Limit Order sets a specific purchase price; the transaction occurs only if the price meets your limit, like preordering a new release.

THE INVESTING PROCESS

	1. Open an account and/or choose existing account.
	2. Contribute money to the designated account.
	3. Select the assets you want to invest in (stocks, index funds, bonds, etc.).
	4. Decide how much or how many shares of each asset to buy.
	5. Choose your order type (Market, Limit, etc.).
	6. Congrats! You're an Investor! Sit Back, Relax, and Enjoy the Ride.

The Financial Abundance Blueprint

6. Press Play! (You're Now an Investor): Congratulations! Your financial playlist is now set to grow over time, much like enjoying your favorite songs. You'll repeat this process for every Playlist you're able to build as you go up the Wealth Pyramid. Remember, investing is a long-term commitment, so monitor and adjust your portfolio regularly to stay aligned with your financial goals.

As highlighted in the Abundant Wealth Chronicle examples, once you initiate your investments and your money begins generating returns, you can seamlessly transition to pursuing other financial objectives. Moreover, achieving debt-free status, coupled

WEALTH PYRAMID
(2024 CONTRIBUTION LIMITS)

Brokerage:
Unlimited

After-Tax 401(k)
(Mega Back Door Roth):
$ = IRS - 401(k) - EM
(employer match)

Traditional/Roth 401(k)
up to Annual Contribution Limit:
$23,000

Traditional/
Roth IRA:
$7,000

Health Savings Account
(HSA): $4,150 (Singles),
$8,300 (Families)

Traditional/Roth 401(k) up to Employer Match

The Foundation:
Prosperity Plan, Savings Goals, Debt Payoff Plan

with income growth while sustaining your lifestyle, accelerates the construction of your wealth pyramid and all the playlists within it!

tFAB in Action: Building Your Prosperity Investing Playlists with the 9-to-5er's Wealth Pyramid

This Track's tFAB in Action moment was about crafting your personalized Wealth Pyramid as a future Financially Free Corporate Queen. Remember, personal finance is just that, personal. Your Wealth Pyramid should reflect your unique circumstances, goals, and financial status. Here are your final action items:

Take Stock of Your Financial Goals: Identify your Abundance Accelerator and calculate your Financial Independence number and desired level of FIRE in alignment with your vision for an Abundant Life.

Visualize Your 9-to-5er's Wealth Pyramid: Utilize the 9-to-5er's WP Framework to map out your current financial structure. Outline actionable steps: specify which paychecks or bonuses will fund each layer, set timelines, and establish SMART goals for each contribution.

Forecast Your Future Wealth: Use online tools such as an investment calculator to project potential growth. Estimate conservative returns (around 7 to 8 percent) over 10 and 25 years to visualize how your investments could compound over time.

Understand Tax-Advantaged Accounts: Differentiate between account types such as Traditional and Roth IRAs, and 401(k)s. Consider the tax implications and benefits of each.

Curate Your Prosperity Investment Playlists: Create multiple investment playlists (accounts) to diversify your portfolio and mitigate risk across different asset classes and strategies. Select investment options such as stocks, bonds, ETFs, and REITs based on your risk tolerance and financial objectives. Explore options for automating your investments to maintain consistency and discipline in building your wealth over time.

Review and Rebalance Regularly: Schedule periodic reviews of your investment portfolio to evaluate performance and ensure alignment with your risk tolerance and long-term goals. Rebalance your playlists (investments) as needed to maintain optimal asset allocation and adjust to market changes.

LIVING OUT YOUR PROSPERITY PLAN

We've covered the essentials of budgeting, saving, investing, and building wealth, but there's more to managing your money. In this chapter, we'll dive into organizing your accounts, getting the most out of your credit cards, handling big purchases, and navigating key financial conversations. These final tools will help you confidently tackle life's financial moments, live out your prosperity plan, and ultimately create your abundant life!

Your Financial iPod: Checking and Savings Accounts

At the heart of every financial journey are your checking and savings accounts, acting as your foundation. Your checking account is where you manage your daily finances, handling everything from bill payments to your morning coffee purchases. This is where your Prosperity Plan from Track 11 comes to life in execution, allowing you to effectively allocate your funds toward your goals. Everyone should have at least one checking account and one savings account, along with as many investing accounts (or "Playlists") as you can build. For some, having multiple checking and/or savings accounts helps keep money in clearly defined buckets, ensuring that nothing gets mixed up.

Personally, I keep it simple with one primary checking account where my direct deposit lands, and from there, some money moves automatically while some money gets transferred manually into different buckets. On the savings side, I'm all about multiple high-yield savings accounts, each labeled with its specific goal. For example, my "House Is a Home Fund"—shout-out to Luther Vandross—is strictly for a home down payment, while my "Emergency Fund" is, you guessed it, for emergencies. And then there's my "Baby JJ Fund" for my son, which will eventually move into his own investing accounts as he grows. Every account serves a distinct purpose, and this system helps me stay organized.

Below, you'll find an example of how this can look in action. Keep in mind, and we'll touch on this again in the Credit Cards section, as your financial journey evolves, your system of organizing accounts might shift, and that's completely normal! Plus, as you get more savvy, you might also take advantage of different bank promos, where you open a new checking or savings account in exchange for a cash bonus. I've done this before myself, but always make sure you have a strategy in place so you don't get stuck with something you don't need after the promo ends. I usually sign up, collect my cash, and go right back to my old faithful accounts. Check out the diagram below to see a visual example of how organizing your accounts can work. Think of it like an iPod (which was a portable music player in the early 2000s) that let you organize your favorite songs. Similarly, organizing your financial accounts helps you categorize your money into different buckets, making it easier to manage and grow your money.

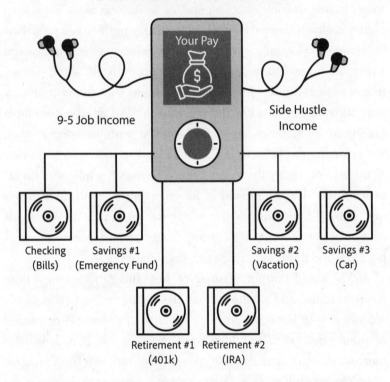

YOUR FINANCIAL iPOD: ORGANIZING YOUR ACCOUNTS

Your Pay

9-5 Job Income

Side Hustle Income

Checking (Bills)

Savings #1 (Emergency Fund)

Savings #2 (Vacation)

Savings #3 (Car)

Retirement #1 (401k)

Retirement #2 (IRA)

Automate Money Movement Based on Your Prosperity Plan

By now, you've taken the Prosperity Plan Quiz back in Track 11 to figure out your preferred budgeting style. For those who landed on the "Pay Yourself First" or "No Budget" methods, here's your moment to shine! Automating your finances could be the perfect fit for you. Set up automatic bill payments from your checking account, schedule transfers to your savings, and even automate contributions to your investment accounts (your financial playlists). This way, your money is working for you, with minimal effort.

On the other hand, if you identified with the Zero-Based Budget, 50/30/20 Method, or the Envelope Budgeting System, manually moving money between accounts may better suit your needs. These approaches give you more hands-on control, which can be comforting if you like to know exactly where each dollar goes.

Whichever style resonates with you, the goal is to keep your system smooth and aligned with your preferences. Whether you automate or manage things manually, what matters most is that Your Process of managing Your Money works for You!

Old School Payments: Throwback on How to Write a Check

Although checks aren't as common these days, they still serve important purposes for certain payments, such as rent, gifts, and charitable donations. They provide a secure and tangible way to manage transactions, especially when dealing with larger sums or specific service providers who prefer this method. We'll reference the example below to make sure you get it right. Here's a quick and easy guide:

1. Date: Pop the current date in the top-right corner: "August 4, 2024" (for example). This just confirms when you're sending the check out into the world.

2. Payee: On the line that says "Pay to the Order of," write the name of the person or organization to whom you are making the payment, such as "Amanda Jane & Co." (for example). Make sure it's their correct name so there are no hiccups!

3. Amount in Numbers: In that little box next to the payee's name, jot down the amount in numbers, like $468.22.

4. Amount in Words: Now, below the payee's name, write out the amount in words (like, "Four hundred sixty-eight dollars and 22/100"). It should match what you wrote in the box. Don't forget to draw a line after it to fill any extra space. Gotta keep it neat!

5. Memo: This part is optional, but it's super handy. Use the memo line to note what the check is for, like "Career Coaching Package" (for example). Trust me, it helps with tracking payments later.

6. Signature: Finally, sign your name at the bottom right as "Alisha Smith" (example). This should of course match the way your name shows up on your bank account, no weird nicknames, so that it's a valid check.

7. Record the Transaction: After you write that check, be sure to jot down the details in your checkbook or personal finance app. Include the check number, date, payee, and amount. This way, you'll know what's in your account once the check clears.

DATE 08/04/2024

PAY TO THE ORDER OF Amanda Jane & Co.

$ 468.22

DOLLARS Four hundred sixty eight and 22/100 ——

MEMO Career Coaching Package

Alisha Smith

53098345367   36749584766   766749

Navigating Credit and Credit Card Rewards

Let's first quickly touch on debit cards. While they can be convenient for daily purchases, allowing you to spend only what you have in your bank account, they don't help you build credit. If you're still getting a grip on your personal finances, it's probably best to start with a debit card. They help you develop budgeting habits by limiting your spending to your available funds, making it easier to track your expenses. However, once you feel more disciplined and confident in managing your finances, transitioning to credit cards can open up new opportunities for building credit, earning rewards, and enjoying benefits that debit cards simply can't provide.

Credit cards work by assigning you a credit limit, which is the maximum amount you can borrow. Each time you make a purchase, that amount is deducted from your available credit. You're expected to pay back the borrowed amount, usually on a monthly basis. If you pay off your balance in full each month, you can avoid interest charges, which is crucial for maintaining good financial health. Responsible credit usage helps build your credit history, which is essential for improving your credit score. Credit scores fall between 300 and 850, with higher scores showing lenders you're a lower risk, and yes, being labeled as lower risk does indeed open up better financing opportunities!

According to Experian, several key factors influence your credit score, which assesses your creditworthiness:

Payment History (35%): Your track record of paying bills on time has the most significant impact on your score. Late payments, defaults, or bankruptcies can really set you back.

Credit Utilization (30%): This ratio shows how much of your available credit you're actually using vs. your total credit limit. For a healthy score, keep your utilization below 30%.

Length of Credit History (15%): A longer credit history can enhance your score, providing more data on your spending habits and reliability.

Types of Credit Accounts (10%): Having a good mix of credit types, such as credit cards, loans, and more, can help improve your score. But again, don't take on more than you can handle!

New Credit (10%): Opening several new accounts in a short time can signal risk, especially if your credit history is brief.

Credit cards are a great tool when used wisely. They come with perks like cashback or travel rewards, but remember: never carry a balance from month to month. Interest charges can drain your finances faster than you think.

If you're new to building credit, you may want to consider opening a secured credit card, which essentially allows you to use a personal cash deposit as your form of credit. Alternatively, you could ask a close family member to add you as an authorized user on their account, which allows you to build credit based on their good credit behaviors. Either approach allows you to learn the ropes around navigating credit in a safer environment.

The Big Three: Credit Card Travel Hacking Strategy

Once you've established good credit, a world of financial possibilities opens up, including the exciting realm of credit card points hacking. This strategy involves using points generated by your everyday spending, whether it's on recurring bills or those big purchases, to pay for a variety of expenses depending on the card issuer. While some cards allow you to redeem points for cash back, gift cards, or merchandise, we're going to focus on travel hacking. This approach lets you redeem points for flights, hotel stays, and other travel-related expenses, making your dream trips significantly more affordable.

My **Big Three Strategy** involves using three types of credit cards to maximize points: a general travel rewards card, a hotel-specific card, and an airline-specific card.

1. General Bank Credit Card: Choose a card that earns flexible points and offers benefits like travel insurance and purchase protection. You can transfer these points to various airline and hotel partners, enhancing your travel experiences and potential savings.

2. Airline-Specific Card: Opt for an airline-specific card that rewards general spending and offers bonus miles for flight-related purchases. Make sure the airline aligns with your frequent travel needs (i.e., don't choose an airline's card you rarely fly)! Frequent travelers should definitely take advantage of this, as they'll quickly accumulate miles, gain status sooner, and enjoy perks like priority boarding or free checked bags.

3. Hotel-Specific Card: A hotel-specific card not only rewards you for hotel stays but also gives you points for everyday spending. You'll likely earn extra bonus points on purchases made at hotel properties, allowing you to redeem points for free nights or room upgrades. This card can significantly enhance your hotel experiences and elevate your travels.

As illustrated in the following visual, my Big Three consists of a Chase Credit Card, an American Airlines Card, and a Hyatt Hotels Card. The Chase card offers numerous perks, including TSA/Global Entry fee credits, access to airport lounges, and excellent transfer options to other airlines! The Chase Sapphire is also a direct partner with Hyatt, allowing for maximized point accumulation. Plus, Hyatt and American Airlines have a partnership that enables you to earn even more rewards. My Big Three for the win!

By strategically combining these three card types, you can optimize your point accumulation and enjoy amazing travel perks. While it might be tempting to open even more cards to take advantage of large bonus point promotions, exercise caution; these cards can be traps for the financially illiterate. Only dabble in what you can handle to maintain control over your finances.

Lastly, a huge shout-out to my brother-in-law for getting me started on this journey! He is the king of points collection; he once booked a week-long trip to the Maldives entirely on points, a trip that, if you know, easily costs thousands of dollars. His success inspired me to explore how I could leverage my own spending to enjoy amazing travel experiences without breaking the bank.

THE BIG THREE:
CREDIT CARD TRAVEL HACKING STRATEGY

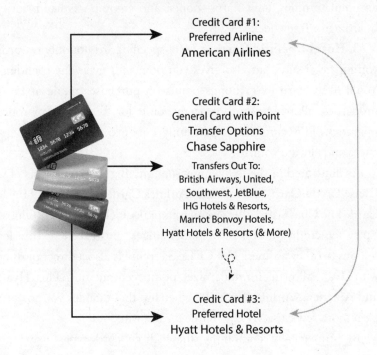

Credit Card #1:
Preferred Airline
American Airlines

Credit Card #2:
General Card with Point
Transfer Options
Chase Sapphire

Transfers Out To:
British Airways, United,
Southwest, JetBlue,
IHG Hotels & Resorts,
Marriott Bonvoy Hotels,
Hyatt Hotels & Resorts (& More)

Credit Card #3:
Preferred Hotel
Hyatt Hotels & Resorts

Buying a Car:
Considering All Factors

Buying a car can feel like a major life upgrade, but it's important to make sure it doesn't derail your financial goals. Your first big choice? New or used. A new car comes with the latest features and a warranty, but it also loses value fast (about 20% as soon as you drive it off the lot). A used car can save you thousands up front, though you might face higher maintenance costs down the road.

Your second big choice? Type of car and brand. Whether you prefer a foreign or US-branded vehicle, I recommend test-driving to get a real feel for the car rather than relying solely on what you see on the dealer's website. Your third big choice? Your preferred way of buying the car, whether that be by leasing, financing, our paying for it outright.

➥ Leasing typically involves lower monthly payments but means you won't own the car outright, which some may feel is akin to throwing money away. However, it ensures you'll always drive a new vehicle.

➥ Financing allows you to eventually own the car, but it often comes with higher monthly payments and interest costs. However, if you keep up with maintenance and take care of the vehicle, you could save money in the long run. There's a reason why folks flock to Toyota, known for their reliability and longevity.

➥ Paying cash can help you avoid debt, but you should consider the opportunity cost of that money; investing it elsewhere could yield better returns.

TABLE 22: MONTHLY CAR EXPENSES EXAMPLE

Expense	Monthly Costs	Notes
Car Loan Payment	$870	Based on a 6% interest rate for a $45,000 loan over 5 years (60 months).
Insurance	$120	Estimated cost varies by driver history, location, and coverage.
Gas	$180	$4.50 per gallon × 10 gallons = $45 per fill-up, 4 fill-ups per month.
Maintenance Fund	$50	Setting aside funds for future maintenance (e.g., oil changes, tire rotation).
Registration & Taxes	$15	Yearly registration and taxes spread out over 12 months.
Tolls	$30	$5 per toll, hybrid in-office 3 days a week, one-way commute for work.
Miscellaneous	$20	Includes items like car washes or unexpected small expenses.
Total Monthly Cost	**$1,285**	**Total of all recurring car-related expense**

When purchasing a car, it's crucial to ensure that all associated costs fit within your prosperity plan, extending beyond just your monthly car payment. While it's easy to focus solely on what you can afford to pay each month, numerous other expenses can significantly impact your budget. As illustrated in Table #22, you must account for costs such as insurance, fuel, maintenance, registration, and potential repairs.

Taking a holistic view of car ownership costs sets you up for success in achieving your objectives, allowing you to transition smoothly from point A to point B on your financial journey. Remember, the right vehicle should be more than just a means of transportation; it should also serve as a supportive asset in your broader prosperity plan.

Buying a House:
Tips for First-Time Buyers

Purchasing a home is a significant milestone and a cornerstone of long-term financial security. Before diving into the housing market, it's vital to carefully evaluate your options to ensure you're making the right choice for your needs. Start by deciding between new construction and existing homes, as both have their benefits and drawbacks. New homes often come with modern amenities and fewer repairs, while existing homes may offer established neighborhoods and lower prices.

Next, consider the type of property that best suits your lifestyle: single-family homes provide privacy and space, while duplexes or townhouses can be more affordable and less maintenance-intensive. Location is another critical factor; homes in good school districts and neighborhoods with low crime rates tend to retain their value better over time.

When determining how much home you can afford, aim to keep your mortgage payment within 28% of your gross income. Additionally, remember to budget for other costs associated with homeownership, including property taxes, insurance, utilities, and maintenance. The example in Table #23 illustrates these monthly expenses, highlighting how they can impact your overall budget.

Getting preapproved for a mortgage can streamline the buying process by giving you a clear budget and demonstrating to sellers that you are a serious buyer. There are various financing options available that you can explore through your personal bank or on real estate websites, which often provide tools to help you find the right mortgage for your needs. Additionally, working with a knowledgeable real estate agent can offer valuable insights into market trends and help you navigate the complexities of home buying.

TABLE 23: MONTHLY HOME EXPENSES EXAMPLE

Expense	Monthly Costs	Notes
Mortgage Payment	$3,835	Based on a 6% interest rate for a $712,500 loan over 30 years (after 5% down payment of $37,500).
Property Taxes	$625	Estimated at 1% of the home's value annually ($7,500/year), divided by 12 months.
Homeowner's Insurance	$100	Estimated cost; can vary based on coverage and provider.
Utilities	$450	Includes electricity, water, gas, trash, and sewer; adjusted for a typical family in a 3 bedroom, 2.5 bath home.
HOA Fees	$50	Estimated monthly fee; varies by neighborhood.
Maintenance Fund	$150	Setting aside funds for future repairs and maintenance (about 1% of home value annually).
Total Monthly Cost	**$5,210**	**Setting aside funds for future repairs and maintenance (about 1% of home value annually).**

While homeownership is often seen as a traditional path to building wealth, it's important to recognize that there are still financially well-off people who choose to rent. Depending on your financial goals and lifestyle preferences, renting can be a smart choice that allows for flexibility and the freedom to allocate funds elsewhere. By thoughtfully evaluating these factors, you empower yourself to make savvy choices that not only fit your budget but also pave the way for lasting financial success and stability. Remember, your journey to wealth can take many forms, and what matters most is finding the right fit for you.

The Financial Abundance Blueprint

Prenups vs. Postnups: Protecting Your Assets, Your Way

Let's shift gears to tackle some of the more challenging financial conversations. Many people believe that prenuptial and postnuptial agreements are only for the rich and famous, but the truth is that these legal tools can benefit anyone seeking clarity and financial protection in their marriage.

Prenups are signed before the wedding, while postnups come into play afterward. Both agreements can outline how assets will be divided in the event of a divorce, as well as address issues like debt, spousal support, and estate planning. They are especially valuable for couples with significant assets, businesses, or children from previous relationships.

Having "the talk" about a prenup or postnup might feel awkward, but it's really an opportunity for open communication and mutual protection. It's far better to discuss these matters when you still care about each other, rather than in the emotional turmoil of a divorce; something we all hope to avoid. Without these agreements, you risk leaving your future in the hands of the courts, your lawyers, and your future emotional state if a divorce does occur.

Recognizing that life can be unpredictable shows that you care about each other enough to want to make sure both of you are set up for success, no matter what happens. It's about having each other's backs and keeping things fair, even in tough times.

Financial Boundaries: Protecting Your Peace and Priorities

Setting financial boundaries is essential for safeguarding both your relationships and your financial well-being. Whether it's with family, friends, or your partner, being clear about your financial limits helps prevent misunderstandings, resentment, and potential financial strain.

Navigating the "Cultural Tax": Black, Brown, and First-Generation Expectations

In many Black, Brown, and immigrant communities, there's often an unspoken expectation to support extended family once you achieve financial stability. This phenomenon, commonly referred to as the Black Tax or Brown Tax, creates significant pressure on individuals to contribute to their family's financial well-being. These concepts reflect both the financial and emotional obligations to support family members, help cover everyday expenses, manage emergencies, or fund larger goals like education, homeownership, and medical care. For immigrant families, these financial obligations can be even more pronounced, especially when it involves sending money back to family members in their countries of origin.

For first-generation graduates or professionals, the First-Gen Tax adds another layer of responsibility. As someone who has likely broken new ground in terms of education and income, you might find yourself not only contributing financially but also serving as the "go-to" for financial advice and decision-making within your family.

Whether it's the Black Tax, Brown Tax, or First-Gen Tax, a common theme emerges: these responsibilities, while noble and rooted in love, can significantly hinder your ability to build long-term wealth. Supporting your family doesn't have to mean sacrificing your financial stability. It's about finding a balance where you can contribute meaningfully without jeopardizing your own goals. *Setting clear boundaries isn't about saying "no" to your loved ones → it's about saying "yes" to your financial peace and long-term prosperity.*

Creating a "Family Care Plan" for Your Loved Ones

Instead of viewing cultural financial responsibilities as burdens, consider framing them as part of a larger Family Care Plan. This plan involves intentionally deciding how much you can afford to give, budgeting for family support like any other financial goal, and ensuring it aligns with your own priorities and resources. By doing this, you maintain control over how you contribute without the guilt or pressure of feeling like you have to give more than you're comfortable with. A Family Care Plan is about building a future for both your family and yourself, ensuring that neither is compromised in the process.

Lending money can be a point of tension for many families that fall prey to the cultural tax. Once you're clear on what you're comfortable lending out (which ultimately you need to be okay with never getting back), it's essential to communicate that clearly and stand firm on those boundaries. This clarity helps prevent confusion and ill feelings.

If you encounter family members who disrespect your boundaries, consider these strategies:

- **Be Direct:** Have a calm, honest conversation about your financial limits and why they are important to you.
- **Stay Firm:** If someone continues to push against your boundaries, reiterate your stance without guilt. You have the right to prioritize your financial health.

↪ **Seek Support:** If necessary, involve other family members who understand your perspective and can help reinforce your boundaries.

Remember, if family members continue to be unreasonable toward your boundaries, you may need to let them go and give it up to God to help shift their mindset, while protecting your peace in the meantime. Hopefully, it never gets to that point, but your peace and well-being come first! Supporting your family shouldn't require sacrificing your financial stability and ultimately feeding into the slippery slope of generational financial struggle. It's about finding a balance where you can contribute meaningfully without jeopardizing your own goals.

Charitable Giving: Financially Uplifting Your Community

As you build financial security, charitable giving becomes an opportunity to put your money where your heart is. Whether you're donating to a cause you care about, volunteering your time, or offering resources, giving back allows you to make a positive impact while staying connected to your values and community.

Tithing and Living off 90%

In many religious communities, particularly among Christians, tithing, which is the practice of giving 10% of your income to the church or charitable causes, holds deep significance. It reflects faith and trust in a higher power, a belief that living off 90% of your income will still provide abundant blessings. For many, tithing is a way to live out their spiritual beliefs through financial action, ensuring that their resources are used to uplift both their spiritual community and broader society. While the 10% rule is a common benchmark adopted by Christians and non-Christians alike, it's not the only path to charitable giving. The most important aspect is giving intentionally and aligning your giving with both your financial situation and personal beliefs.

Budgeting for Impact

To make charitable giving a sustainable part of your financial plan, treat it like any other financial goal by budgeting for it. Allocate a percentage of your income specifically for donations to the causes that resonate with you. Research the organizations you choose to support to ensure they align with your values and effectively manage the donations they receive.

Charitable giving isn't just a selfless act; it can also benefit your financial plan. In many cases, donations are tax-deductible, which can reduce your taxable income. Be sure to keep records of your contributions, including receipts and acknowledgment letters, to maximize your tax benefits. By giving thoughtfully, you're able to uplift others, support causes that resonate with you, and make a meaningful difference, all while securing your financial future. It's a reminder that wealth can be a force for good, empowering you to drive change and contribute to a better, more compassionate world.

tFAB in Action: Living Out Your Prosperity Plan

This chapter's tFAB in action moment emphasizes executing your prosperity plan by organizing your accounts and credit cards, thoughtfully considering big purchases, and balancing key financial conversations. Here are your action items:

1. Audit Your Accounts: Review your checking and savings accounts to ensure they are organized in a way that suits your financial management style. Consider automating bill payments or money transfers to streamline your finances.

2. Leverage Credit Card Rewards: Use credit cards strategically to enhance your lifestyle, but ensure you pay off the balance in full each month to avoid interest while reaping the benefits of rewards.

3. Evaluate Big Purchases: When considering major purchases like a car or a home, think beyond the sticker price to include the total cost of ownership, including maintenance, insurance, and taxes.

4. Set Financial Boundaries: Establish clear, firm financial boundaries with loved ones. This helps prioritize both your relational and financial peace, ensuring that your support doesn't jeopardize your own financial goals.

5. Give with Intention: Align your charitable contributions with causes that resonate with you. Whether through your time, money, or resources, ensure that your giving reflects your values without compromising your financial security.

MAXIMIZING YOUR CORPORATE BENEFITS

Maximizing your 9-to-5 income toward financial independence and abundance means seizing every opportunity your employer provides. Translation: we're not leaving any money on the table! Despite the alarming statistic that most Americans couldn't cover a $1,000 emergency without going into debt, many in the workforce overlook potentially thousands in untapped benefits. If you're new to your career, navigating beyond basic benefits can be daunting. According to CNBC, "fewer than 3 out of 10 workers say they're very confident that they're using their workplace benefits to their fullest potential." Depending on what's offered, neglecting these perks means missing out on significant financial advantages and more.

In this Track, I'll guide you through various corporate benefits worth maximizing; each potentially worth thousands annually for you and your family. While not every benefit may apply equally, even small gains accumulate over time. By the end, my aim is for you to uncover at least $1,000 in annual benefits, helping you avoid financial vulnerability and ensuring you're making the most of what your employer offers.

Employer Contributions to Retirement Accounts (401(k)s and HSAs)

Given our thorough coverage in earlier Tracks, I'll keep this brief. Your priority should be maximizing employer contributions to your 401(k). Understand how much your employer matches based on your salary and their plan percentage, and aim to contribute enough to receive this match. Do what you can so you're not leaving that money on the table. It's a part of your compensation whether you tap into it or not.

When considering health insurance options, note if your employer offers an HSA-eligible high-deductible health plan (HDHP). Some employers contribute to your HSA as an incentive for choosing this plan, which can serve as a wealth-building vehicle through investment opportunities. Assessing this option and the employer's contribution is crucial for making informed health insurance decisions, often outlined in a comparison chart on the benefits site. Personally, I opted for an HDHP that aligned with my family's needs, and one employer even provided a generous annual contribution of $1,000 (Single Plan) or $2,000 (Family Plan) into my HSA, deposited at the start of the year. This contribution was additional money I could allocate freely, maximizing financial benefits without compromising health coverage choices.

The Financial Abundance Blueprint

Health Insurance

Health insurance is pivotal for your financial security and well-being, ensuring you and your family receive essential care without financial strain. Understanding and maximizing health insurance benefits, including comprehensive coverage details and preventative services, is crucial for safeguarding both physical and financial health.

In addition to HSAs, Flexible Spending Accounts (FSAs) are another valuable tax-advantaged option for covering medical expenses. FSAs, offered through employer-sponsored benefits, operate on a use-it-or-lose-it basis within the plan year. Contributions are pre-tax, lowering taxable income. Unlike HSAs, FSAs do not typically allow funds to roll over, limiting their use for long-term wealth building but offering immediate tax savings. Depending on your needs, choosing a health care plan that includes an FSA could be beneficial.

Company Equity

If you're fortunate enough to receive company equity as part of your compensation package, it's not just something to glance over: it's a powerful tool that can significantly impact your financial future. Equity grants, whether in the form of stock options or restricted stock units (RSUs), offer you a stake in the company's success and growth. This ownership can lead to substantial financial rewards, especially if the company performs well and its stock value increases over time.

Understanding the mechanics of equity grants is essential. Typically, these grants come with vesting schedules, which dictate when you gain full ownership of the equity. Vesting schedules often include a "cliff" period where no equity vests until you've worked at the company for a specific period of time (usually one year), followed by gradual vesting increments (monthly or yearly) thereafter. This structure encourages loyalty and long-term commitment to the company, aligning your financial incentives with its performance.

Stock options, a common form of equity compensation, grant you the right to purchase company stock at a predetermined price (the strike price) at a future date. This provides potential for financial gain if the company's stock price rises above the strike price by the time you exercise your options. RSUs, on the other hand, grant you actual company stock upon vesting.

Before taking any action, it's crucial to define your financial goals clearly. If you've followed this book from cover to cover, you've already laid out your aspirations and timelines. If not, I strongly recommend revisiting Track 11 on Your Prosperity Plan, which guides you through setting SMART financial goals and understanding your financial priorities.

Once you've defined your goals, the next step is to evaluate whether holding onto your company stock aligns with your objectives or if selling some shares makes more sense. Here's a practical way to decide: Imagine someone offered you a check for the current value of your upcoming vesting equity. Would you use that money to buy more of your company's stock? If yes, holding onto your equity may be the right move. If not, selling some or all of your vested shares could be a better strategy. Depending on how long you remain with the company, you'll likely receive what we call "equity refreshes" in which you receive more grants of RSUs and/or stock options annually with each performance review. Imagine as an example receiving $30,000 in RSUs upon joining the company and then one year later, receiving another $15,000 in RSUs, and then another $10,000 in RSUs the following year. Eventually, you'll have $1,000s in company stock coming in on various vesting schedules, in addition to your regular 9-to-5 paychecks. This money, should you

The Financial Abundance Blueprint

choose to sell, can be viewed as part of your Abundance Accelerator as well.

There's no one-size-fits-all approach to maximizing company equity. It depends on your personal financial situation, risk tolerance, and long-term goals. For instance, selling some shares could fund a robust emergency fund, pay off debts, or cover a significant life event without impacting your daily finances. Alternatively, diversifying away from company stock by reinvesting in other assets such as index funds can reduce risk and ensure a more balanced investment portfolio.

Personally (and not offering this as investing advice), I've chosen to maintain a set amount of my company's stock while selling any new equity grants and reinvesting the proceeds into diversified investments. As I shared in Track 13, I'm a Buy and Hold Index Fund investor as I prefer to have my portfolio diversified across a lot of companies to enable me to benefit from the gains with moderate risk, and I tend to purchase the same funds over and over again. Put musically, I prefer a diversified playlist with '90s R&B Jams across all my favorite artists so no matter my mood, I know there's a song on there that's going to hit the spot! However, if specific financial goals were to arise that couldn't be covered by my savings/sinking funds, then I'd consider accessing these resources and adjust my strategy accordingly.

Work from Home Benefits

Remember when the pandemic hit in 2020 and workplaces adapted to remote work? Many received a work-from-home stipend, allowing them to set up their home office. Whether you're still remote, hybrid, or back in the office, reflect on how you used those funds. Here's a bold perspective: unless your company mandates specific purchases (like a "Dell" monitor), consider using the stipend to create a workspace that inspires you. Choose the Apple iMac or those AirPods Max in your favorite color; don't settle for generic black or white if it doesn't resonate with you. If your office has a particular aesthetic, find items that fit within those guidelines while also bringing you joy.

Education Reimbursement and Personal Development Stipends

As a leader in the Learning and Development space, this benefit holds personal significance and often remains underutilized. Considering the abundance of free programs available to learn new skills, not to mention such resources as "YouTube University," if I'm investing in further education, I firmly believe my employer should sponsor some, if not all, of the tuition. It's a privilege to have this opportunity, as not all employers offer education or development stipends. If yours does, Corporate Queens, go learn something on their dime! Personally, I pursued my master of science in global marketing management from Boston University part-time while working full-time. The program typically spans eighteen months to two years, and I completed mine from 2014 to 2018 to minimize out-of-pocket costs. Despite switching employers with different education reimbursement benefits during the final semesters, I still paid less than 15 percent of the program's total cost. That's $10,000s put back into my own pocket just by tapping into this corporate benefit!

When considering education reimbursement, people often think of graduate programs or specialized certificates from universities, which are excellent choices if they align with your goals. However, did you know you can likely use these benefits for other nontraditional learning programs as well? Yes, you can invest in courses from your favorite influencers or master minds, or attend industry-specific conferences. Many conferences even provide templates to help secure sponsorship approval from your employer to cover personal costs. Depending on your benefit details, even hobbies like dance or cooking classes might qualify for partial coverage. Reflect on what new skills or experiences you wish to pursue and explore whether they could be funded through your employer's education reimbursement or personal development stipend, if available.

Student Loan Relief

Let's talk about a game-changing benefit: student loan relief. Some companies are stepping up to help employees tackle their student debt. While it might not wipe out your loans entirely, these programs can still put a few thousand dollars back in your pocket each year; again, free money you shouldn't overlook. Even if you're eyeing more education down the road, this benefit can still be a lifeline. Take, for example, a woman I recently spoke with pursuing a doctorate in business administration. She's using her employer's education reimbursement for most of the tuition and strategically using loans for the remainder to tap into this relief program while preserving her savings. It's about maximizing every opportunity, which is literally thousands of dollars in value!

Personal Time Off

Personal Time Off (PTO) isn't just about taking a break; it's a cornerstone of work-life balance and well-being. Whether you're using weekends wisely or taking advantage of flexible schedules, optimizing your PTO can mean ample time for rejuvenation. One of its greatest benefits is flexibility. It's okay to take a mental health "sick" day to recharge when you're on the edge of burnout.

And let's not forget maternity leave and unpaid time off, pivotal for life's milestones. Women should never feel shame for taking their entire maternity leave. Bringing life into this world is intense, and you deserve that time to bond without worry about work piling up.

Moreover, with the rise of remote and hybrid work arrangements, you have even more ways to make your PTO work for you. By being intentional with days off around holidays, you can create minivacations throughout the year. Plan strategically and enjoy well-deserved breaks that enrich your life beyond the office.

Business Travel and International Experience

Business travel isn't just about moving from point A to point B. It's a strategic opportunity to maximize corporate benefits and enrich personal experiences. Aligning trips with desired destinations can turn work travel into an exciting adventure. For instance, prioritizing clients in cities you want to visit can add fulfillment to your professional endeavors. I once strategically planned a trip to my hometown of Buffalo, New York, around Thanksgiving while working with New Era, a sports hat company headquartered locally. If you know anything about traveling during the holidays, then you know I saved quite a few coins having my flight and part of my accommodations covered by my employer.

As you travel for business, establishing loyalty with airlines and hotels not only simplifies booking but also earns valuable rewards such as miles and points for personal travel. Remember all that we covered in Track 14 as it relates to travel hacking with credit cards. It should compliment business travels as well; strategic travel choices can lead to such perks as free flights and hotel nights, enhancing both your professional and personal life travels, as you gain status with frequently used brands.

International experience is another corporate benefit worth seizing, offering opportunities for growth and cultural immersion. Programs such as company rotations provide invaluable experiences in different cultures and work environments. During a professional development program, I spent two months in Milan, Italy, which greatly enhanced my adaptability and cross-cultural communication skills; essential traits for corporate leadership. More importantly, traveling throughout Europe is way cheaper once you're over there. I was able to visit Rome and Venice in Italy and make my way to the UK as well during my time overseas!

Even more rewarding was the fact that the company funded my initial flights to and from Europe and my accommodations in Milan, leaving me responsible only for daily lifestyle expenses. Leveraging opportunities to work abroad not only enriches your résumé but also creates unforgettable life experiences.

Corporate Discounts

Corporate discounts on products and services from other brands are a valuable yet often overlooked benefit that can significantly cut your personal expenses. Whether you enjoy movies, theme parks, electronics, or other types of experiences, there's likely a discount available through your company. Personally, I always take advantage of the rental car discount whenever I travel; it's a small but consistent way to save. I've also enjoyed discounted tickets to popular amusement parks like Disneyland, where ticket costs can really add up. Leveraging corporate discounts for preferred hotels, such as Hyatt in my case, ensures great value for the right price every time I travel. Don't underestimate the power of corporate discounts—they're an easy and effective way to maximize your benefits and keep more money in your pocket.

Random Company-Sponsored Events

Random free events in the corporate world can be unexpected treasures, offering valuable opportunities to maximize your benefits. From networking gatherings with guest speakers to chances to expand your professional circle, these events provide invaluable connections and insights. But the perks don't stop there. Free books from seminars can enrich your library, while swag offers a chance to snag useful items like clothing and accessories. Embrace these hidden gems as part of your strategy to enhance your career and lifestyle while making the most of your corporate benefits. One of my personal favorites was attending a Boyz II Men concert as part of the company's summer festival—an experience tied to my personal history with the award-winning R&B group, but that's a story for another time. Make it a priority to attend these events whenever possible!

Food and Snacks

Saving money can make a significant difference in your budget, especially in high-cost areas like the Bay Area or NYC, where a simple lunch out can easily cost $20. That's why I advocate for making the most of workplace perks, particularly when it comes to food, snacks, and drinks; it's all part of your compensation package. Personally, taking advantage of free office food has been transformative. Arriving a bit earlier in the morning lets me beat the rush and enjoy breakfast, plus I can grab something for lunch. Those late nights at the office? Having dinner available can be a lifesaver when burning the midnight oil. It's not just about main meals either; stocking up on snacks and drinks during office visits has slashed my grocery bill. Whether grabbing extra soda cans or packing leftovers for the weekend, these small actions save big over time.

Now, you might wonder, isn't it opportunistic to take advantage of free office food? Absolutely not. Be reasonable of course, but remember it's part of your compensation package! Look around your office cafeteria; many colleagues do the same. So, next time you're in the office, grab that to-go box of leftovers or stock up on snacks. By maximizing this benefit, you save money for other financial goals, and every dollar counts.

Monetary Gifts, Awards, and Contests

Imagine this: You're excelling in your role, exceeding expectations, and suddenly, an opportunity arises to be recognized and rewarded for your exceptional efforts with more money! One avenue to explore is your company's peer-to-peer recognition program, designed to honor colleagues' achievements. Here, you can highlight outstanding work through formal write-ups, gaining visibility with leadership and often earning a well-deserved bonus.

But wait, there's more! Keep an eye out for additional bonus opportunities, often bestowed by managers and leaders to celebrate significant project wins. Whether achieving sales targets or delivering stellar results on tough projects, these bonuses are tangible rewards for your dedication.

Now, let's delve into contests. If you've worked in sales, you know the thrill of competing in contests that not only boost revenue but also showcase customer success stories. Depending on your company, these contests can potentially offer chances to win monetary bonuses and exciting rewards such as trips to a destination (or different office) of your choosing.

Here's the best part: many of these programs may allow for self-nomination. By raising your hand and sharing your accomplishments, you unlock opportunities for recognition and financial gain. Personally, I have self-nominated and earned $1,000s annually from these types of opportunities alone.

Formal Mentorship and Career Coaching Programs

Formal mentorship and career coaching programs are invaluable corporate benefits that can accelerate your professional growth and development. Job shadowing programs, for example, can offer exposure to different roles within the organization, allowing you to expand your understanding of various teams and career paths without committing fully to a new role.

Additionally, formal mentorship programs provide structured guidance and support, which is particularly beneficial for Corporate Queens from underrepresented communities or those struggling to secure mentors independently. By participating in these programs, you have the opportunity to learn from experienced professionals, gain insights into navigating the workplace, and expand your network within the organization.

Having personally benefited from formal mentorship programs, I can attest to their value. Whether you walk away with a strong mentor or simply a new connection, the experience is what you make of it. Furthermore, my role as a career coach within my organization allowed me to share my knowledge and expertise with others, guiding individuals on navigating the workplace and managing personal finances. If your employer offers any form of free coaching sessions, definitely take advantage! Whether its through peer-to-peer or a collaboration with an external company, these are invaluable resources that can be true game changers as you navigate your career and life in general.

tFAB in Action: Maximizing Your Corporate Benefits

This tFAB in Action moment has focused on optimizing your corporate benefits to strengthen your financial security, elevate career growth opportunities, and enhance overall professional well-being. Here are your action items:

Review Employee Benefits: Thoroughly assess your current employee benefits to know what's fully available to you.

Maximize Retirement Contributions: Evaluate 401(k) and HSA contributions, adjusting for maximum employer matches and benefits.

Assess Company Equity: Review company equity holdings, strategizing for alignment with long-term financial goals.

Take Some Time Off: Consider taking a long weekend off around the next holiday or simply a mental health day to recharge after completing a long project.

Reflect on Business Travel: Align business trips with personal travel goals and explore international work opportunities.

Explore Corporate Discounts: Utilize discounts on products and services to save on purchases.

Maximize Food Perks: Optimize workplace food options to save money on groceries and eating out and redirect funds toward financial goals.

Tap Into Monetary Awards: Proactively seek out recognition by peers and leaders to earn additional money while also expanding your professional brand narrative.

Pursue Formal Mentorship Programs: Assess employer mentorship and coaching for career development and networking opportunities.

TRACK 16

MO' MONEY, NO PROBLEMS

In today's ever-changing economy, relying solely on a single income source can be risky, especially with the unpredictability of Corporate America. Economic downturns, industry shifts, and corporate changes can all disrupt your primary income in an instant. That's why diversifying your income isn't just a smart move. It's essential for securing financial stability and fueling your growth.

Side A of this book focused on navigating the workplace with ease, ensuring you maximize the earning potential of your primary income stream: your 9-to-5. Side B then shifted gears to show you how to manage, multiply, and maximize that income toward financial freedom. Now, in this Track, we're taking it up a notch. With more time on our hands and the knowledge of financial literacy, every dollar of new income brings us closer to our goals, and faster. We've created the system, now it's time to fuel it up and go farther!

The average millionaire has seven streams of income. This strategy not only accelerates your journey to financial independence but also creates a robust safety net. If one stream takes a hit, others are there to support you, opening new doors for wealth-building opportunities. By diversifying your income, you mitigate financial risks like job loss or unexpected expenses. It ensures you're not overly dependent on a single source, providing stability like multiple pillars supporting your financial foundation. This resilience allows you to navigate life's uncertainties with greater confidence.

Moreover, multiple income streams accelerate your path to financial independence by enhancing your savings potential and maximizing compound growth opportunities. This strategy empowers your money to work harder for you, securing your future and enabling a life filled with freedom and fulfillment.

Having extra income unlocks opportunities for travel, pursuing passions, and enjoying a higher quality of life, free from the stress of financial worries. Now to be clear, I'm not contradicting the premise of this book, which is achieving abundance on a 9-5. We've covered how that's possible up to this point. However, between the potential for layoffs/restructuring, evolving industry dynamics, etc., it's imperative to still acknowledge the role multiple streams of income allows you to get to your goals faster if you choose to exert the extra energy to do so!

The Five Main Types of Income Streams

Let's break down the different types of income streams. Diversifying your income isn't just about having multiple sources. It's about understanding how each type can contribute to your financial health and long-term goals. From active income earned through your job to passive income generated from investments, we'll explore how to strategically leverage each type. By the end of this section, you'll have a clearer understanding of which types of income streams you'll want to prioritize adding to your income portfolio to support your journey toward financial independence and abundance.

The Financial Abundance Blueprint

Earned Income

Earned income covers what you get paid for actively working or providing services. This includes your regular paycheck, hourly wages, bonuses based on how well you perform, and commissions from making sales. It's the money you earn from your day job in an office or any extra cash you make freelancing or doing part-time gigs outside of your regular hours.

TABLE 24: PROS AND CONS OF EARNED INCOME

Pros	Cons
Steady and predictable income	Income stops if work stops
Opportunities for skill development	Limited scaling potential
Benefits such as healthcare and retirement plans	Higher taxation rates

Passive Income

Passive income is money you make with little ongoing effort. It includes things like dividends from stocks, interest from savings accounts or bonds, rent from properties you own, and royalties from creative works like books or music. These are income streams that keep bringing in money without you needing to be hands-on every day.

TABLE 25: PROS AND CONS OF PASSIVE INCOME

Pros	Cons
Financial freedom (income continues without active work)	Requires initial investment or capital
Scalability with potential for growth	Market risk and fluctuations
Diversification of income sources	Management may be required (e.g., real estate properties).

Business Income

Business income stems from entrepreneurial ventures or self-employment, representing the earnings derived from launching and managing your own business offering products and services. This type of income allows individuals to exercise creativity, control business decisions, and potentially achieve unlimited income growth.

TABLE 26: PROS AND CONS OF BUSINESS INCOME

Pros	Cons
Unlimited income potential with business growth	High risk of business failure
Creativity and control over business decisions	Time-intensive to establish and grow
Tax benefits for business expenses	Competitive market landscape

Capital Gains

Capital gains refer to the profits you make from selling something for more than what you paid for it originally. For instance, capital gains can come from selling stocks that have increased in value, flipping real estate after renovations or market changes, or selling valuable collectibles such as art or antiques at a higher price than you bought them. These transactions let you benefit from the growth of your investments, giving you extra income beyond what you initially put in.

TABLE 27: PROS AND CONS OF CAPITAL GAINS

Pros	Cons
Potential for significant profit with asset appreciation	Market volatility affects returns.
Diversification of investment portfolio	Timing the market for buying and selling assets can be tricky.
Tax advantages for long-term investments	Requires initial capital investment

Residual Income

Residual income is money you keep getting over time from something you did once, invested in initially, or set up. For example, residual income can come from things like network marketing, where you earn commissions from sales made through a network of sellers you created, or from monthly subscription fees for services that people keep using like paying for access to a community. These income streams keep bringing in money regularly, even if you're not actively working on them all the time, letting you benefit from your initial efforts long after you've done the work.

TABLE 28: PROS AND CONS OF RESIDUAL INCOME

Pros	Cons
Passive nature (Income continues with minimal effort.)	Perception challenges (e.g., stigma in network marketing)
Scalability with growth of network or subscriptions	Initial effort required to establish income stream
Complements other income streams	Market saturation and competition

Abundant Wealth Chronicle: Your Next Income Stream Quiz

Now that you've explored the exciting world of different income streams, you might be feeling inspired or maybe a tad overwhelmed. Remember, it's all about focusing your energy where it counts. Whether you're keen on mastering one income stream before moving to the next or you're tempted to tackle them all at once (though we don't recommend that!), this quiz will help pinpoint your ideal next pursuit. Let's find out which income stream aligns best with your goals and aspirations for financial success!

1. What is your current employment situation?

    A) I have a stable job with benefits and regular income.

    B) I freelance or have a side hustle for additional income.

    C) I am self-employed and manage my own business.

    D) I am actively investing in assets like stocks or real estate.

    E) I am exploring ways to generate income with minimal ongoing effort.

2. How do you view financial risk and effort?

    A) I prefer steady income with lower risk, even if it means less potential for high returns.

    B) I am willing to invest time and effort up-front for potential long-term gains.

    C) I am comfortable taking on higher risk for the possibility of significant income growth.

    D) I am strategic about managing market risks to maximize capital gains.

    E) I seek opportunities that provide ongoing income without constant active involvement.

3. What is your long-term financial goal? To:

    A) Maintain financial stability and security

B) Build wealth steadily over time through diversified investments

C) Achieve financial independence through entrepreneurial ventures

D) Grow wealth by investing in appreciating assets

E) Create multiple streams of income that require minimal ongoing effort

4. How do you prefer to allocate your time for income generation?

A) I prioritize my primary job and stable income.

B) I dedicate time to grow my skills and side income opportunities.

C) I invest heavily in building and expanding my own business.

D) I actively manage investments and explore new opportunities.

E) I seek passive income streams that complement my current activities.

5. What excites you most about income generation?

A) Stability and benefits from steady employment

B) Potential for scalability and growth in various ventures

C) Creativity and control in entrepreneurial pursuits

D) Profiting from asset appreciation and market opportunities

E) Generating income that continues with minimal ongoing effort

Congratulations on completing the Your Next Income Stream Quiz to discover which new income stream is most ideal for you to curate next to achieve your financial goals and ultimately achieve a life of financial abundance! For those who:

Mostly Checked A's: Prioritize Earned Income. Congratulations, Queen! Your focus on maximizing your primary job is spot on. You're already slaying in your career—now it's time to amplify it. Think about how your skills and expertise can light up a side hustle that brings in extra cash. Whether it's freelancing in your field or starting a passion project, you've got what it takes to turn your hustle into major gains.

Mostly Checked B's: Prioritize Passive Income. Girl, you're all about building that financial future with a smart and savvy mindset. Diversify your income with investments that keep the money flowing while you focus on what matters, like turning that side hustle into a powerhouse or diving deep into dividend stocks and rental properties. Your hard work now will set you up for that Queen lifestyle you're dreaming of.

Mostly Checked C's: Prioritize Business Income. You're a visionary, ready to carve out your path and own it. Dive headfirst into your entrepreneurial dreams and watch your empire grow. Whether it's launching your own business or taking your current hustle to the next level, your creativity and determination will make waves. Get ready to make your mark and build that business empire like the future CEO you are.

Mostly Checked D's: Prioritize Capital Gains. You've got your eyes on the prize, wealth building through smart investments. Whether it's stocks or real estate, your knack for spotting opportunities and navigating the market will pay off big time. Get ready to level up your financial game and secure that wealth you've been dreaming of.

Mostly Checked E's: Prioritize Residual Income. You're all about that steady flow of income with minimal effort. Explore opportunities like network marketing or creating subscription services that keep the money coming in while you focus on what you love. Your drive to create multiple income streams will ensure you're living your best life without being tied down. Get ready to enjoy that financial freedom you've been working toward.

The Financial Abundance Blueprint

Strategies to Create Multiple Streams of Income

Let's dive into five effective ways to start building multiple income streams. Each strategy aligns with a different income stream category, giving you flexibility to focus on what suits your goals best. Keep in mind these strategies aim to provide some quick next steps for you to explore building an income stream in these categories. More research and execution will be required as you dive deeper in your selection(s). There's no such thing as overnight success, Rome wasn't built in a day!

Leverage Your Skills and Talents

Begin by identifying the skills, hobbies, and areas of expertise that you excel in. Once you've pinpointed these strengths, research the market demand for them. Consider options such as freelancing, creating online courses, offering coaching services, essentially marketing your expertise and packing it up to reach more people beyond your 9-5. To attract clients, build a portfolio that showcases your work, and actively network through social media and professional events.

Invest Wisely

Start by assessing your financial goals, risk tolerance, and investment horizon. With these factors in mind, diversify your investments across stocks, bonds, mutual funds, and real estate to effectively manage risk. Consulting with a financial advisor can help you tailor a strategy that aligns with your unique needs. As you track dividends and capital gains, you'll strategically grow your wealth, ensuring your investments work toward securing your financial future.

Start a Side Business

Brainstorm business ideas that align with your interests and meet market demand. Once you have a solid idea, develop a comprehensive business plan that outlines your product or service, target market, and marketing strategies. Next, register your business, obtain any necessary licenses, and set up a separate bank account. With these foundations in place, launch your website or online store, implement marketing campaigns, and continuously refine your offerings based on customer feedback to turn your passion into a profitable venture.

Develop Passive Income Streams

Create digital products such as eBooks or online courses that can generate income over time and set up sales funnels or distribution channels to reach your audience. Simultaneously, research real estate markets and investment opportunities for rental properties. To maximize returns with minimal daily involvement, utilize automation tools to streamline operations and scale your passive income ventures. Additionally, seek professional advice on tax implications and property management to ensure your investments are optimized for long-term success.

Join Affiliate Programs

Choose products or services that align with your interests and resonate with your audience. After selecting, research and join reputable affiliate networks, then create content and promotional strategies to effectively market these products on your platforms. Monitor performance metrics, optimize campaigns based on data insights, and continually explore new affiliate partnerships to diversify your income streams. By participating in affiliate programs, you can earn commissions without the need to create your own products, expanding your income potential.

The Financial Abundance Blueprint

These strategies offer actionable steps to create diverse income sources that align with your preferences and financial goals. Whether you're leveraging your skills, investing wisely, starting a side business, developing passive income, or joining affiliate programs, each approach provides unique benefits to enhance your financial stability.

Abundant Wealth Chronicle: My Journey with Living In The Abundance (LITA)

Let me take you back to how Living In The Abundance (LITA) began. It all started as an Instagram account where I tracked my debt-free journey. As I shared my progress and tips, I realized there was a bigger need for guidance, especially for young women like you and me navigating the corporate world. Early in my career, I didn't have mentors to show me the ropes or explain the unwritten rules of corporate life. Through LITA, I aimed to bridge that gap for the next generation of Corporate Queens.

During the pandemic, everything changed. One day, I received a message asking if I offered money coaching. At that time, I didn't, I was just putting out information for free! But I thought, "Why not?" Plenty of folks were already monetizing their side hustles, so why not me? This moment was a turning point. I realized that the knowledge and experiences I had been sharing for free could be the foundation of a real business. As a senior corporate trainer and volunteer career coach at my company, I've always had a passion for helping others. It was a valuable skillset that my employer at the time benefited greatly from, but clearly was worth so much more than my bi-weekly paycheck. I officially decided to turn this passion into a side hustle and created the business side of LITA, where I get paid to do what I love: empowering young women like you to thrive in their careers and build a secure financial future.

What started as a simple Instagram account sharing my debt-free journey has now become a platform making a real impact.

By leveraging my skills and experiences, I'm able to bridge the gap for the next generation, providing mentorship and guidance that I wish I had early in my career while making some coins on the side! Through LITA, I've cultivated several income streams that leverage my skills and passion:

→ **Speaking Events:** I get invited to speak at conferences and events, both in person and virtually, sharing my knowledge and inspiring others while getting paid for my expertise.

→ **One-on-One Coaching Sessions:** I offer personalized coaching sessions where I work one-on-one with clients to help them achieve their career and financial goals. This direct interaction is incredibly fulfilling as I see the immediate impact of my guidance.

→ **Team Workshops:** I conduct workshops for teams, helping them develop their skills and improve their performance. These workshops are a great way to reach a larger audience and make a significant impact within organizations.

In the future, I plan to expand my income streams with new ventures such as:

→ **Digital Products (eBooks, Online Courses):** Offering self-paced learning materials to reach a broader audience and provide valuable resources.

→ **Brand Deals:** Monetizing my social media presence through partnerships with brands that align with my values and mission.

→ **Group Coaching Programs:** Creating community learning experiences that foster growth and support among like-minded individuals.

That's six potential streams of income, all stemming from one central theme: helping young women succeed in their careers and personal finances. In addition to the income generated through LITA, I also have other streams of income through passive investments in the stock market and savings accounts, providing a steady flow of income without ongoing effort.

You don't necessarily need seven streams of income to become financially secure! Having multiple streams can accelerate your financial goals, but it's more about generating consistent, repeatable income, whether passively from earlier efforts or actively from direct work. LITA has shown me that by leaning into my strengths and passions, I can create diverse income streams that not only boost my financial stability but also allow me to live a life of abundance.

Managing Multiple Income Streams

Now that we've explored various income streams and identified which category would be most optimal based on our Income Stream quiz results, let's consolidate our understanding and transition to effective management strategies. Managing multiple income streams can vary in complexity depending on your current setup. Whether you're prioritizing earned income from your 9-to-5, passive income from investments, or building foundational streams like starting a business or investing in real estate, these tips will help you establish and optimize your ventures from the outset, empowering you as Corporate Queens to navigate and thrive in your financial journey:

➡ **Stay Organized:** Maintain detailed records using accounting software or a bookkeeper to track income, expenses, and ensure tax compliance.

➡ **Automate Where Possible:** Use technology to automate recurring tasks such as buying and selling stocks or running marketing funnels, freeing up time for strategic activities.

→ **Monitor and Adjust:** Regularly assess performance metrics such as revenue growth and investment returns. Adjust investments and scale successful ventures while cutting back on underperforming ones.

→ **Balance Time and Effort:** Delegate non-core tasks to freelancers or assistants to focus on high-impact activities and maintain work-life balance.

→ **Manage Taxes Efficiently:** Understand the tax implications for each income stream, keep thorough records of deductible expenses, and consult with a tax professional to optimize tax strategies.

By implementing these streamlined strategies, you can effectively manage your income streams, ensuring financial security and maximizing growth opportunities.

tFAB in Action: More Money Should Lead to Less or No Problems

This Track's tFAB in Action moment centered on diversifying your income streams to enhance your financial resilience and abundance. Instead of relying on a single source of income, the focus is on leveraging existing skills and interests to create multiple revenue streams. If you haven't already, take the "Your Next Income Stream Quiz" to discover which type of income stream suits you best. Once you have clarity, consider the relevant action item(s):

Utilize Your Skills and Interests: Monetize hobbies and skills through freelancing or coaching based on market demand.

Build Passive Income: Invest in stocks or real estate for steady income with minimal effort.

Brainstorm Business Ideas: Develop and launch business ideas that align with your passions and market needs.

Leverage Affiliate Programs: Promote relevant affiliate products to earn commissions from sales on your platforms.

Implement Effective Management: Use software or a bookkeeper to organize finances and automate income tasks.

Monitor and Optimize: Regularly review and adjust income streams to maximize profitability and consult tax professionals for optimization.

OUTRO: THE FINAL PLAY

tFAB in Action

Dear Corporate Queens,

While Top 100 Billboard might be a stretch for this Deluxe Album of a book, The Financial Abundance Blueprint: A Black Woman's Guide to Achieving Financial Literacy, Building a Successful Career, and Breaking Boundaries making it onto your personal best-read list is more than enough for me!

In the Introduction Track, I shared my vision for readers who fully engage with the lessons and complete all the tFAB action items to walk away with (1) confidence and self-awareness, (2) a corporate playbook, and (3) a realistic financial plan. Like any smooth album, each track took you on a journey and left you with memorable lyrics, tools, and techniques to achieve that vision. Here's a recap of each track, highlighting the key message to unlock the future financially free Corporate Queen in you who thrives in your career and maximizes your money toward your abundant life:

⇥ **Track 1:** Begin by visualizing and documenting your abundant life across core elements. This vision serves as your North Star, guiding every decision and goal.

➤ **Track 2:** Conduct a Personal SWOT Analysis to align your role with your strengths while addressing areas for growth, ensuring that your career is both fulfilling and strategically positioned.

➤ **Track 3:** Define your Personal Brand Statement and elevator pitch, thoughtfully deciding how much of your authentic self to bring into the workplace while remaining true to your values.

➤ **Track 4:** Optimize your work environment and daily workflow using tools like the R&B Hit List Prioritization Matrix and time management strategies to work smarter, not harder.

➤ **Track 5:** Navigate the unwritten rules of corporate life effectively with the EMBODY Framework, simplifying your path to career success without compromising your identity or well-being.

➤ **Track 6:** Master workplace performance with PAGES, documenting your Abundant Accomplishments to shine and stay protected.

➤ **Track 7:** Build your Personal Board of Directors (i.e., your supportive Tribe) through intentional networking, leveraging the Drive-Thru Method to Networking to foster meaningful connections. Always remember to follow up.

➤ **Track 8:** Create positive brand experiences with your colleagues by aligning communication, collaboration, and storytelling to build trust and influence.

➤ **Track 9:** Navigate workplace challenges by focusing on what's within your control, building industry relationships, practicing gratitude, and maintaining resilience.

➤ **Track 10:** Create your own version of a CMJ Map to track and visualize career and money milestones annually, allowing you to connect the dots between these achievements.

➥ **Track 11:** Align your money with your values through your Prosperity Plan and constantly adjust, refine, and execute to bring your vision to life, as needed.

➥ **Track 12:** Set and achieve SMART Financial Goals, starting with building an emergency fund, then tackling savings goals or paying off debt systematically through the "snowy methods."

➥ **Track 13:** Prioritize your Prosperity Investing Playlists (accounts) and select the right songs (investments) using the 9-5er's Wealth Pyramid Framework to guide your wealth-building journey.

➥ **Track 14:** Live your Prosperity Plan out daily with intentional money organization, financial boundaries, and value-based spending on items and experiences that bring you joy.

➥ **Track 15:** Maximize your corporate benefits by uncovering opportunities—aim to extract at least $1,000 annually—by reviewing your employee handbook and/or benefits hub, if available.

➥ **Track 16:** Cultivate streams of income that align with your gifts and passions, accelerating your journey to financial independence and a deeply abundant life where you have more than enough to enjoy your life's desires.

Now that you've made it through each track, you've almost completed your journey through this deluxe album of a book. Each track had its own vibe, rhythm, and, most importantly, a message for you to carry with you. But just like any great album, there's an underlying story that ties it all together. As you moved from one track to the next, you probably noticed how each one built on the other, guiding you toward leveling up in both your career and personal finances. This carefully curated album of a book is more than just a vibe, it's a playbook, designed to help you align your career, finances, and personal goals so everything flows effortlessly. You now know the life you want to live, and you're holding the keys to make it happen as a Corporate Queen, ruling over her career and finances to create the life she deserves. Before we close, I want to share one final Abundant Life Chronicle: my own personal wealth-building journey. This peek behind the scenes will show you exactly how I've applied these strategies in my own life

Abundant Wealth Chronicle: The Evolution of My Personal 9:5er's Wealth Pyramid and Playlist Prioritization

Today, my Abundance Accelerator is ~$50,000 annually, which includes ~$13,500 in employer matches, meaning only $38,000 comes from my paychecks and bonuses. That's my goal every year, and the majority of it happens in the first quarter of the year, which grants me the freedom to enjoy some value-based spending the remaining months, knowing that my future self is taken care of. Based on my financial independence goals set in 2019, I was forecasted to reach FIRE by my late thirties, assuming a modest 7% return on my investment, given my goal was a little north of $1M at the time. That forecast didn't include any additional income coming from company equity (RSUs) or any side hustles I'd explore in the meantime. My ability to provide myself the freedom to be work-optional and achieve financial independence was calculated solely from my 9-5 income. Because again, it should be possible to be financially secure without having to extend yourself into multiple lanes, if you so choose. Of course, given those additional streams of funding, I'm on track to achieve my FIRE goals much sooner. However, it's now 2024 as I write this. It's been a 10 year journey. Just as we saw Alisha's 9-5 WP strategy evolve over time as her career progressed and life circumstances shifted, so has my journey, as will yours.

I graduated with over $60,000 in debt and spent my early career (2014–2018) focused on paying it off and building an emergency fund. My first job in the telecom industry kickstarted my wealth journey with a 401(k) plan I didn't fully understand. Thankfully, auto-enrollment at 6% and profit-sharing bonuses helped me save $25,000 in three years, which was a big surprise for someone earning $54,000 annually. When I transitioned to the tech industry in 2017, I became a top salesperson, directing those sales bonuses toward student loans, which accelerated my payoff journey. In maximizing one of our corporate benefits, I had the privilege of speaking with a financial advisor at Vanguard, where I learned about 401(k)s, IRAs, and the Mega Backdoor Roth more comprehensively, which inspired my 9-to-5er's Wealth Pyramid Framework, because not everyone has access to nor the time to have someone break down this financial lingo in an easy-to-understand way. I calculated my Financial Independence number at the time with a goal of being able to support myself at California's high cost of living prices. As an ambitious first-generation aries and married woman, I will always maintain and encourage other women to have their own sense of financial security, because life can happen at any time. Take that advice however you want, but as for me, "I plan to stay ready so I never have to get ready."

Post my newfound financial understanding, I walked away empowered to work my Prosperity Plan because it was truly worth it. Initially, I focused on eliminating debt, reclaiming nearly $800/month in minimum payments. As my income grew, I was able to max out retirement accounts and secure promotions and raises using the EMBODY Framework, becoming more confident and authentic in how I showed up in the workplace. If you recall my CMJ Map in Track 10, each time I made a major move in my career, I saw parallel growth in my wealth-building journey too! Furthermore, with each milestone as life went on, I was gaining greater clarity on what brought me joy as it relates to how I spent my money. I prioritized experiences such as traveling/vacationing a few times a year and being able to eat out as I desire over materialistic things because that's what mattered to me, and I aligned my prosperity plan accordingly. Peer pressure has no place for my bank account because my peers share different goals and aspirations and should be spending differently as a result. Jones Who? I don't know them, so why am I trying to impress them?! #NoThankYou.

Although I'm further along in my journey now, I want to illustrate the power of compound interest over time. Let's assume I was starting at ground zero with my current Abundance Accelerator. If I were to consistently invest that ~$50K over 25 years, assuming a 7% return, I'd be looking at a portfolio of $3M. Seeing nearly two-thirds of that money would be due to just leaving it alone and letting the market do its thing never ceases to amaze me!

TABLE 29: MY 2024 PERSONAL WEALTH PYRAMID & PLAYLIST PRIORITIZATION

Layers	Playlists (Accounts)	Amount ($)	How I Actually Contribute
1 &3	401(k) Elective Deferral	$23,000	Allocate annual bonus via traditional 401(k) (pre-tax).
	Employer Match	$11,500 (50% contribution)	Investing in my 401(k) up to the employer match requires me to do the full annual limit!
2A	IRA	$7,000	Contribute from my bi-weekly paychecks via Backdoor Roth IRA method.
2B	HSA	$8,300 (Family Plan Limit)	Employer contributions $2,000 automatically at top of the year. Remaining $6,300 I allocate funds from the extra checks received during three-paycheck months.
4	Mega Backdoor Roth	TBD (Depends on other financial goals)	Contribute from my bi-weekly paychecks.
5	General Brokerage		
My 9:5er's Wealth Pyramid		**$49,800 + TBD**	**Maximizing My Abundance Accelerator**

MY WEALTH FORECAST

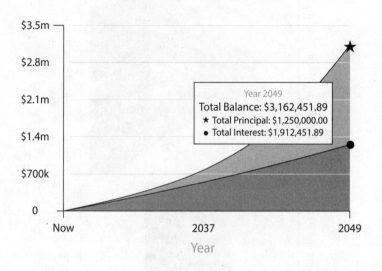

INVESTMENT DETAILS

Initial Investment	$0
Additional Investment Contributions	$50,000
Frequency of Investment Contributions	Annual
Years to Grow	25
Expected Rate of Return	7%
Compound Frequency	Annual

Note that I've been conservative in all our examples using a safe 7% rate of return to show what's possible, but of course, your personal rate of return could be higher or lower, depending on your level of risk and chosen investments. With a higher return, your timeline accelerates. With a lower return, your gains will take longer. Build up your playlists accordingly!

TABLE 30: THE EVOLUTION OF MY PERSONAL WEALTH PYRAMIDS (2014–2024)

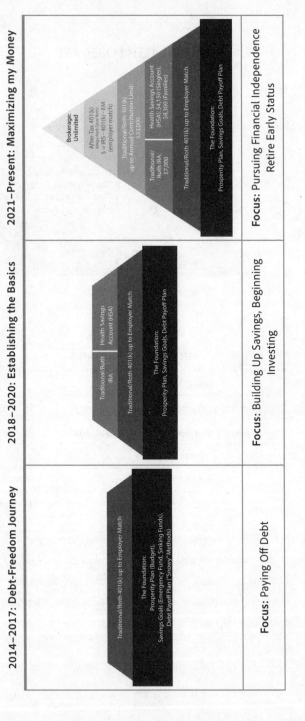

2014–2017: Debt-Freedom Journey

2018–2020: Establishing the Basics

2021–Present: Maximizing my Money

2014–2017:

Traditional/Roth 401(k) up to Employer Match

The Foundation:
Prosperity Plan (Budget),
Savings Goals (Emergency Fund, Sinking Funds),
Debt Payoff Plan ("Snowy" Methods)

Focus: Paying Off Debt

2018–2020:

Traditional/Roth IRA

Health Savings Account (HSA)

Traditional/Roth 401(k) up to Employer Match

The Foundation:
Prosperity Plan, Savings Goals, Debt Payoff Plan

Focus: Building Up Savings, Beginning Investing

2021–Present:

Brokerage:
Unlimited

After-Tax 401(k)
$ = IRS – 401(k) – EM
(employer match)

Traditional/Roth 401(k)
up to Annual Contribution Limit:
$23,000

Traditional/Roth IRA:
$7,000

Health Savings Account
(HSA): $4,150 (Singles),
$8,300 (Families)

Traditional/Roth 401(k) up to Employer Match

The Foundation:
Prosperity Plan, Savings Goals, Debt Payoff Plan

Focus: Pursuing Financial Independence Retire Early Status

Looking back, my journey from small contributions early in my career to contributing to every account I can now 10 years later highlights the importance of starting, no matter how small. Each stage of my pyramid has evolved alongside my career and priorities. As a first-generation everything, Black Millennial Woman in Corporate America, my story is proof that anything is truly possible with a strong sense of self-awareness and confidence in who you are, a playbook on how to navigate the workplace effectively, and a realistic you-based prosperity plan for managing your money. Let this be your motivator: just begin. *As Melanated Corporate Queens I urge you to be done with accepting limits because someone says they're so. Yes, there are some things you cannot change, but many that are in your control! And until you try, you'll never know. It's truly time to try defying gravity. Just you and I, defying gravity.*

As this final track comes to a close, know that you've got the tools and the skills to thrive into adulthood as the Corporate Queen you are. Navigating the workplace and maximizing the money that comes with it to enjoy your abundant life is all I wish for each and every one of you reading this. Now is the time to take the mic, hit play, and let your Financial Abundance Blueprint make its way onto your greatest hits playlist, because living your abundant life is now guaranteed.

With love, empowerment, and plenty of R&B vibes,
Amanda

REFERENCES

Akin, Jim. "What Affects Your Credit Scores?" July 29, 2023. https://
www.experian.com/blogs/ask-experian/credit-education/score
-basics/what-affects-your-credit-scores.

Covey, Steven R. 2004. *The 7 Habits of Highly Effective People*. New York:
Free Press.

Cornfield, Jill. 2019. "Try a Snowball, an Avalanche or a Blizzard to
Crush Credit Card Debt." CNBC. https://www.cnbc.com/2019
/12/27/try-a-snowball-an-avalanche-or-a-blizzard-to-crush-credit
-card-debt.html.

Curtis, Tiffany, and Tiffany L. Curtis. 2024. "Debt Snowball Method:
What It Is and How to Use It." NerdWallet. https://www.nerdwallet
.com/article/finance/what-is-a-debt-snowball.

Davis, Chris. 2024. "Investment Calculator." NerdWallet. https://www
.nerdwallet.com/calculator/investment-calculator.

Investopedia Team. 2024. *Roth vs. Traditional IRA: Which Is Better for You?*
Investopedia. https://www.investopedia.com/retirement/roth-vs
-traditional-ira-which-is-right-for-you.

Kesmodel, David, and Peter Pyhrr. 2015. "Meet the Father of Zero-Based
Budgeting." WSJ. https://www.wsj.com/articles/meet-the-father-of
-zero-based-budgeting-1427415074.

Konish, Lorie. 2024. "Many Americans can't pay an unexpected $1000
expense from savings. 'We're just not wired to save,' expert says."
CNBC. https://www.cnbc.com/2024/01/24/many-americans
-cannot-pay-for-an-unexpected-1000-expense-heres-why.html.

Mangla, Ismat S. 2016. "The History Behind the Financial Wisdom of
Paying Yourself First."

Mendelow, Aubrey. 1981. "Stakeholder mapping." In *Proceedings of the 2nd International Conference on Information Systems*, pp. 10–24. Baltimore, MD: Association for Computing Machinery.

Northwestern Mutual. 2024. "Planning & Progress Study 2024." Northwestern Mutual. https://news.northwesternmutual.com /planning-and-progress-study-2024.

O'Shea, Bev. 2024. "How to Use Debt Avalanche." NerdWallet. https://www.nerdwallet.com/article/finance/what-is-a-debt -avalanche.

Pope, Karla. 2022. "40 Best Maya Angelou Quotes to Live By." *Good Housekeeping*. https://www.goodhousekeeping.com/life/g39178842 /maya-angelou-quotes.

Porter, Kim, Katherine Haan, Casey Bond, and Ivana Pino. 2024. "Is the Envelope Budgeting Method Right for You?" *Fortune*. https://fortune.com/recommends/banking/envelope-budgeting -method.

Puyt, Richard W., Finn Birger Lie, and Celeste P. M. Wilderom. "The Origins of SWOT Analysis." *Long Range Planning* 56, no. 3 (2023): 102304. https://doi.org/10.1016/j.lrp.2023.102304.

Quartz. 2016. "The World's Most Popular Money Tip Came From a Mapmaker Who Business Got Crushed by the Great Depression." https://qz.com/813644/the-worlds-most-popular-money-tip- came-from-a-map-maker-whose-business-got-crushed-by-the-great -depression.

Ramsey, Dave. 2024. *The Total Money Makeover Updated and Expanded: A Proven Plan for Financial Peace*. N.p.: Thomas Nelson.

Roman, Madalina. 2024. "The 4 Quadrants of Time Management Matrix [Guide]." Timeular. https://timeular.com/blog/time -management-matrix.

Warren, Karon. 2024. "Roth 401(k) vs. 401(k): What's the Difference?" Investopedia. https://www.investopedia.com/roth-401k-vs -traditional-401k-8599695.

Whiteside, Eric. 2024. "The 50/30/20 Budget Rule Explained With Examples." Investopedia. https://www.investopedia.com/ask /answers/022916/what-502030-budget-rule.asp.

ACKNOWLEDGMENTS

To my husband, Jonathan, for being my biggest cheerleader, my partner, and my rock. Thank you for supporting all my wild ambitions, for stepping up on daddy duties so I could grind late into the night, for holding me accountable to my dreams, and always reminding me to "make that money, don't let it make me." I couldn't ask for a better teammate in life or love.

To my parents, thank for you doing the best you could with the tools you were provided. They were more than enough and established a strong foundation for me grow and thrive from.

To my brothers, thanks for making it easy to be the eldest sister LOL. Keep hitting 'em long and straight and giving Tiger a run for his money.

A special shoutout to my cousin Majid, who always said I was the smartest person he knew. Gone from us too soon, and I never got the chance to share the good news. I hope I'm making you proud, cousin, and that you continue to RIP.

To my In-Laws (Luvs), thank you for welcoming me with open arms and becoming the additional family I never knew I needed. Your support means the world to me.

To my Loved Ones and Friends, thank you for being my support system and rooting for me through it all. I'm so blessed to have a core group of ride-or-dies who've been with me through thick and thin. Y'all are the real MVPs.

The Financial Abundance Blueprint

To my corporate aunties and uncles, y'all saved me when I was on the brink of giving up. I can't thank you enough for all the wisdom, pep talks, and encouragement you gave me. You all walked so I could run, and I'm committed to finishing this race so those behind us can fly!

To my Living In The Abundance community, you inspire me every single day. I promise to continue showing up for y'all and educating future Financially Free Corporate Queens so we all can experience an abundant life on a 9-5.

Last, but certainly not least, thank you, God. You've been with me from start to finish, and I can't take credit for a single thing without acknowledging Your favor and grace. I'm so thankful for the opportunity to be a living testimony of what's possible when you stay obedient to the Word and strive to be salt in this earth. Your blessings have made all of this possible, and I'm forever grateful.

ABOUT THE AUTHOR

 Amanda Henry is a Black first-generation Ivy League graduate, Wife, Mom, Author, Corporate Trainer, and Mrs. Arizona US 2024. While paying off $65K in debt, building a thriving corporate career, and reaching the brink of financial independence, Amanda discovered a powerful truth: abundant living is achievable on a 9 to 5. She coined the term *Financially Free Corporate Queen* to embody a woman who navigates the workplace authentically and confidently, using her career to create financial stability and a life of freedom and joy. Through her platform, Living In the Abundance, Amanda empowers ambitious women to thrive professionally and financially, helping them design a life on their own terms.

Dedicated to closing the wealth gap and helping women confidently navigate work and life, Amanda has been featured in multiple media outlets and speaks at events nationwide. Amanda holds a BS in Economics from The Wharton School, University of Pennsylvania, and an MS in Global Marketing Management from Boston University. When she's not inspiring others, she enjoys spending time with her husband and son, relaxing at all-inclusive resorts, and vibing to '90s R&B. Learn more about Amanda and her work at www.AmandaJHenry.com.